TOO FAST, TOO SHORT

HOLLYWOOD LEGENDS SERIES

CARL ROLLYSON, GENERAL EDITOR

TOO FAST, TOO SHORT

The Life of Diana Barrymore

◆ ◆ ◆

JENNIFER ANN REDMOND

UNIVERSITY PRESS OF MISSISSIPPI / JACKSON

The University Press of Mississippi is the scholarly publishing agency of the Mississippi Institutions of Higher Learning: Alcorn State University, Delta State University, Jackson State University, Mississippi State University, Mississippi University for Women, Mississippi Valley State University, University of Mississippi, and University of Southern Mississippi.

www.upress.state.ms.us

Frontispiece photograph by Arnold Genthe, 1941. Library of Congress, Prints & Photographs Division, Arnold Genthe Collection, LC-DIG-agc-7a01247

The University Press of Mississippi is a member of the Association of University Presses.

Publisher: University Press of Mississippi, Jackson, USA
Authorised GPSR Safety Representative: Easy Access System Europe - Mustamäe tee 50, 10621 Tallinn, Estonia, gpsr.requests@easproject.com

Library of Congress Cataloging-in-Publication Data

Names: Redmond, Jennifer Ann, author.
Title: Too fast, too short : the life of Diana Barrymore / Jennifer Ann Redmond.
Other titles: Hollywood legends series.
Description: Jackson : University Press of Mississippi, 2025. | Series: Hollywood legends series | Includes bibliographical references and index.
Identifiers: LCCN 2025025144 (print) | LCCN 2025025145 (ebook) | ISBN 9781496858665 (hardback) | ISBN 9781496858672 (epub) | ISBN 9781496858689 (epub) | ISBN 9781496858696 (pdf) | ISBN 9781496858702 (pdf)
Subjects: LCSH: Barrymore, Diana, 1921–1960. | Actors—United States—Biography. | Motion picture actors and actresses—United States—Biography. | LCGFT: Biographies.
Classification: LCC PN2287.B377 R43 2025 (print) | LCC PN2287.B377 (ebook) | DDC 791.4302/8092 [B]—dc23/eng/20250627
LC record available at https://lccn.loc.gov/2025025144
LC ebook record available at https://lccn.loc.gov/2025025145

British Library Cataloging-in-Publication Data available

TO MOM
FOR EVERYTHING

In the massive volume that one could write about the big-screen history of the Barrymore clan, the life of Diana Barrymore would scarcely merit more than a couple of pages.

—GARY CAHALL, REVIEW OF *TOO MUCH, TOO SOON* (1958)

CONTENTS

ACKNOWLEDGMENTS

MANY PEOPLE HELPED ME BRING DIANA'S STORY INTO THE WORLD, AND FOR that I am eternally grateful. Thank you to:

Emily Snyder Bandy and everyone at the University Press of Mississippi for their direction and guidance.

Joana Avillez, John Blyth Barrymore, and Vivian Thomas Trimble for access and insight into your remarkable family.

The amazing Nailah Holmes, Associate Manager of Research Access Services at the New York Public Library for the Performing Arts, without whom my research would not have been possible—particularly during a pandemic.

Luke Vilelle, librarian at the Wyndham Robertson Library, and the late Beth Harris, archivist, both of Hollins University, for their kindness and hard work.

Sue Kupcinet, for sharing some of Essee and Diana's correspondence.

Kenzie McPhie and Nora M. Plant, A/V Archives, American Heritage Center, University of Wisconsin; Rebecca Smith and Heather M. Szafran, Williams Research Center, the Historic New Orleans Collection; Bree Russell, Curator of the Warner Bros. Archives at USC School of Cinematic Arts; and Sharon Rork, Reference Librarian for the NYPL's Billy Rose Theatre Division, for your generosity and willingness to help.

Everyone who contributed in some way, especially: Denise Barrymore, Claire Cohen, Deena Ecker, Edward Engel, Julia Fine, Nathaniel Frank, Amy Gary, the late Donna Hill, Orin Kennedy, Charles Lieurance, Roy Mauritsen, Eric Melzer, Philip Mershon, the late Joan Myers, Terry Chester Shulman, David Stenn, Mélanie Tartoué, Laura Wagner, Jeffrey Weissman, and Tom Zimmerman.

My family and friends for their love, support, and patient endurance of my Barrymore obsession.

Special thanks to Sam Amorese (1956-2023), my "third biggest fan," who was so excited about this book. Hope I made you proud.

TOO FAST, TOO SHORT

CHAPTER 1

NEWPORT, PHILADELPHIA, MANHATTAN

IT WAS AUGUST IN NEWPORT, RHODE ISLAND, "AMERICA'S FIRST RESORT," and the town was thick with Nobs and Swells. Nobs, said Ward McAllister, were old money, families from New England or the South with fortunes that went back at least three generations. They never had to work. The largely New York-based Swells earned their way into The 400, the list of elites created by McAllister with empress of society Caroline "*the* Mrs." Astor, as oil barons, railroad tycoons, newly minted millionaires eager for the "conspicuous consumption" that defined the Gilded Age.

Theresa Fair was an unlikely Swell. She was born in 1871 to an Irish immigrant miner and the keeper of a boarding house her father met in Nevada. Two years later, James Graham Fair and his three stock brokerage partners made millions as the "Silver Kings" after the Comstock Lode "big bonanza"— one of the largest silver discoveries in North America. Theresa Rooney divorced James over his drinking and infidelity in 1883, receiving a handsome settlement as well as custody of their two daughters, Tessie and Virginia. The three moved to San Francisco and regularly summered in Newport, where nineteen-year-old Tessie caught the eye of shipping magnate Hermann Oelrichs during a tennis tournament. The two married in 1890, and Theresa Fair Oelrichs rose quickly through the ranks to become one of three ladies who ruled over the upper class after Caroline Astor's death in 1908.

Alva Vanderbilt Belmont oozed extravagance. Mrs. Stuyvesant (Mamie) Fish loved practical jokes and possessed a biting sense of humor. And formidable Tessie, stickler for society mores, tolerated nothing less than perfection. For approximately six weeks every year, the "Great Triumverate" organized and oversaw Newport's European-flavored activities, calibrated for the maximum "see and be seen" effect: "bathing" at Bailey's Beach, leisure rides in opulent coaches with liveried footmen, sports (lawn tennis at the

Casino for the ladies, yachting for the men), and dinner parties or balls in the evening. At night all retired to their Bellevue Avenue "cottages," sprawling mansions modeled on European palatial estates. Tessie's was "Rosecliff," modeled after the Grand Trianon at Versailles in France.

Hermann Oelrichs's brother, Charles, a broker and "clubman," married Blanche de Loosey ("Tibi"), one of two surviving daughters of the Austrian Consul to New York, Chevalier Charles F. de Loosey. The other, Emilie, married American Sugar Refining Company heir Theodore Havemeyer, who also served as Austro-Hungarian Consul-General to New York City and cofounded the Newport Country Club. Hermann and Emilie generously shared with their siblings; in fact, it was the Havemeyers who bought Charles and Tibi the yellow wooden house on Newport's Kay Street, just north of Bellevue and across the street from their own, to spend summers in with their children. They had four: classically beautiful Natalie, called "Lily"; serious, brown-eyed Charles (whose daughter, Marjorie, married bandleader Eddy Duchin and died six days after birthing their son, Peter); Henry, nicknamed "Harry," the freckled prima donna; and "the baby," Blanche Marie Louise Oelrichs, born October 1, 1890. The family resided in a townhouse on Madison Square in New York City.

"It seemed to me in the year of my first impressions of Newport that my parents led a gay and happy life," Blanche wrote, a contrast from her Aunt Tessie's "Society as a business." Charles easily switched from cowpunching in Wyoming to throwing costume balls with Tibi, whose "sumptuous" Viennese upbringing influenced everything with "a waltz-time aura of romance." Tall and blonde, Lily was the star of the family. Blanche described herself as a "gnome" in comparison—"wretched-looking," according to her cousin—but she didn't care. She had better things to do: get muddy with the servants' children, learn a new piece to recite at the next charity function, or antagonize everyone by blacking out her teeth and dressing in rags. The rest of the time, when not spying on Lily and her many suitors, she spent happily lost in her imagination.

The death of her beloved Uncle Harry on May 28, 1902, shattered that dream world. Blanche once asked her mother how the former athlete and American polo pioneer became bedridden. A cryptic tale followed about Henry Oelrichs's close friendship with the controversial Mr. James Gordon Bennett Jr., whose father founded the *New York Herald*. A hard partier and passionate yachter known as "the Mad Commodore," the two sailed around the world with the Jersey Lily herself, actress Lillie Langtry, on Bennett's sumptuous 314-foot *Lysistrata*, complete with library, saloon, full-time masseur, and a cow to provide fresh milk and butter. Something sickened Harry on that voyage, progressing to dropsy,[1] Bright's disease,[2] and finally paralysis. Only during his final, feverish days did his geniality and impish sparkle fade; Blanche remembered him calling out, begging her to send the doctors away. The next time she saw him, it was to leave flowers as he lay in state, "hoping he would now say something in spite of the grown-up people being there whom I knew he had never really liked." Two months later, on July 24th, Lily married star polo player Peter Donahue Martin in a church resplendent with flowers and finery. Martin's late father, Edward, was president of the First National Bank of San Francisco and thus an excellent catch. Blanche beamed for her sister but wept at the thought of losing her. Besides, she wasn't interested in beaux yet—her interests were decidedly more rebellious.

The exclusive, upper-class Brearley School expelled her for organizing fake fire alarms, lacing a teacher's soup with whiskey, and other pranks with her friends. Manhattanville Convent, where Lily attended for a time, expelled her for throwing midnight snack parties with foie gras sandwiches and chocolates she had hidden in her underwear drawer. At fifteen, she was an olive-skinned, dark-eyed beauty, still blissfully unaware of encroaching adulthood. Society gently suggested she stop wearing juniors' shoe-top skirts and wear her famous dark tresses in a proper updo instead of "tossing about with only one gigantic black bow to hold it in place." Uncle Hermann died in 1906 and left his entire estate to Charles, which Tessie vigorously contested; the resulting fifty-fifty split afforded the family greater financial comfort. Tibi held an unofficial "coming-out" small dinner-dance for Blanche at the Park Avenue apartment in February 1909, just before they sailed to Europe with Emilie, with her official debut planned for Newport in May.

The highlight of Blanche's trip was visiting Lily and Peter at their Paris home. A last-minute guest switch at one of their dinner parties led to Blanche meeting Leonard M. Thomas, diplomat and son of Drexel banking firm head George C. Thomas. She liked him immediately—and even more after he sent a gift of books. Blanche surprised herself by falling for Leonard. She usually leaned towards the Byronic type, like Lawrence Perrin, a former beau of Lily's too intense to pass muster with Charles and Tibi. Blanche was heartbroken when he died by suicide in 1917, after years spent in and out of asylums. Leonard was blonde, blue-eyed, blandly proper . . . until Blanche overheard Tibi and Lily whispering about a scandal in his past.

It's tame by today's standards: Leonard's fellow diplomats threw him a party to celebrate his transfer from Rome to Madrid. Drunken colleagues hoisted the dancing girls up on tables and pelted them with bread, flowers,

1. Edema.
2. Nephritis.

anything in reach. Dancer Vera Sylvas lost her temper after getting salt in her eyes and brained the secretary to the Spanish Embassy to the Vatican with a champagne bottle. Chaos followed as paramedics rushed a bleeding Señor Diaz to the hospital with a fractured skull. Pope Leo demanded resignations of every Vatican representative present, Leonard and Vera Sylvas fled Rome immediately, and poor Señor Diaz—who lost an eye in the debacle—received the bill for damages, "the hardest punishment of all." After lying low for a few months, the scandal was forgotten, and Leonard returned to public life.

Charles and Tibi announced Blanche and Leonard's engagement on August 21, 1909, at the Newport Clambake Club. "My daughter and I are supremely happy," Tibi said, waving away rumors of a $200,000 diamond necklace Len gave Blanche as an engagement gift. "[Leonard] is not looking for stage money notoriety. He is all right." Golden candelabras and floral urns transformed the Park Avenue apartment into a chapel for the wedding on January 26, 1910. Blanche walked down an improvised aisle of white ribbons in white chiffon embroidered with roses, masses of gardenias and white orchids in her arms. Kathleen Vanderbilt and her nephew Charles Martin carried her train, and diamonds indeed glimmered at her throat. "I was fantastically spoiled by everyone," wrote Blanche, remembering how all Newport embraced them that summer. When the days shortened, they left their Narragansett Avenue home for a lovely apartment on East 81st Street in Manhattan. Their first child, Leonard May Oelrichs Thomas, was born there on May 2, 1911. Four years later, on April 26, 1915, Meredith Michael Thomas joined the family. Leonard disliked their names and petitioned to have them changed, and on September 15th, the boys became Leonard Moorhead Thomas and Robin May Thomas.

Blanche also changed. She bobbed her hair, smoked in public, and supported the burgeoning suffrage movement. She wasn't the only society woman to do so; in 1914, Alva Belmont inaugurated the Chinese Teahouse at her Newport "cottage," Marble House, with a Women's Vote conference, and later helped found the National Women's Party. Tibi adopted the cause while in the UK and invited women's rights activist Alice Paul to lecture at the house. Afterwards, believing only "frumps, fools, and knaves" would oppose such progress, Blanche led thousands up Fifth Avenue during the "monster" October 1915 Votes for Women parade. Bearing "the white and gold banner of the International Suffrage Alliance," she passionately declared: "it is not enough to believe in suffrage in a passive fashion; we must stand up and be counted for our convictions." Her women's rights work scandalized her father, "paragon of conventionality," into not speaking to her for a while. "He was terribly against her modernity," said a family friend.

She wrote copiously, sometimes for suffrage, but mostly meandering Whitmanesque verse occasionally published as a society curio. National syndication of "Insaroff," her Russian short story based on Turgenev's *On the Eve*, caught the eye of Mitchell Kennerley, an editor and art dealer who enjoyed the avant-garde and wanted to issue a book of her poetry. It was he who first suggested she use a nom de plume for anonymity. Something shifted once she changed her name: it brought confidence, maturity, and gravitas. Though quickly rendered pointless by headlines like "Mrs. Leonard Thomas Takes up Poetry,"[3] she was now and forever Michael Strange.

The indefatigable Louisa Lane was a seven-year-old superstar by 1827, the same year she left London and moved to New York with her singer/actor mother Eliza. A year later, she played five adult roles in the same play, *Twelve Precisely*. By ten an accomplished actor, and by thirteen a highly regarded leading lady, she achieved her greatest fame as the first woman to manage a major American theater. Louisa's third husband, Irish comedian/actor John Drew, was part lessee, but he neglected his duties and in 1861 shareholders appointed Louisa. Renamed "Mrs. John Drew's Arch Street Theatre," it boasted, until her retirement over thirty years later, "one of the most brilliant repertory companies in the history of the American stage." Her children all found success on the stage, and the lovely Georgie also found a corker of a husband: the clever, handsome, and talented Victorian matinee idol Maurice Barrymore. Born Herbert Chamberlayne Blyth, "Barrymore" was a stage name he took to avoid shaming the family with his chosen profession. They had three children: Lionel (1878), Ethel (1879), and John, born in Philadelphia on February 14 or 15, 1882.

To the public, Louisa was Lady Teazle of *The School for Scandal* or Mrs. Malaprop of *The Rivals*. To her grandchildren, especially little Jack, she was Mummum (accent on the second *mum*). "Of those days in Philadelphia I have few memories," Jack wrote, but the ones he did were of the grandmother who raised him and his siblings while his parents were off on tour. He didn't remember much of Georgie, who died of tuberculosis when he was eleven, but he worshipped the autodidactic Maurice, whom everybody loved.

Unfortunately, he loved them right back, sparking frequent fights with Georgie about his womanizing. Only his fondness for the bottle eclipsed his adoration of the fairer sex. Not the best role model for an observant boy, so while the older Lionel and Ethel joined the family business on stage, Jack was sent to private school.

---

3. Several versions of this in papers around the country. One florid example, from the *San Francisco Chronicle*, December 31, 1918: "Mrs. Leonard Moorhead Thomas Puzzles and Thrills New York's '600' by the Publication of Verses Rich in 'Atmosphere.'"

A tussle with a classmate at the Convent of Notre Dame introduced Jack to *Dante's Inferno*. He was supposed to read of the horrors awaiting disobedient nine-year-old boys but the grotesque Gustav Doré illustrations fascinated him. "This incident," he later remarked, "accounts for much that is macabre in my character." After his eventual expulsion, he attended Seton Hall Prep, which he disliked, and a series of New York public schools. Georgetown Prep followed in 1895, as did another expulsion. Jack, at fifteen, "seemed to be thrown in with a disreputable lot more and more," charged with smoking, drinking, visiting a brothel, possibly all three at once. There was also another woman around the house: Mamie Floyd, whom Maurice married a year after Georgie's death. Mamie was a twenty-eight-year-old theater owner's daughter who'd done a little acting herself and had crushed on Maurice for years. She also had an eye for her underage stepson, and in 1897, she lured him into his first sexual encounter. He drank to numb the confusion and shame, and when Mummum died that summer, alcohol brought welcome forgetfulness.

He tried to find his own way in the world. "I didn't want to be an actor," he wrote. "I wanted to be a painter." He loved drawing and his talented sketches convey the ghoulish influence of Doré. He attempted art school after a short stint at King's College School in the UK, but dropped out and spent his remaining time in London amusing himself. By 1900, he was back in New York and illustrating Arthur Brisbane's editorial page for the *New York Evening Journal*. Brisbane was a newspaper editor, public relations coach for the biggest businessmen of his day, and writer called "the greatest journalist of his day" by friend and colleague William R. Hearst. Jack ventured on stage with his father (*A Man of the World*) and sister (her hugely successful *Captain Jinks of the Horse Marines*) but never seriously considered acting until Brisbane fired him, legend says, over shoddy work he did while hung over. "I only went back to the theater because there is hope—at least money . . . [t]he indifferent painter usually starves." Later that year it became evident to everyone that Maurice could no longer work. Dementia caused by tertiary syphilis sent him into uncontrollable rages, and by 1901, he was institutionalized at the Long Island Home for the Insane (now South Oaks Hospital) in Amityville, New York, where he died in 1905. Watching his brilliant father disintegrate was the most traumatic experience of Jack's life and imprinted him with a lifelong fear of "going mad."

After his father's death, Jack worked his way up to leads in light comedies like *The Boys of Company B* (1907) and the comic opera *A Stubborn Cinderella* (1909). He and actress-model Evelyn Nesbit fell hard for each other—Jack proposed marriage and Evelyn seemed ready to accept—but her mother disapproved, as did architect Stanford White, Nesbit's "benefactor." They sent Evelyn to a New Jersey boarding school, where an "appendectomy" may have been forced termination of a pregnancy. Jack dated other popular stage performers like Bonnie Magin, Elsie Janis, and Vivian Blackburn, until the producers of *The Fortune Hunters* approached him with a promotional idea: they would insure his "bachelorhood" with Lloyd's of London for one year. The play opened in September of 1909 and ran 345 performances, helped by hordes of starry-eyed girls who sent "mash notes" to his dressing room. It ended at the Gaiety Theatre in May 1910, and in September, just after his insurance expired, Jack married Katherine Corri Harris. He and the teenage socialite met over the summer but their relationship was ill-fated from the start: Katherine loathed his drinking and night-owl habits, and Jack hated her constant badgering for him to start her acting career. He managed to get her a role in the touring production of *The Fortune Hunters*, a couple of other plays, and two of his films (now lost), but they were too incompatible. They separated and officially divorced in 1917 but remained friendly enough that Jack was at her bedside when she died of pneumonia in 1927.

He probably would've continued making light comedies on stage and in films—of this early output, only his fifth film, *The Incorrigible Dukane* (Famous Players, 1915), survives—if his closest friend and roommate, Edward Sheldon, hadn't convinced him to try drama. Ned was the much-loved genius playwright and dramatist behind hits like *Salvation Nell* (1908), *Romance* (1913), and *The Song of Songs* (1914). Though later blinded and paralyzed by what is now believed to have been ankylosing spondylitis, he wrote, doctored scripts, and advised luminaries like Helen Hayes, Thornton Wilder, and Ruth Gordon until his untimely death in 1946. Ned knew Jack had more in him, and after minor successes in *The Yellow Ticket* (1914) and *Kick-In* (1914–15), he hit pay dirt as William Falder in *Justice* (1916). This was definitely no comedy: Falder serves three years hard labor after forging a check to help Ruth, the woman he loves, flee her abusive husband. He is offered his old business position after release, with one condition: he must agree to never contact her again. He discovers Ruth is behind the arrangements; the law provided no rights for a woman or her children after separation, and poverty forced her into sex work for them to survive. Devastated by the system's cruelty, he hurls himself out a window. Jack stopped drinking, shaved off his trademark mustache, and committed himself 100 percent to the role. On opening night, April 3, 1916, critics and audiences alike marveled at the change. Alexander Woollcott, the acerbic critic, writer, and head of the Algonquin Round Table called Jack "vivid and exquisitely sensitive" in the *New York Times*, Falder's final scenes of madness suffused with "the monstrous nightmare quality that he could put into his drawings years ago." This John Barrymore was "a being transformed . . . step[ping] forward into a new position on the American stage." After 103 performances and touring the following season, he followed it with *Peter Ibbetson*, Ned's rewrite of John N. Raphael's drama. His brother Lionel was in the cast, as were acclaimed actresses Constance Collier and Laura Hope Crews.

Raphael's play was based on the George du Maurier novel, one of Maurice's favorites. A man, serving life in prison for murder, discovers he and his beloved can meet in their dreams. After "dreaming true" for forty years, they die a day apart and are reunited in the afterlife. Everyone's performances were praised, Jack's called "finely imaginative" by the *New York Times*. Many were moved to see both brothers together on stage, especially the family; "at its great moments the Barrymore-Drew box wept as one tear duct." It ended its run after seventy-one performances, and after making *Raffles, the Amateur Cracksman* (States' Rights, 1917), Jack prepared for a play that, this time, would change his life personally as well as professionally.

CHAPTER 2

A UNION OF GENIUS

ARTHUR HOPKINS WAS THE KING MIDAS OF BROADWAY: EVERYTHING THE successful theater director and producer touched turned to gold. He caught a production of Tolstoy's *The Living Corpse* in Germany and immediately planned an American version, one he hoped would lure the new dramatic John Barrymore. Ned Sheldon pushed Jack to take the bait, since he'd coveted the role of Fedya ever since seeing Jacob Adler in a 1916 Yiddish theater production. The character was certainly his friend's speed: Fedya flees his unhappy marriage and embeds himself in a group of traveling Roma. After learning his wife has renewed an old romance, he fakes his death, freeing her to marry; once Fedya is discovered alive, he dies by suicide rather than have his wife face bigamy charges. The actor and producer met and agreed to hold things until the end of *Peter Ibbetson*. Hopkins had long wanted to open a theater devoted to meatier fare like Shakespeare and Ibsen as an antidote to all the Broadway fluff. *The Living Corpse*, tentatively retitled *Redemption*, would be the first of two classical productions a year, with sets and costumes by "leading designer of the New Stagecraft in America," Robert Edmond Jones. It was backed by the Shubert brothers, successful theater producers and managers themselves. The next step was adapting the play, and Jack recommended an acquaintance who had knowledge of Russian literature: Michael Strange.

Michael turned to friend Rachel Rosenbaum for help translating. Ray was an activist well-liked by the artistic community described by her brother, sculptor Jo Davidson, as a "vivacious creature with sparkling, snapping eyes." They spent the summer in the basement of Rosenbaum's restaurant the Russian Inn, Michael taking notes as Ray read aloud. It was a progressive group: Fania Mindell, their costume and prop designer and the proprietor of the Greenwich Village import boutique Little Russia, helped Margaret Sanger and Ethel Byrne open the Brownsville Clinic in 1916. It was the first birth control clinic in the United States and the blueprint for what would become

Planned Parenthood. Cast member Ruza Wenclawska, under her Anglicized name Rose Winslow, fought for labor unions and women's suffrage and was once jailed with Alice Paul. It was a project rich with creative energy, and Michael, Ray, and Jack met frequently to check progress and brainstorm.

Michael claimed she first saw Jack when she was fourteen and having lunch at the Hotel Knickerbocker. He looked "dazed," with a "drooping mustache" and garish older lady on his arm. Years later, a different impression during a chance meeting at Cartier's: "he looked elfin and forsaken, an intriguing combination," she remembered, "immense fascination" in his eyes and a coiled grace to his walk that Diana later described "as if he were at sea . . . an assurance of a man who knows the deck." Grand lady of the stage Cathleen Nesbit insisted it was she who introduced the two when he begrudgingly accompanied her to one of Michael's luncheons. "My God, that's a fascinating woman," he gushed. "What eyes, and did you notice that cute little hole with her elbow peeping through?" After so many "society bitches," he was besotted by the eccentric in velvet, "like a mast on a ship with the hair flying back," smelling like "somebody put lemon on their hair and added sugar." The holey gown was indicative of her wardrobe. "She wore outrageous clothes. She would put on a beautiful evening dress and if she didn't feel like it, she'd wear a pair of sneakers with it . . . nothing matched."

Jack (sans Katherine) often visited his Uncle John Drew at his home in Easthampton, Long Island, when the Thomases vacationed there; he would meet with Michael (often sans Leonard) and the other "smart clans of the beach" for "neighborhood tea." Their rapport in public was cordial, guarded, but they were falling in love.

Opinions were split on Michael's poetry. Literary editor George Keppel Thomas liked, if misgendered, her: "The work of this young man contains much beauty of expression but more promise . . . [i]f one reads his verses, bearing in mind at the time that the poet in this age of great spiritual chaos is in the throes of bereavement, the understanding ought to be clear." Critic Gordon Ray Young wrote of "his [sic] soul, a troubled, fluid and vaguely colored soul" in the *Los Angeles Times*, the poems "being made of various forms and not the most intelligible of utterances . . . this poet is given to much morbidity, wearisome introspection, being much troubled about himself and the aforementioned soul." The *Santa Barbara Daily News and the Independent* called her "unconventional in her thinking and in her methods of expression, but her phraseology frequently shows much beauty, and there is often evident keen spiritual divination into the significance of ordinary things." They printed a snippet of her poem "A Poem to Poets": "We are an unhappy lot, / We guessers after the infinite, / And as we run naked amuck through the halls of truth / Bleeding like pigs from the pricks of real experience."[4]

Language like that—and worse—befuddled almost everyone else, who sided with this unnamed critic: "And we are all sure we will like Michael now that he [sic] tells us that he [sic] smells of the moon. We rather suspected from one or two things in the early pages of the book that there was something looney somewhere."

Redemption was a sterling accomplishment. "Mr. Barrymore is distinctly arriving," wrote critic Arthur Hornblow in *Theatre Magazine*, "[and] shows the wonderful and impressive strides that he has made in his profession." It received excellent reviews, except for one Michael distinctly remembered: "During the first entr'acte, when the lights went up, I saw a very stout man sitting in the stage box angrily searching the program and waving his arms in controversy with the usher . . . '[h]e is Count Tolstoi [sic]! He is the son of the author,' [Ray] replied, 'and wants to know immediately who adapted the play. He cannot find a name on the program.' *He'll have to wait some time, thank God!* I thought to myself. . . ." It closed in March 1919 after 204 performances.

Jack filmed the comedy *Here Comes the Bride* and his first onscreen drama *The Test of Honor* for Famous Players-Lasky/Paramount, then back to Broadway with Lionel for the English-language debut of *The Jest*. Translated and adapted by Ned Sheldon from Benelli's "La cena della beffe," the tale of two very different men whose rivalry over a beautiful woman descends into cruelty, revenge, and madness won over the brilliantly caustic Dorothy Parker. "Once again the Barrymore brothers have shown what they can do when they try," she wrote for *Vanity Fair*. "They have easily outclassed all comers in this season's histrionic marathon . . . any better seems impossible." It ended in February 1920 after 179 performances.

Michael's second collection of verse, *Poems*, was released by Brentano's in May 1919. The *New York Times* found her poems "so unusual and so outstanding that they strike the attention at once and remain in the memory." The one constant dark spot: Michael's marriage, which was getting harder for Jack to bear. "I am waiting so patiently for the time when I can put my arms around you and keep you safe and happy," Jack wrote, aching with "a more or less continual pain [like] something crustacean was forming around my heart." He left daily letters for her to pick up personally at the Colony Club, Michael's women-only social club on Park Avenue. In many of them, he lamented the subterfuge, feeling "horribly sorry" for wanting another man's wife. Len, who left for the French battlefront perplexed by the "restless poet

---

4. Michael Strange, "A Poem to Poets," Miscellaneous Poems (New York: Mitchell Kennerley).

who had not been to the slightest degree visible in the girl he married," now returned to find that his wife no longer wanted him.

Len suggested that Michael take a short solo trip to California to shake the affair out of her system. No sooner had the train left the station when a porter delivered Jack's gift: camellias and a little bejeweled self-portrait he designed at Cartier's. Len never had a chance. He tried again with a second honeymoon, asking Charles to speak to his daughter on behalf of the boys, but it was no use. A hopeful Jack wrote Michael after news of her separation: "It is terrible to think how much our happiness depends on Len but if there is a God at all—you will in a very few months be starting a divine peaceful—free—and utterly new existence." The last few months were anything but peaceful for him. All through November and December 1919, he was occupied with principal photography for Paramount-Artcraft's *Dr. Jekyll and Mr. Hyde* during the day, with *The Jest* at night (and matinees). During January and February 1920, he shoehorned in lessons with esteemed vocal coach Margaret Carrington in preparation for *Richard III*, his first attempt at Shakespeare.

The combined abilities of Hopkins, Edmond-Jones, and Barrymore created a fresh, exciting Bard for the twentieth century, and much of what they experimented with carried over to *Hamlet* two years later. It opened at the Plymouth Theater on March 6th, only two weeks after *The Jest* closed, and was a critical success almost instantly.

It drained Jack emotionally and physically to play Richard night after night. He was onstage for all but a few moments, often wearing "heavy armor in which he was required to engage in several energetic scenes of stage combat . . . [it] grew so hot under the lights that it had to be hosed down before it could be removed." After each show, Jack hopped the train from Penn Station to Atlantic City, New Jersey, where Michael isolated herself to work on a new play. After a night of passion, he caught the dawn train back to Manhattan to start all over again. Edmond-Jones worried about him: "[H]e gave so much, revealed so much, that I said to myself, this can't last! . . . It isn't human to drive yourself like that!"

On Wednesday, March 31st, he startled audiences by fumbling his lines and nearly collapsing. The box office refunded tickets for Thursday night and production officially halted on Friday. After only twenty-seven performances, John Barrymore suffered a breakdown. "I could play [Richard III] a great deal better now, I am certain," he wrote in 1926, "but never again would I undertake to play it eight times a week." The press pinned Jack's exhaustion on his commitment to excellence. They fooled no one. "[I]t is no secret that many of Barrymore's friends lay the blame for his breakdown on anxiety over Mrs. Thomas's affairs. . . . Mrs. Thomas is a very temperamental young woman."

"Michael was always on a play on [the] stage of her own life," said a source close to the family. "She was elegance itself . . . [b]ut toward the end of the day, sometimes this control wore thin . . . she would flush and bridle and become almost a frightening human being." Another source, one of the domestic help, remembered her tantrums: "She had been snubbed, or something simply didn't work out. Then, suddenly, she would burst loose . . . [s]he'd smash dishes, pull [the] tablecloth off [the] table, hurl chinaware [at] the wall. We'd hold our breaths, feeling almost a physical danger—while she was besieged by this strange, terrible violence."

Reporters inundated Arthur Hopkins with phone queries about Michael's marital status. *Variety* noticed how often she attended *The Jest* and *Richard III*, throngs of rubberneckers in her wake. "Indeed, there is something almost ludicrous in the shameless peeking and preening that has gone on among distinguished women of the stage—that has gone on in the effort to catch a glimpse of this slender, willowy poetess, so long a queen among the fashionables." They also doubted she was divorced—at least not yet.

Jack spent a few days at home, then left in early April for William Muldoon's health retreat near White Plains, in Westchester, New York. "Billy" Muldoon was a wrestler and friend of Maurice; they had acted together in *As You Like It*. His farm promised to whip the ailing Jack (and those like him) into shape with cold showers and ten-mile hikes, farm work, horseback riding, and gym workouts. "Muldoon conceives his job to be the rebuilding of constitutions," wrote the Brooklyn *Daily Eagle*. "John Barrymore is up there with him now, regaining his health by meekly doing what he is told, and, unless Billy Muldoon has changed of late, not daring to talk back." Muldoon's advice, as interpreted by Ada Patterson in *Photoplay*:

"My boy—ye seem that to me because I knew your father and mother before you were born," said the granite remoulder [*sic*] of men, "I believe you are in love. Nobody told me. I know the symptoms. When a man is in love he is at his worst in every way. His reasoning is defective. He is whimsical. His judgments are bad."

He went home on May 15th, invigorated after six weeks of milking cows and medicine balls and absolutely no alcohol, cigarettes, or telephone. Invigorated, but not relaxed; that was impossible for him. "A very nervous sort of man," remembered Margaret Huston Walters, Margaret Carrington's niece. She was fourteen when she met him. "[N]ot a comfortable type at all."

He took a hiatus from work, per doctor's orders, giving him plenty of time to think about Michael and her divorce, which went public in late April while Jack was incommunicado. Jack had a black belt in obsessing. From his West Fourth Street rooftop garden that almost caved in his landlady's roof to playing ping-pong incessantly for almost four months straight, when he became interested in something, it consumed him completely. Imagine that up against Michael's "huge ego, supreme self-confidence, [and] iron will." The maelstrom approached.

On August 5, 1920—"in spite of the Four Horsemen shouting 'Don't'!"— John Sidney Blyth and Blanche M. Thomas were married in a friend's flat at the Ritz-Carlton Hotel in Manhattan. Blanche's father, Charles, did not attend ("entrenched in the Reading Room at Newport, with, I dare say, a stiff drink") but Tibi did, as did Ethel, Lionel and his first wife, actress Doris Rankin, and a couple of friends. Using their legal names dissuaded no one—by the next morning papers celebrated this "union of genius" alongside ads for *Dr Jekyll and Mr. Hyde*—but it confused and upset Tibi, who tearfully took Lionel aside after the ceremony and asked, "But has he married the Baby at all? I heard no mention of the name Barrymore!"

Jack broke family tradition by not marrying a trouper, said the public, but they forgave him since she was a poet (dubbed the "Fifth Avenue Ella Wheeler Wilcox") and "America's Most Beautiful Woman," according to artist Paul Helleu. "I am the happiest man in the world today," beamed a robust and completely recovered Jack. "I have just married the most wonderful woman, so why shouldn't I be happy?" Reporters wanted a few words about his bride. What was she wearing? "I'll be hanged if I can tell you. All I can say is that she looked just wonderful—as she always does." Secretly, the public awaited the collision of their infamous "temperament[s] with a big T," but they were still happy newlyweds seven months later when Joan Strange Blyth, their only child, entered the world on March 3, 1921.

CHAPTER 3

JOAN STRANGE BLYTH

JACK LOVED WATCHING HIS DAUGHTER IN HER CRIB. "MR. B WAS A WORSHIP-ping father," said nurse Mary Dempsey, but anything more hands-on caused instant panic. Once she handed him the baby for a few minutes while she attended to something and returned to find him frozen in terror and holding Joan like a live grenade. "Now and then Michael would sweep in—Mrs. High and Mighty," said Dempsey. She was far from an attentive mother. During one family trip, she and Jack fought so bitterly they woke Leonard, then eleven, who climbed out his window on a rope of bedsheets and "wandered the dark, lonely streets of Biarritz in tears" through the small hours of the morning. He returned later to find everyone sleeping soundly—unaware he was even missing. "She did not visit the nursery often," Dempsey recalled. "Barrymore was there more often than she. He would say, 'How's my little Dingle—how's my little Treepee?'" Since the baby's birth, he called her Treepeewee—Treepee for short—the meaning a lifelong secret between father and daughter.

In the taxi en route to Joan's christening, Michael decided her daughter's name sounded too much like John. They shared the news at church with godparents Lionel and Doris that she would now be named Diana Blanche Barrymore instead. After the ceremony, they resumed pouring all their attention into Michael's upcoming play, *Clair de Lune*. She spent the last year on the loose adaptation of Victor Hugo's novel *L'homme qui rit*, a bitter critique of the aristocracy disguised as a swashbuckling romance. Gwynplaine is a nobleman's son disfigured by agents of the king, forced into carnival work as his only means to survive. He travels with Dea, the blind girl he rescued as a baby and with whom he is secretly in love, and Ursus, philosopher and fellow performer. Since its publication in 1869, the novel has inspired many film adaptations; the best-known is Universal's *The Man Who Laughs* (1928), with Conrad Veidt, whose chilling rictus grin became the blueprint for DC

17

Comics' character The Joker. In 1921 only two foreign-language versions existed, and none for the stage. Michael's would arguably be the first.

Clair de Lune starred Jack as Gwymplaine (why she changed the spelling, no one knows) during his time at the court of Queen Anne, played by Ethel Barrymore. The large and varied cast included prolific British actors Henry Daniell and Violet Kemble-Cooper. Michael took great liberties with the story, most notably reducing Gwymplaine's horrific Glasgow smile to a gentle slash of red greasepaint. Jack designed costumes and sets, and took ballet classes to improve his form; Michael composed music to accompany her Maeterlinck-style interpretation. It opened at the Empire Theatre on April 18, 1921, and broke box-office records during the first two weeks playing to packed houses for almost the entire run. There were three reasons why: one, both Jack and Ethel were impossibly beautiful, especially the latter in her white or near-white ball gowns; two, a price cap of $5.50, which meant average Joes, not just the wealthy, could afford tickets; and three, the biggest reason of all—everyone enjoys a good trainwreck.

The sets reminded humorist and Algonquin Round Table member Robert Benchley of "the play-room of an institution." The "clumsy . . . at times grotesque" story drew unintentional laughs and a parody by *Snapshots of 1921*, the *Forbidden Hollywood* of its day. Ethel stumbled over the dialogue, which Patterson James of *Billboard* called "decaying rose leaves on a sodden corpse." Michael believed for years that she did it on purpose. Jack's exuberance (and leaping choreography) amused James Whitaker of the *Chicago Tribune,* who said he must have done it "for the love of Mike." The poor reviews hurt him as much as Michael. "[H]e wrote a long letter to the *Times* and the *Tribune* [that was] never printed. . . . John remarked in his letter that [critics] must have dipped their pens into acid, using their hearts as ink-wells . . . he could not help wondering why critics could not do two simple things at one time, such as think and write." Jack later admitted the play was "maimed by loving kindness." G. P. Putman's Sons published it in book form; "it reads better than it acts," said the Brooklyn *Daily Eagle*. It did not tour. "[*Clair de Lune*] wore itself out," wrote *Photoplay*, "[and] will probably never be revived. (A French film based on the play was made by Films Diamant in 1932.)

They spent the summer in Europe, nursing their wounds. The boys stayed with their father, and Jack and Michael rented a seaside bungalow for Diana and Mary Dempsey about forty minutes from Manhattan in Long Beach on Long Island. "Diana was quite a celebrity as Jack Barrymore's daughter, and I could never take her down to the beach without being swamped by people, so I would spend much of the day with the baby on the veranda in the sun. She was completely naked and brown as a berry. I would bring up pails of salt water and bathe her in a tub of it. The water had minnows in it and Diana would try to catch the little fish." Jack traveled with Michael to Paris and Venice until Goldwyn Pictures needed him in London for *Sherlock Holmes* exteriors. Michael continued touring Europe until October and the release of her new poetry collection, *Resurrecting Life*, bearing a gorgeous full-color frontispiece painted by Jack of an ethereal woman slipping the bonds of Earth and ascending to heaven. He joined her back in New York that month to film *Sherlock's* interior shots.

"When they returned from Europe, Mr. B brought me a blue shawl," said Nurse Dempsey, who had a clear favorite of the two. "He was very sweet and very quiet. Michael attracted men like honey attracts flies and she was fatal to any man she possessed . . . she was a spoiled beauty."

The first few years of Diana's life coincided with her father's legendary *Hamlet*. Months of intense preparation, innovative sets, and a modern Oedipal interpretation culminated in what is still considered the finest Hamlet of that generation, if not all time. "If John Barrymore fails to establish himself as the Hamlet of his generation, fit successor to Forbes-Robertson and Edwin Booth," wrote the *New York Times*, "it will not be for the lack of endowment in physique and in inward genius . . . [h]is is a performance to which the lover of acting must return again and again." It opened on November 16, 1922, played 101 performances, and ended its tour in January 1924. "[H]e hasn't had time to think of the small fat trepie [*sic*] at all," he wrote. Michael was in Europe avoiding her husband's Broadway success—she was too bitter over *Clair de Lune* to attend—but happily accompanied him to London when *Hamlet* played the Haymarket Theater in 1925. Diana remembered the "frightening[ly] high ceilings" while staying at the "White House," built for artist James McNeill Whistler in the 1870s. Her parents were relaxed and genial, in a good place following a brief separation the year before, and Jack called preparing for his sixty-eight sellout shows "more fun than anything I have ever done." Fun until, as was typical for him, he grew bored repeating the same role nightly and resumed drinking heavily. By the time they returned to New York, their quarrelling was worse than ever.

"I don't suppose two people have ever been so strangely alike in almost every way," Jack wrote in a love letter to Michael. They were such equals in everything—their egos, their jealous anger, their flair for the dramatic—that the simplest disagreements exploded into broken furniture and shredded nightclothes. Diana later wrote these "violent clashes of temperament" turned their home into "something out of a Russian novel." Both regularly threatened to drink poison or throw themselves into traffic, and Diana remembered a time her mother sported a shiner and a sling when kissing her goodnight—she blamed tripping over one of the multiple champagne cases piled up by their bedroom. After witnessing one knife-wielding row, writer and raconteur Mercedes de Acosta wondered who would kill the other first. Iris Tree famously called their marriage "a tennis game in hell, darling, where nobody misses a ball." Leonard Thomas was forced to intervene when Jack returned from a short separation, "in a strangely exhilarated state of mind" and "proceeded to express his affection for his wife according to the precepts of the stone age." A frantic Michael called Len then left, weeping, "on the arm of her former husband."

In that same love letter, Jack concluded: "I know that just over the edge of our communion is Heaven or Hell." He was right. This time there was no reconciling. He swore off the stage and left for Hollywood, and Michael took the children and moved into the Hotel Madison. "If ever two egotists crashed down in one field it was Jack and I," she wrote in her memoirs. "The spectacle we presented was both tragic and comic . . . the acrostic of two superlatively immature people."

Diana's first clear memory was their new daily routine: from the twelfth floor maid to the elevator porter to Louis the doorman, who walked her once around the block and sent her back up. The five-year-old was thus "aired" twice a day while Mummy focused on her work. Jack had encouraged this: "you cannot devote your *life* to your children entirely . . . you will defeat *their* purpose and your own as well if you do not at the same time make with calmness and great sanity an irrevocable time for your work." Nothing would come between her and Art. "Love and marriage and motherhood interrupted for a short time her ambitions," wrote *Theatre Magazine*. "But only for a short time."

Michael's acting debut was as Sally Negly in the American Theatre's 1924 summer stock production of the Civil War drama *Barbara Frietchie.* The supportive, mostly "North Shore summer colony" audience whet her appetite for more, and she was eagerly searching out her next role when the esteemed lawyers of Sackett, Chapman, Brown and Cross sent a letter to Jack accusing her of plagiarism.

Sophie Treadwell was a playwright, journalist, poet, actor, writer, and women's rights activist who frequented the same circles as Michael and Jack. Her acting mentor was the great Shakespearean interpreter Helena Modjeska, who later hired her to write her biography; Maurice Barrymore worked closely with Modjeska, and chose her to be goddaughter to Ethel. She wrote prolifically, and in 1921—her masterpiece, *Machinal*, still seven years away—she wrote a play based on the life of Edgar Allan Poe.

"Miss Treadwell wrote it with John Barrymore in mind as the star. In fact, he wrote it for him, as she explained in a letter dated January 20, 1921, which accompanied the delivery of the manuscript to the actor . . . [f]or more than two years Miss Treadwell had worked to turn out what she called 'indeed an American play in which every character existed and every situation happened'—a play to fit John Barrymore."

Jack loved it and sent an exuberant reply to Treadwell: "I think it is a very beautiful play, and I am very glad and very proud that you had me in mind when you wrote it." He was not certain when he could produce it, "but this play, I think," he added, "has too many elements of beauty and power to let go." Jack sailed to Europe in June to meet Michael, and for the next three years Treadwell heard nothing from him, even after writing him several letters asking him to at least return the manuscript. Then, September 1, 1924, Treadwell gets a letter from Jack wanting to meet with her.

Jack "announced he had another Poe play, one he felt was just what he wanted and which was the only Poe play he cared to do"—one written by his own wife. He read Treadwell *The Dark Crown* and "she became convinced that the play was not an original written by 'Michael Strange,' but a copy and imitation of her own play." She expressed this to Jack who, after a short discussion, said he himself would not produce Michael's play. (Arthur Hopkins announced shortly after that he wanted nothing to do with it.) He still didn't return Treadwell's, however, resulting in the letter from her lawyers "demanding the return of the Treadwell manuscript, and also a note of warning that the rights of their client would be protected if Barrymore tried to produce the Poe play attributed to his wife." When Jack *still* didn't return Treadwell's *Poe*, the Supreme Court issued a writ of replevin stating Jack return it or pay restitution of $2,500 (almost $46,000 in today's money). The Barrymores' response? A countersuit.

In late October 1924, Michael sued Treadwell for $200,000 damages "charging libel and slander." Her lawyer, Nathan Burkan, "asserted that Mrs. Barrymore's suit was designed to compel Miss Treadwell to prove her allegations . . . [t]he suit asks $100,000 damages for the alleged injury to Mrs. Barrymore, and an additional $100,000 for alleged slander of title." He agreed with Jack, who said, "[T]he only reason for Miss Treadwell's complaint may be her disappointment over her failure to obtain the production of her play." Neither side flinched, and it was months before the case was finally settled in Treadwell's favor and *Poe* was returned to its author. (It was staged in 1936 as *Plumes in the Dust*.) Unfortunately for Sophie Treadwell, sparring with a couple like the Barrymores "subjected her to withering attacks by the usual stage-door journalistic toadies who smeared her as an unprincipled gold-digger." It took some time for her to be welcomed into the world of Broadway again. Michael, however, was ready for her official debut there with The Stagers at the Princess Theatre, March 19, 1926.

In *Easter* by August Strindberg, a family suffers "gloom, trouble and strife": financial problems, incarceration of the family patriarch, and institutionalization of the daughter, all of which comes to a head over the course of the Easter holiday. Hope arrives with the dawn of Easter Sunday itself. The son, Elis, was portrayed by Warren William, future King of the Pre-Codes and whom Ray W. Harper of the *Brooklyn Citizen* thought was a "fortunate choice for leading man." Harper thought Michael, as the daughter Eleonora, gave a "very capable showing . . . [t]rue, there were some points to quibble on but for the most part she was quite excellent." The *Brooklyn Times-Union* said Michael "performed last night with a skill that must have contented her watching relatives." Alexander Woollcott felt differently, and expressed it in his inimitable style:

> [Michael Strange] made her New York debut last week in her own rearrangement of Strindberg's "Easter" an art event which, as far as I could tell, left the temperature of our town about what it was before. I would give a good deal to know what John Drew and Ethel Barrymore thought as they watched the proceedings on the first night. . . .
>
> Her gnawing interest in the theatre has been manifested in sundry ways, notably by marrying John Barrymore.

Due to Michael's newfound love of society, Diana socialized little, and only with certain handpicked playmates. Innes James's mother, Marion, was an Eliot, one of the oldest families in New York; distant cousin and future actress Cobina Wright Jr. had a stockbroker father and actress/opera singer/columnist Cobina Wright Sr. for a mother; Gloria Caruso, daughter of opera great Enrico Caruso; Brenda Frazier, destined to become Queen of the Debutantes and the most famous socialite of all time; and Gloria Vanderbilt, heir to the massive Vanderbilt fortune and subject of a scandalous custody case that dubbed her the "Poor Little Rich Girl" until reinventing herself as model, occasional actor, and fashion heavyweight in the 1970s and '80s (everyone wanted a pair of her jeans). Each friend offered a glimpse into the socialite life Michael always shunned but now craved for her daughter, but Diana was happiest when alone and lost in her daydreams, not unlike Michael as a child.

Diana's circle of friends shrank further when she was sent to school at Couvent des Ouiseaux (now Ensemble Scolaire Notre-Dame Les Ouiseaux) in Paris with her governess, Margaret Gerdes, a petite steel-haired woman who had served various Oelrichses for twenty years. Apart from a visit from Cobina, Diana's only friends were her Catholic "holy cards," lithographs of Jesus and the saints with whom she imagined talking and playing games, something the girls at school would not. "The wonderful colors fascinated me and my over-fertile imagination brought the figures to life . . . [p]erhaps this is a child's religion and a bigger better religion than anything we know as we pretend to 'grow up.'" Her school often gave the cards as academic rewards, and Diana greedily pilfered them from unattended desks. When later she dropped her missal, spilling the ill-gotten gains, she was shunned with "the native cruelty with which and by which all children can be so brutal." It was in France that Michael permitted Diana to see her first movie, a Lon Chaney Sr. picture—either *Hunchback of Notre Dame* or *Phantom of the Opera*, she couldn't recall—that gave her nightmares.

The self-absorbed Michael was incapable of loving her daughter unconditionally, and Jack was verboten—only after confronting Miss Gerdes with a found copy of *Confessions of an Actor*, her father's 1926 memoir, did she learn her last name of Blyth[5] meant she was a Barrymore.

Michael filed for divorce as publicity ran rampant about Jack's romance with his costar from *The Sea Beast*, Dolores Costello. Diana returned home and, Leonard away at school, she, her mother, and Robin moved into a three-story home overlooking the East River. Michael created the "Captain's Cabin," a nautical bedroom-cum-office where she would lie on her "bunk"— a bed chained to the wall—for hours brainstorming poetry. She was to be disturbed only for emergencies, and each household member had their own "knock." Diana wondered how many of the other children at the elite Miss Hewitt's School needed a signal to see their mommies. She couldn't even say "Mummy" in public; it was always Miss Strange, as in "Miss Strange is expecting you." Since Leonard spent his vacations with his father in Palm Beach, Florida, and Robin escaped to "Greystock," his paternal aunt's house in Pennsylvania, Diana was pressed into being the welcome wagon. "If Robin had been there, he would have been sent, of course, to be the official greeter. I never would have been allowed if he was there." Watching her mother transform into Michael Strange almost made up for the smiles and curtsies. She obliterated everyone else in the room with what Gene Fowler called "the face of a Romney portrait and the spirit of a US Marine," the same energy she later brought to her performance as the lead in *L'Aiglon*.

---

5. While most sources use *Blythe*, I've chosen to use the proper spelling of *Blyth* throughout the book.

It took being the most famous person on the planet to excite Diana about a guest. Context in *Too Much, Too Soon* puts Charles Chaplin's visit sometime in late 1927, when tawdry front-page details about his divorce from Lita Grey turned him from the whimsical, beloved Little Tramp of *The Kid* (1921) and *The Gold Rush* (1925) into a licentious, cruel villain. Chaplin escaped Los Angeles for the East Coast, where a Manhattan doctor prescribed a week's bed rest for a nervous breakdown.

He spent months rubbing elbows with the upper crust of New York, and soon Michael got her turn. "You're going to meet a genius this afternoon," she told Diana, who watched for him from the window. Imagine her surprise when the little man exiting the car wore an ordinary coat and hat! "How frenzied the neighborhood of East End Avenue would become over Charlie's visits," Michael wrote. He greeted the waiting throng of boys (members of the Sea Wall Savages gang, he and Michael joked) and handed out movie passes, most likely for the January debut of the problem-riddled *The Circus* (1928). Chaplin chatted a bit with Diana and Robin, who was home on school break, then flashed his impish grin and joined Michael inside for tea. The two discussed many things, including a low opinion of Hollywood—"It's the deadest, dullest hole in the world," Chaplin said—and Jack, a great friend of Chaplin's and the subject of one of his most viciously funny impressions, reciting the *Hamlet* soliloquy while picking his nose.

After he left, Diana confessed to Robin her disappointment at the missing trademark bowler and baggy trousers. Robin laughed and jangled his pockets. Who cared what he wore? He made a mint charging the kids 25 cents each.

Where to start with Robin? He was out of a fairy tale: skin clear and pale as marble, bright blue-grey eyes, and ash-blonde hair Michael kept in glossy ringlets well past toddlerhood. While the other kids played marbles or kick-the-can, he shouted decrees dressed as Nero, complete with gilded laurel wreath, a swift rescue by Mummy the only thing between him and a pop in the nose. This old soul who "worshipped the epoch of Marie Antoinette" was Michael's clear favorite and she spoiled him rotten, obliging his demands for fancy meals, fine clothes, and his own playroom stocked with one of everything sold by FAO Schwarz. (Diana could not enter unless expressly invited.) Michael's friends marveled at him. "When did I realize that my brother was a little different than other boys?" Diana wrote. "I never thought Robin was any different. I just thought he was gayer than most people." Writer Gertrude Stein once inscribed one of her books to "a nice Robin, a good Robin, a sweet Robin," not typically the first adjectives that came to mind about him. He insulted the "peasants" around him, tormented his sister, frequently threw tantrums—shades of Uncle Harry—and got into mischief, like lowering Michael's birdcage (furious bird still inside) out the window suspended by a rope of her ball gowns and fur stoles. Robin's angel face let him get away with murder and he reveled in it.

"I should have been the girl instead of you because I'm so much prettier," he once gloated, and Diana agreed. "I was the ugliest child I knew," she wrote, convinced she held no trace of her parents' beauty. All she saw was a little girl with baby fat, "jaundice," and a lank Dutch bob. Despite similarly describing her own appearance at Diana's age as "dank-haired" and "sallow-faced," her mother never tried to build her daughter's self-esteem. She was around six years old when Michael took a month's trip to Europe just before the holidays, leaving her with Charles and Tibi. Diana people-watched from her grandparents' living room window, local girls with velvet ribbons tied around their silky curls, and suddenly Diana hated her "stringy bangs" more than anything on earth. She sneaked upstairs, pocketed Tibi's sewing scissors, and hacked them off, stuffing them into the Christmas tree. It made sense to her: what better place for her "devil's hair" than under the angel hair tinsel? It didn't take long for Tibi to notice, and Diana tearfully confessed: the girls, her hated bob, the ache to be pretty. Tibi promised to keep it secret; they'd grow back before Mummy returned home anyway. They made a game of cleaning up the tree, then shared Diana's favorite treat, Viennese "coffee" (mostly milk with whipped cream). Charles told her a bedtime story, tucked her in, kissed her, and told her she was beautiful. They showered her with compassion and unconditional love, something Diana desperately needed.

The night after Christmas, Diana got to do something Gerdes always promised her: see her mother on stage. Michael had the lead in a revival of *L'Aiglon*, the Edmond Rostand play about Napoleon II written expressly for Sarah Bernhardt, who originated the role in March 1900; the English translation premiered that October at the Knickerbocker Theatre with Maude Adams as "The Eaglet." She sat next to her governess in their box at the Cosmopolitan Theatre, wide-eyed, as her mother entered, dressed in a boy's white suit and shiny, knee-high black leather boots. "I think she played boy's parts because she always looked like a little boy," Diana later wrote. "She didn't look like a woman. She looked like a healthy little country boy [from] the 18th century." She watched, transfixed, until the Duke—"L'Aiglon"—succumbed at play's end. "She lay there without moving. I became panic-stricken. In the absolute silence of the theater I screamed, 'Oh, Mummy's dead!' and burst into tears." Gerdes hurried her backstage to her mother's waiting embrace, scented with "something that was to become so familiar to me in later years—greasepaint and powder." It was Diana's first lesson in the spellcraft of the theater.

Critics were divided about the illusion. Michael's "understanding of meanings and subtleties" was "charming," wrote the *Brooklyn Daily Times*, but she "never for an instant" truly became the character. The *New York Times* thought her "very—and obvious—lack of command of that technique" actually gave a "childishness" and "wistfulness" to her Duke "of which a perfected technique might have robbed it utterly. . . . Miss Strange may easily become a greater actress, but when she does she will probably not play L'Aiglon half as well."

Jack and Dolores tied the knot in November 1928. Dolores's father, actor and former matinee idol Maurice Costello, didn't trust Jack and vehemently opposed their marriage. Michael insisted she found "the perfection of love in the maternal urge" and needed no one other than her three children. Six months later, on May 23, 1929, she quietly wed attorney Harrison Tweed in London. "Harry" was completely different: laidback, pragmatic, devoted to equity. He supported legal aid for the disenfranchised and ran a "fresh air camp" on Long Island for inner-city boys. The family moved into 10 Gracie Square the following year and spent summers at "Tick Hall," the McKim, Mead, and White-built Tweed estate on Montauk Point. Diana recalled her mother introducing Tweed to her lifelong ritual of saluting the setting sun: "[W]hen we were at Montauk Point I remember watching those two silhouettes watching the sun, she and Tweed, like two soldiers, and they used to hold their hands against their brow till the sun went down and then they'd go for a walk."

Meeting Harry's daughters inspired a rare bit of introspection from Michael, the "pathos" of watching children of divorce denied the "clear and consoling" image of their parents' happy marriage. It quickly passed and by autumn she was herself again, back at her desk. Leonard returned to Yale, Robin back to private school, and Diana to the prestigious Brearley School, just across the street from home.

Diana was an uneven student, bright and gifted in art, but easily distracted and careless. Her mood swings and belligerence drove away potential friends, and she had few confidantes. Robin was running around in London with a group of sophisticates including photographer Cecil Beaton, artist and stage designer Oliver Messel, and art collector Peter Watson. They inspired the privately circulated sex spoof *Girls of Radclyffe Hall* by composer Lord Berners, a friend of the group (Robin's character was named May). The title was a wink at lesbian author Radclyffe Hall and her notorious 1928 novel *The Well of Loneliness*. Harry meant well, but outbursts of any kind ruffled his

English reserve. Harry never got upset or snapped at anyone. Even his break-fast was predictable: corn flakes and soft-boiled eggs, every morning for twelve years. Grandma Tibi was growing infirm, and Grandpa Charles passed away in January 1932, a year after Lily died in San Francisco of pneumonia. She definitely couldn't talk to Michael, hard at work on her play about the Byrons. "She wasn't like a mother—she was like a beautiful satyr—to look at, be admired and be afraid of all in one . . . [s]he'd say oh, catkin dear, and it was all very charming but it was so damned surface and children know those things. I finally got to the point where I'd only ask her about her writ-ing, and when I did that she'd talk to me. If I'd asked her anything about the family she'd say, 'Don't talk to me. I don't want to talk about it.'"

Dolores wrote Michael the summer of 1932, wanting Diana to stay with them in Los Angeles a couple of months and get to know her new baby brother, John Jr., but Michael immediately declined. Diana was much too young and innocent to be anywhere near Hollywood. However, this was purely a power move on Michael's part; Diana was born mature. Back in 1928, Jack wrote Ned that his seven-year-old daughter need only grow taller, "as she is quite grown up enough as she is."

Diana's reaction was straight out of her parents' playbook: she sprinted to the window and threatened to hurl herself seven stories to the ground. Michael calmed Diana down, but the decision stood, and she had window safety bars installed the next day. Undeterred, Diana teamed up with Michael-approved banker's daughter Marjorie Willer[6] to concoct a Plan B. The two girls packed some things—Diana included some drawings she did for her father—and they sneaked out, determined to get to Hollywood. "I thought, *well, I'm like this man—I must get to him. We're alike*." They crept through Central Park for half an hour before a sharp-eyed policeman collared them.

Diana stood quietly as her mother paced the room. Did she think life with her father would be idyllic? Suddenly she stopped and, ramrod straight, launched into her Cole Porter story. Yes, that Cole Porter, the composer, lyricist, and Broadway genius, and Diana had the story burned into her brain by adulthood. "When you were about two or three years old, Linda Porter came to me when I was quite broke and said, 'Look, Michael, I love the child. She's perfectly enchanting. Why don't you let me have her? You won't have to worry about her. Not necessarily adopt her—but let me take care of her until later on in years.' Mother didn't give me much of the conversation . . . [she] went into a big thing how she could never give up her daughter. She said, 'Well, I didn't give you up. You think you would have had a home life?'"

---

6. Marjorie later was assistant to columnist Dorothy Kilgallen.

Diana was sent to see Brearley psychiatrist Dr. Florence Powdermaker, later an expert in pediatric psychiatry, and it was a surprisingly healing experience: "For the first time an adult was interested in me and listened to me." She purged herself of her loneliness, her pain over her father, her disconnected mother. She described how Michael slapped her for wanting gaudy red slippers and ridiculed her in front of friends for wearing a frilly dress. Any deviation from Michael's way of thinking brought swift rebukes about her "Barrymore streak."

Then there were the tall tales. "I guess I was just acting all the time, the truth was so plebeian, such a bore that I had to make something up. I made [up] one thing that I got caught on and my mother said, 'Your father was a consummate liar and you're just like him' . . . [t]hat was another slap." Diana secretly relished the comparison. She had so little of her father to hold on to; she confessed that almost all the stories she told her classmates about him came from fan magazines. Dr. Powdermaker let a few session details slip during her weekly phone call to Michael, and Michael was *furious*. How dare Diana complain about her home life! Harry reminded his wife the whole point of therapy was to let Diana be honest about her feelings, but he could tell what was on her mind: Robin. He and a friend made a suicide pact while away at school; Robin swallowed his sleeping pills, but the other boy panicked and ran for help. They pumped Robin's stomach and sent him to a Phoenix, Arizona, hospital to recover. Harry saw the same anguish in Michael's eyes and promised to speak with Dr. Powdermaker the next day. A few weeks later, saying she needed to be less with adults and more with girls her own age, Diana transferred to the "small, proper, exclusive" Garrison Forest School in Maryland for the 1932–33 term. (Dr. Powdermaker went on to write the critically acclaimed *The Intelligent Parents Manual* in 1940.)

She didn't see her father before she left, and only saw him once in all the previous years, a brief stop while he was in town. The tall, thin man who smelled like "peppermint" sat on the floor and smoked while he and Diana discussed art. A few minutes later he left with a kiss and remark of how beautiful she was, just like her Aunt Ethel. "She had a very engaging smile," said B, a close family friend unnamed in available records. "[S]he had a way of hopping and dancing a little. She was a remarkably well made child, lovely skin, sort of a mocha tinge . . . remarkably observant and she seemed to watch everyone closely."

Ivan Moffat, Iris Tree's son, said thirteen-year-old Diana was stunning. Lustrous dark hair, almost black eyes, "mulberry-colored lips" . . . her beauty intimidated him and she enjoyed flustering the shy Ivan by snuggling next to him or holding his hand. Their mothers "betrothed" them at birth and

Diana reminded him at every turn, constantly demanding compliments. Michael rolled her eyes at the impertinence. "If I am pushy, Mother," Diana replied, "it's your fault. Because Robin's pushy too." Ivan cringed recalling the afternoon Robin took him to the movies, pushing past everyone else on line. "I'm John Barrymore's son and I don't have to stand in line," he crowed at the ticket booth. Robin and Diana frequently went to the movies to see her father on the screen. During *A Bill of Divorcement* (1932), she watched his tenderness with Katharine Hepburn and thought, *Others may play his daughter but I'm the real thing.* It comforted her until three weeks shy of her fourteenth birthday, when Jack came to Garrison Forest.

Jack was not in a good place. He'd had a breakdown in May 1934, and he and Dolores separated that August after a failed attempt to save their marriage with an extended family cruise. After trips to the UK and Italy, he took a two-month health sabbatical in India, the last week of which he blew in a brothel. Now back in New York and recovered after a brief February 1935 hospital stay, he wanted to visit his daughter while still on the east coast. Michael agreed this time but with one condition: under no circumstances were they to leave the school grounds. She emphasized that last point with everyone, especially headmistresses Miss Nancy J. Offutt and Miss Jean Marshall.

Jack arrived, smartly clad in a grey flannel suit and tan coat. Diana shook her usual ennui and rushed into his gift-laden arms. He delighted everyone at tea before retreating to Diana's room for presents: a copper kettle, exotic jewelry, and a portable Victrola with records. Diana chattered about the recent school play as he put an Indian ballad on the turntable, then paused for a moment, listening to the singer's wistful voice. "They've saddled you with the Barrymore curse," he replied. "Pillows and false faces, like your father." At dinner he sat with the headmistresses, Diana, and two VIP friends: Alice Fox, daughter of *Toonerville Trolley* cartoonist Fontaine Fox, and Diana's roommate, "Pamela Gardiner," an older girl of good breeding whose mother Michael knew.

Pamela was a pseudonym for Audrey Gray (1918–84), a debutante of the 1936–37 season and the daughter of New York assistant district attorney Henry G. Gray. Her mother, the former Edith Deacon, was one of the three celebrated "Deacon sisters" of Boston—Audrey's aunts were the Dowager Duchess of Marlborough and Princess Radziwill. In her memoir, Diana describes Pam as "seventeen and always ready for fun." Audrey was seventeen. Her nickname was "Giddy."

Jack, the picture of charm and propriety, convinced Misses Offutt and Marshall that one little off-campus trip couldn't hurt. They relented and even allowed Diana and Jack (and Audrey) to go to Baltimore, usually reserved for alternate weekends. He would come back the next evening to pick up the girls.

Jack met Diana and Audrey with two friends, "Will," a drummer, and "Lou," a nightclub entertainer. Their first stop was a fancy restaurant where they dodged photographers and ordered cocktails. Diana hesitated, but Jack knew what she'd like: a Brandy Alexander. "It's exactly like a milkshake." She drank two with gusto before dinner was over. A soused Jack asked the girls over coffee where to go next. The movies! *Les Misérables* was playing at the Century and Fredric March was dreamy and could they please go? He roared with laughter and promised Diana March's autograph. Treepee amused him, a wobbly kid in borrowed high heels. He clearly thought differently of lovely blonde Audrey, necking with her through the whole movie while Diana stared blankly at the screen. It ended a half-hour before midnight curfew, but Jack wasn't ready to call it a night. He steered the party towards a club for a little music and a lot more brandy.

They rolled up to Garrison Forest at around one in the morning, Jack passed out, Audrey dozing on his shoulder. Diana scrubbed Audrey's lipstick off her father's face and asked the driver to take Daddy back to the hotel while she and her friend slipped quietly inside. The problem: Jack never told the driver where he was staying. Unable to rouse him, the girls had no choice but to let him sleep it off. The next morning, Miss Marshall brought him inside and poured black coffee into him until his head cleared enough to go home. Photos of their escapade made the papers, and Michael melted the phone telling both headmistresses exactly what she thought of them, exasperated at how easily they were played by her charismatic ex-husband. She ensured there would be no scandal, and Diana would transfer to a new school. Jack's "biographer" Alma Power-Waters spun it differently: "John visited [Diana] at a boarding school in Baltimore, and once took her and a party of school friends to a night club in New York," she wrote in 1941's *John Barrymore: The Legend and the Man*. "One can imagine the excitement of the young ladies in question, being the guests of John Barrymore, the handsomest man in the movies!"

In April, Jack was again hospitalized and spurned visitors, aside from his daughter and a new friend, college student Elaine Jacobs, whom he met during his earlier hospital stay. She requested an interview, he unexpectedly granted it, and the result was a meeting of kindred spirits. During one of Diana's visits, accompanied by Michael and Harry, he invited her and a friend to spend Easter break with him on the *Infanta*. Michael agreed if Harry came along as chaperone, and both men agreed—they liked each other, and both looked forward to the fishing in Bermuda. Jack would arrange everything. All they had to do was meet him down in Miami once he was discharged. Down in Florida, Jack greeted Harry, Diana, and Innes James[7]—about as different from Audrey Gray as one got—with $100 to spend on clothes for the trip. Not that they needed them: they were abandoned to sunbathe or ogle the cabin boy while "Barrymore, Doc [Dr. Kenneth Taylor, Jack's physician], and I would get up seven in the morning, get in a row boat and fish all day," as Tweed recalled. "The only time Barrymore saw Diana was a little while in the evening. He never talked about her on the boat with us."

A gregarious Jack—"more mettlesome," Tweed called it—appeared only once, after siphoning and ingesting a pint of engine coolant; outfoxing his doctor and a "dry" ship required ingenuity. A crew member was stationed at the engine room door, and back to fishing it was. Diana remembered Michael's odd reaction when she got home: "When I came back from that yacht trip she said, 'Did you have a nice trip?' I started to talk to her . . . [s]he didn't want to hear about it. You had a nice time—fine." The unspoken worry hung thick in the air. "She didn't want me alone with [Daddy]. She never did . . . she probably figured that if I got really close to that man. . . ."

Diana started that autumn at the Thomas School in Norwalk, Connecticut. Her father wrote her in mid-September in a sheepish state about money troubles, as evident in this excerpt from Gene Fowler's *Good Night Sweet Prince*:

Dearest Diana—
It's a long time since I have seen or heard from you, although I suppose you know that some weeks ago I tried my best to see you—or didn't you know?
You probably know I have been having some "domestic trouble" . . . even all through this lean period, I have done my best to see that you should be well provided for . . . [d]on't you think that in view of *that* and of the fact that it is *I* who now need some consideration, that you would do without any further payment from me, at least until I can get to work again and begin to earn once more?
As you can imagine I have felt very reluctant to write you in this fashion . . . I hope you will understand the spirit of this letter, my dear baby, my own dear funny thing, and that you will—as they say in the classics—"drop me a little line," saying that *do*. This will mean a *great deal* to me, and I know damn well this is all I need to say to you.
All my love—fuzzy dear one.
Daddy

---

7. Also aboard was college student Marion Kelly; why (and with whom) is unclear.

According to Fowler, "[n]o reply to this appeal ever reached her father."

Life was pleasant but unremarkable for Diana until December 1935, when locals and journalists alike packed Rowayton First Methodist Church to see Diana's stage debut as a Wise Man in the annual Christmas play. She, Jane Shaw, and Carol Case followed the star to Bethlehem, hyperbolic reports confirming Diana "display[ed] much of the ability that has made her family name internationally famous." She looked forward to celebrating Christmas at home and wondered if there would be guests like last year, when Aunt Ethel joined them for Christmas Eve dinner and midnight Mass. Michael and Ethel were cordial but distant: Michael was still angry over *Clair de Lune*, Ethel over Michael's treatment of her brother during the divorce. Ethel was so regal Diana curtsied when she welcomed her. There were martinis before dinner, wine during, and brandy after. Ethel stumbled and fell as they readied for Mass, and Michael asked Robin to stay behind and help her settle into the guest room for the night. Robin, who didn't want to go to church anyway, was elated, but Diana worried about her aunt and asked her mother on the way to St. Patrick's if Aunt Ethel was sick. No, she replied. It was only a "Barrymore headache." Ethel hid her drinking problem better than her younger brother, but it surfaced publicly in 1931 when she staggered and flubbed her lines during the Denver opening of *The School for Scandal*. Actress and friend Ruth Gordon stumbled on her hidden brandy stash when Ethel stayed with her in 1933, but she kept mum out of respect. Diana barely spoke with her aunt that night, and she was gone by Christmas morning.

In September 1937, Michael allowed Diana to travel abroad alone for the first time. Well, not completely alone; she went with a chaperone, and Michael joined them a bit later. Diana and "Fanquie" sailed on the *Ile de France* and checked into Vienna's historic Hotel Imperial, "the last word in luxury," with its magnificent red velvet drapes, marble foyer, and gilded wrought iron.

Robin lived in Vienna and Diana popped in to see him. "His place was lovely. A large room filled with books and papers, facing one of the great cathedrals." After, she and Fanquie had lunch at the Hotel Imperial's sidewalk restaurant, "the chic place to eat." Diana was struck as the populace walked by in worn clothing, hungry, looking "as if they wished us all in hell for eating beautiful meals in front of them . . . [w]e must have looked like the definition of capitalism to them." One man not much older than Diana stopped and hurled insults "about rich people gorging themselves" until the police led him away. "I felt sorry for him," she said later. "He was so young and believed so passionately."

Travels took them next to Mondsee, an upper Austrian lakeside town home to Mondsee Abbey (now the Basilica of St. Michael, famous for the wedding scene in 1965's *The Sound of Music*). Diana claimed the picturesque village was where she met Fritz, "[a] tall dark young man in lederhosen and green socks," with whom she had her first kiss. "It was very nice . . . [w]e got back to the pensione and said a tender '*Gute Nacht, Liebchen*.' I felt wonderful. This was love!"

Michael arrived later that week and they readied for their next stop, Salzburg. Diana, mentally dressed in her wedding dirndl, dragged Fritz to meet her mother. Everyone was very polite and made small talk—as much as possible, since Fritz spoke no English and Diana's German was limited to menu items—until, kissing Michael's hand, he made his exit. Michael smiled. "He looks like an anteater," she said. *Auf Wiedersehen*, Fritz.

Being almost sixteen, she was ready for the joys of adolescence, which, as far as Michael was concerned, consisted only of what befitted a lady: no lipstick, no heels, and her own tasteful velvet dresses, retailored to fit. Diana dreaded the unfashionable castoffs and took matters into her own hands when she scored an invite to the annual Groton–St. Mark's holiday dance, thrown by the two poshest boys' schools in Connecticut. (They went co-ed in the 1970s.) She packed her new dress, a prim pink taffeta Michael bought at Henri Bendel, and exchanged it for a friend's backless, low-cut number with heels to match. Add a dab of rouge and lipstick, and the entire school was aroused. The sweating headmaster sent her to change, the news of which reached home before Diana did. Diana's mouth was a defiant line as her mother raged over the phone. This was her declaration of independence, and the dress was only the beginning. She informed Michael that, despite enjoying the horseback riding, she was done at Fermata and would be enrolling at the American Academy of Dramatic Art in New York. All right, said Michael, but it would be as Diana Blyth. If she wanted to be an actress, it would be on her own merits, not a famous name. Also: her society debut. *Not* up for debate.

Diana spent summer 1938 in the south of France boarding with the Comtesse Germaine de Guitaut. The Comtesse struggled financially since her husband Philippe's death in 1932 and opened her seaside home to well-connected society to support her four children. "I'm having a good time here as it's the season and Madame Guitaut's friends are so charming . . . a marvelous life—better time than at Monte Carlo." Based on Diana's description of a "rose and white" villa, La Baule historian Melanie Tartoué believes it may be Villa Ker Souveraine in Pornichet, known as the "Rose Villa," built in 1925 in the Italian neoclassical style and declared a historic monument in 2002. With Diana was Mlle. Eloise de Veitelle, a companion so skittish Diana nicknamed her "Bunny." The schoolmarmish de Veitelle, a private tutor from the Bronx, spoke fluent French and would serve as chaperone while her charge soaked up sunshine and culture. Diana met others in Guitaut's circle, like the Comtesse de la Peyrouse-Vaucresson, the mayor's wife, and a boy she referred to as "Count Edouard," who became her summer boyfriend. They spent a lot of time together, including a picnic where they both drank too much wine and Diana rode her bike into traffic, injuring her ankle. At the station, Bunny untangled the young lovers so that she and Diana could board the train to Leonard and Yvonne's. Who he was exactly is unclear; she was linked with Gianni Agnelli of the Fiat family, called the "Kennedys of Italy," but in her personal files puts that in 1937; she was photographed on the beach with Prince Guido Pignatelli di Monticalvo, who had a proclivity for socialites, but that happened in Monte Carlo.

The Navellos were from Nice, in southeastern France, and emigrated to the United States when Yvonne was a teenager. They settled in Boston, where the artistically gifted Yvonne attended the Boston Museum School, and frequented New York and Rhode Island, where she crossed paths with Leonard Jr. They married in Philadelphia in August of 1938, and by Diana's visit, lived on Quai d'Orleans in Paris.

After hugs and greetings, the pregnant Yvonne stayed behind so brother and sister could tour the museums and stroll the Latin Quarter. They chose the Edward Molyneux salon for Diana's debutante gown, the tastefully understated British *styliste* a favorite of Greta Garbo, Marlene Dietrich, and Michael herself, who approved—as long as they stuck to her design parameters, of course. Cobina Jr. came to visit, and Diana couldn't wait to tell her how she'd met handsome actor Jean-Pierre Aumont at a function. He'd even escorted her home! Cobina, who just left London, had news of her own: she was involved with the dashing Prince Philip, the future Duke of Edinburgh.

The advancing threat of war curtailed their trip, and they readied to leave France. Back at the Hotel Pierre, buzz: Bruce Cabot and Errol Flynn were staying there. Diana wrote that she waited outside their room, "like any girl waiting who stands on a corner to be picked up," until Flynn came out. If Diana's version is to be believed—and a good rule of thumb with Diana, according to everyone who knew her, was to take only about 50 percent of what she said at face value—he invited her into the room and introduced her to Cabot; they she was Diana Barrymore, and she without a doubt belonged on the big screen. She said she wasn't interested.

Edouard proposed marriage and Diana accepted. A tearful, lovesick Edouard promised he would come to America as quickly as possible. Diana promised to write every day until he arrived. Their romance for the ages lasted until October.

CHAPTER 4

PERSONALITY DEB OF 1938

SUB-DEB DIANA BLYTH WAS A *LOT*. MOM AND DAD COMBINED TO PRODUCE what the columns called an "electrical nymph" with "windblown hair, sparkling brown eyes and an aura of enchantment," if "nymph" meant loud, impulsive, and exhausting. "Exaggerated as the early silent movie heroines," sniffed British journalist C. V. R. Thompson after watching her run back and forth between chairs in a breakneck game of backgammon—against herself. She drank her soup through a straw (or ladled it directly into her mouth from the tureen), slapped or dumped ice water on her friends for fun, fired cap guns or blew police whistles to create chaos. "Wasn't here also an audience?"

She made the "magnificent discovery" of boys, and if six beaus asked her to dinner, she showed up with all of them. Most society boys, like future actor Montgomery Clift, thought her tolerable in small doses. Not tobacco heir Anthony Drexel Duke. He met Diana through mutual friend Julian Gerard and, amazingly, wasn't put off by her antics. He became Diana's first "real" boyfriend, accompanying her to the Stork Club and those functions at which, as a debutante-in-training, she was expected. She didn't hide her scorn. "Society's all right," Diana said, "if you're only interested in marrying a rich husband. Otherwise it's deadly." Dirt-dishing phone calls, boozy brunches, and half-hearted stabs at philanthropy, which Brenda Frazier famously called "disgusting." Peter Arno, years before his revolutionary cartooning at the *New Yorker*, called the debs "vain little girls with more alcohol in their brains than common sense." A society debut wasn't like a sweet sixteen party; one eased into it, assisting—"pouring"—at other girls' debuts, attending various charity events like the Velvet Ball and Debutante Cotillion, held three days before Halloween 1938 to benefit the New York Infirmary for Women and Children. Arno portrayed the Sun King in silver and gold, and future Renaissance man and sartorialist Lucius Beebe acted as emcee. Society columnist Nancy Randolph joked the modern dance steps at the Brenda Frazier-chaired fete would've had Ward McAllister—*the* Mrs. Astor's right-hand man and official gatekeeper to the Four Hundred—"revolving in his grave."

It was around that time Diana first publicly announced her intentions to study acting, something everyone wondered about since she was an infant in Jack's arms. Theatrical producer, director, and Tony Award founder Brock Pemberton pounced on her for her father's upcoming stage project, *My Dear Children,* but she declined. She did accept an invitation to Paramount Studios in Astoria, where M-G-M producer David O. Selznick was holding the hottest leading lady search since *Gentlemen Prefer Blondes'* Lorelei Lee a decade before. Diana joined scores of young hopefuls descending on Queens, New York, to test for Scarlett O'Hara. She read with actor Richard Carlson as her Ashley Wilkes, but neither made it to *Gone with the Wind* callbacks.

Diana formally entered society at the River Club on December 3, 1938, sharing her "coming out" with her cousin Eleanor vom Rath, related through the Mays on her mother's side. "[She] is a very nice, sweet, fairly attractive girl. She isn't attractive enough to completely take the light away from me," Diana wrote in a letter home from La Baule that summer, "and she is attractive enough to make a very decorative picture at the receiving [*sic*] line. That is all very blunt—but true." The warmly bedecked ballroom (for young people) and dining room (for older friends and family) featured yellow snapdragons and yellow and brown chrysanthemums. Cedar trees beckoned from the corners. Both girls wore traditional white, Diana's gown off-the-shoulder with "a hooped skirt and Marie Antoinette fichu."[8] Tony Duke, Innes James, and cousin John Drew Colt shared her VIP table, and Mrs. Cornelius Vanderbilt, Harry's escort for the evening, said Diana was the spitting image of Michael at her own debut. At dinner, Tony toasted her as "the most beautiful, the most talented, the most exciting debutante of 1938!" Diana laughed about this later: "[L]ike a young lawyer trying to save his client from the chair, making an inspiring plea to the jury." Hearst columnist Maury Paul, who as "Cholly Knickerbocker" reported on what he coined "café society," crowned her that year's "Personality Deb." As lovely as it was, the people she longed for most were absent: Michael still in Palm Springs, Florida recovering from a canoeing injury, Robin in Paris, Daddy in Hollywood . . . even Leonard was away in London. She pushed it out of her mind and prepared for Brenda Frazier's debut, likely the event of the year.

Diana left for Palm Beach with twin goals: to visit Mummy and transform into a bronzed goddess for Brenda's party. She broiled herself for hours each day and when some idiot kicked sand in her tanning oil she jumped up to give

---

8. Small lacy shawl.

them a piece of her mind. The idiot was incredibly apologetic—and incredibly handsome. Diana recognized Errol Flynn immediately and knew how much he admired her father. She asked about actress Lili Damita, Errol's wife and one of Robin's good friends, and before long their chance meeting turned into three weeks together on the beach—and in the bar. Errol loved her earthiness, suggested darker lipstick and heavier eye makeup to accentuate it. The two drew looks running in from the beach for a drink, laughing raucously, bathing suits wet and clinging. The two shared a sensuality that Diana (or perhaps ghostwriter Gerold Frank) termed "vitality"; she insisted Errol treated her like a sister, yet later: "You're a society girl, but by God, you're alive! You've got blood in your veins." Sex was coded this way often throughout her memoirs.

When she wasn't with Errol, she accompanied Michael to sedate brunches with radio pioneer Atwater Kent and his wife or Hope Diamond-owning heiress Evelyn Walsh Mclean. Cobina Wright Sr. was at one and pulled Diana aside. People were talking, she said, and she would do well to curb her alcohol intake. She hugged the older woman and laughed. Yes, she knew her family history, but Michael taught her to take a teaspoon of olive oil beforehand so cocktails wouldn't hit as hard—and hadn't Michael joked how she needed a martini or two to endure the get-togethers at the Sun & Surf Beach Club? It was all in fun, and soon they'd be headed back to New York and to her beloved Tony.

Anthony Drexel Duke was the younger son of Angier Buchanan Duke, whose family founded the American Tobacco Company, and Cordelia Drexel Biddle, descendant of the prominent Philadelphia Biddles and banking Drexels, who founded Drexel University. Tony was smart and affable and adored being on the water in Princeton crew or sailing between semesters. Diana got on well with his family and friends, especially his mother and older brother Angier, and spent countless weekends at the family home in Old Westbury on Long Island, New York. "Tony is marvelous," she wrote Michael. He kept her impetuousness in check. "I think of his sweetness and kindness and then all temptation disappears." Michael approved, as did Cordelia. "[Tony] loves you very much, and Cordelia told me that you made him very happy . . . she is the most kind and understanding woman in the whole world." Diana's first sexual experience was with Tony, during a winter vacation at Angier's home in Tuxedo Park, New York. "Tony was to be my husband," she wrote, and Michael always said sex was off the table unless engagement was imminent. It wasn't quite perfect: the two were interrupted, Tony fleeing out the window, his clothes thrown to him by Diana's friend, actress Joan Wetmore.

That Christmas she attended Brenda's debut with a blue fox cape on one arm and Tony on the other. She told everyone they'd be engaged by spring.

"Dark, pert Diana Blythe, John Barrymore's daughter," observed columnist Mary van Rensselaer Thayer, "wiggles the most distracting rhumba in New York." But by April, their relationship was over. Tongues wagged about family disapproval, which a deeply hurt Diana blamed on pearl-clutching over Palm Beach rumors and pressure for Tony to choose a more profitable match.

Tony's son, Washington Duke, remembered his father speaking fondly of the Barrymores. Tony just wasn't as deeply in love with Diana as she was with him, he thought. The Dukes, especially Cordelia, were "progressive," unconcerned with gossip. "Country club life had lost its allure," he wrote in his 2007 memoir, *Uncharted Course*, which showed a young man acutely aware of the socioeconomic divide. Ed Sullivan noted in a May 1937 column that Tony planned to "devote all of his fortune to social uplift of the poor," and that year Tony founded Boys' Harbor, a sleepaway camp for inner-city youth. (It expanded in the 1960s to a year-round, coed program, merging with Supportive Children's Advocacy in 2019 to form the youth services organization SCAN-Harbor.) He felt privilege was pointless if not shared with those less fortunate, and it drove a wedge between him and some of his society friends, in particular a girl he called "Catherine." She couldn't understand choosing philanthropy over fun and questioned his love for her. "I didn't know if I loved her. I liked kissing her. But I must've loved camp more," he admitted. It wasn't until he met Alice Rutgers that he thought seriously about romance. Diana took the breakup hard and wrote her mother for guidance. "[L]ast night, when all those people were at dinner, a tereffic [sic] loneliness for Tony came over me," she wrote. "[A]ll this unhappiness I'm going through will make me what is called 'a woman who has lived'— concerning I'm only 18 I think I've had my share of experience for awhile." Leonard Jr.'s wife Yvonne blamed Michael in part for the breakup. "Michael was always against Diana's decisions. Diana was engaged to Tony Duke . . . she was against it. 'No, no, you're a Barrymore,' she told Diana. 'You must never forget who you are [and] you'll never be able to act if you take upon the life of a Mrs. Tony Duke.' And when Diana acted, Michael would sort of bungle that, telling her that she belonged to society." Michael's advice this time was to forget Tony and go to the upcoming Princeton dance with debonair undergrad Francis Kellogg, and soon Fran edged out other society boys like "Jimmie" Clark or "Hobie" Hare Cook for her affections. He liked sailing, too.

Diana kicked off 1939 with a show-stopping entrance at the premiere of *The Importance of Being Earnest*. She and Robin attended the Broadway revival's January 12th opening night to see his friend, actress Estelle Winwood, starring opposite Clifton Webb. She was gorgeous in powder blue and gardenias, and Robin cut a figure handsome enough to make the National Association of Merchant Tailors' list of "America's 20 Best-Dressed Men." She spent the first half of the year balancing classes at the American Academy of Dramatic Art with obligations like judging the "Little Sisters Beauty Contest" for the Boys' Club, chairing the Russian Easter Ball committee, and opening the Brazilian Pavilion at the World's Fair. Fran threw a June 12th luncheon at the Stork Club to celebrate Diana's entry into summer stock. Dressed in black with summery seashell jewelry, she welcomed guests and chatted excitedly about Ogunquit, Maine; her first play, *You Can't Take it With You*, opened on June 28th. Walter Winchell called the young couple an "excitem," the column running three days after Tony Duke and Alice Rutgers's engagement notices. "That [Duke] has picked a bride of equal, if not greater, ancestral background must be a source of satisfaction to his family and friends," wrote columnist Nancy Randolph.

A swimsuit-clad Diana smiled awkwardly from the July 31st cover of *Life* magazine, a cute teenager with a slight overbite kneeling in the Ogunquit sand. She rented a small cottage with her governess and papillon Moka, and when not in rehearsals she enjoyed the beach—though it couldn't compare to European resorts. The short interview ran opposite a full-page photo of Aunt Ethel made up for *Whiteoaks*. She had her stepfather to thank for being featured at all: "Mother said, 'Be very very careful . . . they're just going to use the name of Barrymore and they're not going to think of you as an actress.' I think Harry talked her into it. I said, 'It's very good publicity for the theatre, Mummy.'" Critics liked her in *The Philadelphia Story*, agreeing with the *Boston Globe:* "A subdued, winsome Tracy Lord—charming, provocative and impulsive." In August, her eyes "inflamed from artificial eyelashes," she played Juliet to actor William Haversham's son Philip as Romeo, a role she wanted to play on Broadway while young and "not a middle-aged actress of 45 or so." (A dig at Norma Shearer, perhaps, who was in her mid-thirties when she played the role for M-G-M.)[9] She kept her program, circled her name, and wrote "this is me!!!!" in tiny, curled letters. "She IS theater," wrote the *Buffalo Evening News*. The most effusive praise of the season came from Diana herself, who proclaimed, "I am simply marvelous!" while zipping around town on her scooter.

Diana's photo was in newspapers and magazines before, but regional to New York or Rhode Island. *Life*'s circulation was over a million copies by March 1937, bringing nationwide attention to anyone featured, like fellow

---

9. Leslie Howard (Romeo) was in his early forties, and Jack (Mercutio) in his early fifties. Teenaged love indeed!

deb Brenda Frazier in November 1938. Jack and Michael were at their physical and creative zeniths when Diana was born, a bittersweet yardstick by
which Diana grew up being closely measured, especially by herself. Not that
beauty standards were easily achievable for any girl: you must be attractive,
but not bland; natural, but not plain; distinctive, but not different. Gloria
Vanderbilt was described as "pudgy, plain and pug-nosed" only a few years
before her debut, while Brenda Frazier—already anorexic and bulimic by
age 14—possessed a "round, saucy-lipped" face.

   "When I'd see a pretty girl in a café, I used to get excited and say, 'There's
a girl I'd like to take a picture of,'" said New York commercial photographer
Arthur O' Neill in 1937. The higher each hopeful scored on his points system—each facial feature rated on if it would "take well"—the better their
chances of landing a toothpaste ad or magazine cover. Score low, and, well,
"[they] photograph looking like Donald Duck."

   Diana's weight was also under scrutiny. "The ideal figure," advised *Life*
in an August 1938 article, "must have a round, high bosom, a slim but not
wasp-like waist, and gently rounded hips." They illustrated their point with
twenty-year-old June Cox, almost 5 foot 7 inches and 124 pounds, similar
to Brenda Frazier, 5 foot 6 inches and 116 pounds at the time of her *Life*
cover. Opinions varied on Diana, whose weight fluctuated since childhood.
"[N]either too slim or too ample," read one article, "she doesn't diet, easts
what she likes and is fond of outdoor sports." Another thought she was
"scrawny." Ed Sullivan, the charmer, remarked "a diet would help . . . she'd
be gorgeous with ten pounds off her bustle."

   That fall, she joined the road production of Broadway's hit revival *Outward Bound.* Six weeks earlier, actor-turned-star-making producer William
A. Brady directly contacted Diana with an offer to read, a "good start" with
a touring company of which Michael approved. It was for Ann, one of the
suicidal lovers doomed to limbo, played by Helen Chandler during the New
York run (and in the 1930 film version). She bought and devoured the play
but, not wanting to appear desperate, pretended she hadn't prepared at
all, and the formidable Brady upbraided her. "Young lady, people very big
in the theatre study before they read. When they get really big, when they
are stars, they are not asked to . . . [y]ou are an unknown quantity. Nobody
knows what you could do." Diana dropped the charade and got the part,
replacing Chandler, who declined to tour. Chandler's husband, Bramwell
Fletcher, the play's Mr. Prior, also chose not to tour, disappointing Diana;
he supported Jack in *Svengali* (Warner Bros., 1931) and she enjoyed the idea
of working with someone who costarred with her father. Laurette Taylor
and Florence Reed reprised their roles, and Diana's friend Poopsie, fellow

society kid Harry Ellerbe, took over the role of Mr. Prior. It was her first Equity contract, $150 a week. "I wanted to make good. I took the theatre seriously . . . [I] wrote [a] study of [the] girl, why she killed [her]self . . . I really worked at it. I was terrified the night of the opening. This was the first time a professional audience was going to see me . . . I sweated right through the [dress] shields."

Philadelphia cheered the return of a Barrymore to the Locust Street Theatre on October 9, 1939. "Diana Barrymore as the pathetic 'half-way' Ann holds up the high tradition of the famous Drew-Barrymore family," wrote the *Evening Sun*. "Genuinely affecting," said the *Philadelphia Inquirer*. "When I heard that applause," wrote Diana, "I said, *I want to hear this the rest of my life*. There's no sound like it in all the world." On to Boston, where Michael chided her for staying at the Ritz: "'Where are the actors staying?' I said, those who can afford it are staying at the Touraine. She said, 'Pack your bags and go to the Touraine—it's a theatrical hotel. Go and be with your fellow actors.'" The *Boston Globe* said Diana "[held] her own against the veteran players . . . heartbreakingly dramatic." They played the Harris Theater in Chicago at the end of November, where Jack was in his hit farce *My Dear Children* right next door at the Selwyn. Written by screenwriters Jerry Horwin and Catherine Turney and directed by the great Otto Preminger, *My Dear Children*—the title a nod to King Lear—featured Jack as Allan Manville, an aging former matinee idol shocked by the sudden Christmas Eve appearance of three previously unknown daughters. He attempts to make up for lost time by "fixing" their problems, particularly for youngest daughter Cordelia, "the only one of them to inherit her father's electric personality." The show's New York opening sold out ten months in advance, thanks to press coverage of Jack's behavior during the pre-Broadway tour. Actress Dorothy McGuire (*A Tree Grows in Brooklyn*, *Gentleman's Agreement*) was dismayed watching a man she admired "make a fool of himself" and left before Broadway, replaced by Patricia Waters. Preminger thought Jack "beneath human dignity" some nights. "He has such a wonderful sense of humor," said Diana of her father. "*My Dear Children* is a good time. It may even be a good play," said Jack in his preface to the print edition. "If the reader of the printed script will imagine he is a person enjoying himself and not picturing himself a critic he may find all the fun in it that I have found." Jack met her at the Illinois Central Railroad, tired but bursting with pride. "She's the best thing I ever produced," he boasted while flashbulbs popped.

"We went to my apartment first, then he took me to dinner at Ricardo's," Diana wrote. "Ricardo was a great friend of his, a sculptor and painter who worshipped him and really tried to take care of him, watering his drinks . . .

[b]efore we left my apartment, he said, 'would you like to ask Laurette to join us?'

"'No, I certainly would not.'

"He raised an eyebrow. 'Ooooooh, has she been behaving badly?'"

Laurette Taylor's "illness" forced *Outward Bound* to postpone its November 27th opening night; a lifelong alcoholic, she'd fallen and injured herself while drunk.

The next day at his "modest, rented" house, he teased her about the "two charming men" touring with *My Dear Children*. "'[D]o you like them tall, dark and handsome?' I laughed. 'I like them if they've got pants.' I was 18, and flip." Jack chuckled but reminded her the importance of "discipline, discipline, discipline." After all, he said, "Look what happened to me." Diana called her mother and to her surprise, found her receptive to hearing about Jack. She mentioned his jaw surgery due to an impacted wisdom tooth. "Did it give him pain?" she asked, concerned. Michael laughed when Diana relayed some of his comments. "How typically Jack." Marvel of marvels, just before they hung up: "Give him my love . . . I'm glad you two got along."

Outward Bound opened that Wednesday matinee instead, and Jack closed his show that day to attend. "I gave my best performance . . . [b]ecause he was there I was never so good." Afterwards, in her dressing room, he had tears in his eyes. "Oh, my God, Treepee, you have it. Now all you must do is work like a[n] S.O.B." Her reward was *My Dear Children* for an audience of one: a special performance "In Honor of Diana Barrymore."

Afterwards Jack took his daughter out to his favorite Windy City watering hole, Harry's New York Bar. It was the kind of place he loved, noisy and boisterous, with a bouncy cabaret. One of the dancers, twenty-two-year-old Winnie Hoveler, gamboled over and perched in his lap. She was Jack's "constant friend and companion" in Chicago, one he stopped by to see nightly. Diana's stomach knotted watching the blonde kiss and pet her father and she stood, adjusting her furs. Best to leave before this turned into another Audrey Gray situation. Jack pushed Diana back into her chair, one arm still around Winnie. "You-will-leave-when-your-father-tells-you-to-leave." Rarely had the Barrymore glare been so terrible. But shortly after, according to Diana's memoir, he took her to a more suitable nightclub and apologized, "almost like a little boy."

Jack privately enjoyed Diana's reactions to his outbursts. Critic Ashton Stevens went to dinner one night in Chicago with Diana, Laurette Taylor, and Jack, who told an old chestnut about teetering on the tenth story cornice of a hotel room in order to sneak in a sweetheart's window. Stevens heard the story before, the hotel and sweetheart changing over the years, but like all good yarns, the listeners' faces were the payoff. Jack thought the yarns of his "wastrel youth" might reset Diana's "infantile worldview"; after seeing his daughter act, he quipped to critic Ashton Stevens, "he thought her more realistic on stage than off."

Robin had a surprise for Diana when she got home. *Greta Garbo* was coming to tea and she was invited of course and she needed to get there a half-hour early and help Rene set up and isn't it divine?! His good friends Gaylord Hauser, the health and diet "nutrician," and his partner, producer Frey Brown, chatted Robin up to Garbo, and she wanted to meet the "nice young man in New York who was a gentleman." Diana got there at 5 p.m. and plated hors d'oeuvres with Rene, Robin's butler who "looked like everyone's idea of Arsene Lupin." Just before 5:30, Garbo arrived with Hauser and Brown.

"I saw a woman in a brown coat and [Vietnamese-style] hat, with black shoes and black stockings, and she came in like a frightened doe . . . she rushed upstairs [for] at least 15 minutes—seemed as if she had to do something extraordinary to pull herself together in order to meet strangers. She had a page boy bob, long, no makeup, except her eyes—mascara and eyebrows. The eye was unbelievable . . . Robin nearly made a court curtsy. I said, 'how do you do, Miss Garbo,' and I didn't say one more word the entire afternoon . . . [a]ll I could do was look at her." Garbo made the rounds in Manhattan, and everyone was smitten, even Fefe's Monte Carlo, where they allowed her into the main room in street clothes—usually banned. She left for Florida on the night of February 3, 1940.

Diana began 1940 back at the Academy. Her nineteenth birthday at the Monte Carlo was "hilarious"—the cake was an icing-covered hatbox filled with "matchboxes that buzzed, cigarettes [that] squeaked, bottomless spoons." March and April had her on the road with the Resident Theatre as the lead in *There's Always Juliet*, then her second summer season in Ogunquit, "a little quieter, a little more sure of herself." Michael, whose memoir *Who Tells Me True* was published by Scribner's in May and declared both "readable" and "pretentious" by the *New York Times*, visited that summer and "consented to make a one-week appearance in 'Amphitryon.'" Leonard also came up and worked at the apprentice theater while Yvonne, now a student at the prestigious Art Students League in New York, painted at Goose Rocks Beach in nearby Kennebunkport. She wrote Fran that her favorite production was *The Greeks Had a Word for Them*, her "tough" character refreshing "after those sweet ingénues I play." Diana's letters to Fran were warm and funny. The two remained close friends after their romance ended, and Diana enjoyed teasing him about other prospects: "Anything crawl out of an oil well?"' When he wrote her about Fernanda Wanamaker Munn, whom he would eventually marry in 1942, she turned wistful. "I shall always love you in my own way," she wrote, admitting she could've been nicer and more patient during their time together. "I respect you for being such a fine person and such a gentleman . . . [d]on't ever lose that old world charm." Later she wrote that Kellogg's parents wanted her as a daughter-in-law, and Michael pushed for the marriage, "but I couldn't do it. I adored him but I wasn't in love with him."

In January 1940, *My Dear Children* reached Broadway, and Manhattanites awaited with perverse delight. Seventeen years after Jack left, most knew him not from *Hamlet* or *The Jest* but from his belching, snorting caricature on Rudy Vallee's radio show. They gleefully followed coverage of the "Caliban-Ariel" drama, Jack's shameless cross-country pursuit of twenty-four-year-old Elaine Barrie (née Jacobs), by now his on-again, off-again fourth wife. He arrived from Detroit with Patricia Waters, Portia in the play and the daughter of its producer, Captain Pierce Power-Waters. (His wife, Alma, was Jack's "authorized" biographer.) Backstage he joked about he and Elaine's pending divorce—given ice to cool his throat between acts, he quipped, "I haven't experienced such a chill since Elaine left"—but in truth he missed her terribly. "Hope springs eternal in the human heart," he mused to reporters. He wanted to reconcile. Not if Diana could help it.

She and Doris Dudley met for lunch the day before opening and brainstormed how to keep Elaine away from Dad. Jack had also wanted Diana as one of Manville's daughters—"[t]wo Barrymores in one play should be a knockout"—but Doris got the job instead, replacing Elaine in Omaha after another lovers' spat. Both ladies felt she'd worm her way back into the play. "I'm in the peculiar position of trying to fight sex with talent," Doris said. "You got to hand it to her . . . she's got guts—she'll stop at nothing."

The glitterati of Hollywood and New York shoehorned themselves into the Belasco Theater, wondering if they'd get the same liquor-soaked Great Profile as Chicago. Only one person declined. "I can't bear to see Jack debase himself," Michael told Diana. "You go . . . I can't." Diana did, in black velvet and diamonds, along with Robin, her cousin Jack Colt, and several friends. The plan: surround John backstage as soon as the curtain rang down, escort him to the Monte Carlo, then finish the evening with a late supper at Robin's apartment.

The standing-room-only crowd welcomed him with a forty-five-second ovation. "The theatre is a strange cruel depressing place really, like a shellaced [*sic*] and painted harlot with a face of brass," Jack once wrote Michael. "The older one gets in it instead of being enriched one is impoverished. . . . I must make enough money at it or movies to leave it before I get old—There really is something about it my beloved that goes awfully against my grain and makes me unhappy."

The audience howled with laughter as critics wept. "Hamlet comes home a clown," Burns Mantle famously observed. "[Y]ou who have tears to shed over the loss of the American theatre's one-time leader may prepare to shed them." Arthur Pollock felt "Mr. Barrymore ceased to be an artist of any kind long ago," but when Allan Manville turned to his own portrait and recited Hamlet's "To be or not to be" soliloquy, the theatre became quiet as a chapel . . . then the spell broke and he resumed "thumbing his Grecian profile" at the world. Harold Cohen found the silver lining: "at 58, the star looks 45 and acts 30." *Life* magazine's impression of him was "that of a fine virtuoso burlesquing his own incomparable art."

Elaine, who was indeed in the audience, strongly disagreed. While some joked the former matinee idol suffered "stenographer's spread," to her, Jack looked "like Death itself," gaunt, exhausted. There was no way in hell she was leaving without checking in on him.

Laughter spilled from Jack's dressing room, packed with well-wishers properly vetted by the Anti-Ariel League (Diana Barrymore, President). Lucius Beebe noticed Elaine headed towards them in a low-cut gold lamé-and-mesh evening gown topped with red fox furs. "She's dressed for battle," he muttered to Diana. "Watch out!" "If it comes to blows, it will come to blows," she muttered back. "I'm willing to fight it out with her." Elaine approached the doorway. "Nobody wants you here, Miss Jacobs," Diana growled. She went inside and slammed the door. Elaine pounded repeatedly, then jammed her foot in the door when Diana cracked it. "Please allow your father to dismiss me, my dear," she said. "It's your father's decision." Jack, sipping his drink, perked up at Elaine's voice. "Treepee," he said, "perhaps we should permit her to come in and state her business." Elaine swept in and shut the door. Out in the hall, Diana crumpled to the floor and wailed. "I can't stand it anymore . . . this is the end!" Jack couldn't stand it when she acted like this. "Stop trying to be a Barrymore!" he'd snap.

Voices rose. Elaine began sobbing. Diana barged back in, emerging with "the satisfied smile of a tiger which has just eaten a missionary." Once the shouting was over, however, a tenderness crept back in. "One would've never thought we had such a bitter breakup," Elaine remembered. The old chemistry reignited. Jack invited her to dine with them at the Monte Carlo and refused her protests that she was unwelcome: "Goddam[n] it, I'm asking you . . . [t]hey'll try to keep us apart, but I'll expect you, baby. We have to have a long talk." Diana and her entourage swept Jack from the room as columnist (and C. V. R. Thompson's wife) Dixie Tighe of the *New York Post* sent Elaine to the Stork Club as a decoy.

The Monte Carlo reception was a who's who: the Jack Warners, editor and critic George Jean Nathan, Pulitzer Prize-winning journalist (and Algonquin Round Tabler) Herbert Bayard Swope, and Tyrone Power, now an A-list actor with his new bride, a French actress named Annabella. Diana confidently led Jack to their fortress of prearranged seating, then screamed: Elaine, not fooled for a moment, waited for them at the table across from theirs. She hugged Jack tight and kissed his cheeks while Diana threatened bodily harm to anyone with a camera who dared document it. Conversation quieted and the crowd edged as closely as they dared. Elaine nestled against Jack, begging him for just "twenty-four hours of bliss." He fiddled with his scotch and soda in reply but did not send Elaine away. Diana huffed her way to the dance floor, scowled, pouted, swore, shot daggers at Elaine, and returned to the table slightly more controlled. "Miss Jacobs: you will do us all a favor if you get lost. Just go away." Diana glared at her father, who turned to Elaine. "This is like the gentle rain from heaven," he said softly. Elaine took his arm. Diana transformed into the Miss Newport her father loathed. "We are Barrymores." Ice crackled in her voice. "You have nothing in common with us. Please leave." Elaine looked startled. Jack, "confused and torn," turned to Elaine for aid. "Maybe so," said Elaine, "but I know him better than any other Barrymore. I'm staying." Diana drew herself up grandly and balled her fists. "Daddy, either this woman leaves or I do." Jack thought for a moment. The air between them trembled. "Well, you leave," he told Diana, quietly, blandly. "Goodnight, Treepee." Diana fought back tears. "Very well," she said. "I am not responsible for anything that happens now." Jack and Elaine canoodled after Diana's exit, then went to Elaine's room at the Navarro to consummate their reunion (and void the divorce decree).

As her father's "self-appointed protector" Diana stayed neutral in public. "Everybody knows what happened," she told reporters. "Let them form their own opinion." Privately, she called her mother and Doris to "21" for a damage control lunch. Daddy hadn't called and now was in the hospital with a "vitamin deficiency"—surely that woman wasn't taking proper care of him! Maybe Uncle Lionel and Aunt Ethel would get involved? A long shot at best. Doris knew her days as a Manville daughter were numbered and shrugged with resignation. "I am very definitely being fired," she told the press, harboring no ill will towards anyone involved—except for Elaine, whom she thought "crude." As for Jack, she both "hated and loved" him: "he's not a person you can be on an even keel about."

The tabloids covered it like a Louis-Schmeling prizefight, some devoting more space to the confrontation than the play:

"DIANA LOSES TO PAPA BARRYMORE'S 4TH 'EX' IN NIGHT CLUB TANGLE"
"ELAINE AND DIANA TANGLE OVER JOHN; ELAINE WINS"
"ELAINE WINS—DAUGHTER FURIOUS"

Jack's young, dark-eyed daughter versus his young, dark-eyed wife playing his daughter? That was as profitable as it was Freudian. Even Elaine acknowledged the juiciness of the "public squabble." Many expressed shock over Diana's behavior, forgetting she was behaving like any impudent eighteen-year-old desperate for her father's love and approval. Meanwhile, at nearly sixty, Jack was everyone's favorite dotty uncle, forgiven no matter how childish. His nurse, Karl Stuever, called him "a genius—therefore a little abnormal." Dolores Costello vigorously challenged any negative press about him. The same critics who lamented the lost actor begged the man to take care of himself. The result was ebullient support of the Barrymore-Barries and a raspberry to Diana, the "Barrymore Brat." Even Winnie Hoveler, who flew in to see Jack, claimed she was happy over the reconciliation. She didn't add how she'd been turned away in tears, allowed only a brief phone call with the man who had promised to nurture her dramatic career. "Everything is just fine," she said, and leaving was "the best thing under the circumstances." "We are still very good friends," she added.

Yet somehow, despite—or perhaps because of—the publicity, Diana was a hot commodity. She hawked Woodbury Soap ("Take a tip from the 'personality girl' of the season!") and Nobility Silverware ("Nobility of the American Stage!"), buying new clothes with the money—and sending the bills to Harry if she overspent. She donned a platinum-blonde wig for the Allied Relief costume party, lady-in-waiting to Brenda's Mme. Pompadour. (Robin, "garbed as a Turk," was Brenda's escort.) In Washington, DC, for Fight for Freedom, she tried to smooch Pennsylvania Senator Gaffney during a photo op, and bonded with "Hobie" Clark's ex, actress Anne Francine. Her best friend, aside from Robin, was actress Yvonne Castle. "Vonny," who was seven years older, was once leading lady for the WPA Federal Theatre. They whispered and giggled their way through summer stock and spent hours on the phone together after it ended. Sadly, Castle fell overboard the ocean liner Monterey after an "attack of vertigo" and was declared "lost at sea" in late June 1941.

Thank God for her dear Robina. "No half-brother and sister ever got along more famously." Robin had friends everywhere, from every color, creed, and economic level, and boasted to all of them how his divine sister Diana was "on the threshold of theatrical success." Robin wanted to be an actor himself and joined the Manhattan Repertory, debuting in December 1935's *At Marian's* while staying with his father in Palm Beach, Florida. The play faltered due to headliner Laurette Taylor's drinking, but their second show, *Daisy Mayme* with actress Blanche Ring, fared better. Various theater productions followed, including the homoerotically charged drama *The Green Bay Tree*, once considered "too decadent to be sent on tour." The Broadway original starred Laurence Oliver as Julian, a handsome bachelor forced to choose between an average life with his fiancée or luxury with his male "mentor" (Leo G. Carroll). Robin, beautiful and conflicted himself, was a perfect Julian, though his diction remained in the "hot-potato-in-the-mouth phase" and would have benefitted from Michael's elocution lessons. Aside from that, wrote the review, he was "a promising rookie." After false starts in music, writing, and art, Robin finally found his calling. Even more exciting: he found someone special while touring with the Dahlberg Stock Company. As soon as he got home, he pulled a photo out to show Diana. "Mother had a bust of Apollo in the sitting room," she wrote later of the stunning dark-haired man with piercing eyes. "This was him come to life." His name was Tyrone Power Jr.

Ty worked as a movie house usher and read comic strips over the radio before following his father into show business. Tyrone Power Sr. worked with Diana's grandfather, Maurice Barrymore, and starred as Claudius opposite her father in *Hamlet*. Acclaimed on the stage, he easily shifted to silent films and was poised to work in talkies when, in 1931, he died of a heart attack in his son's arms. Ty was only seventeen. As their relationship progressed, Robin invited Ty to stay at the Tweed house in New York while looking for offseason work. Michael forbade anything unpleasant around Robin—not even World War II, when she insisted he "take the first battleship home" after enlisting in 1939—and so her home was a safe, welcoming space where Ty and her son "showed their affection openly . . . with no secret or apology." Robin, "with endless rolls of bills in his pockets," made sure Ty lacked for nothing until a job with actress Katharine Cornell's acting troupe led to *Saint Joan* at the Martin Beck Theater, then a screen test at 20th Century Fox. After his big breakthrough role in *Lloyd's of London* (1936), the studio image-makers erased not only Robin but any evidence of same-sex attraction. In private, he cared deeply for Robin and Diana, and remained in touch with them for years.

Diana waited backstage at the Plymouth Theater during the winter of 1939–40 to compliment Bramwell Fletcher on his performance in Claire Boothe Luce's anti-Nazi comedy/mystery *Margin for Error*. She never forgot his smile and bright blue eyes, and Bramwell, who never forgot her either, immediately invited her to dinner. He gushed over her work, her potential, implored her not to sell out to Hollywood. They met again for supper after the last show, then back to his place for a nightcap. He read to her from Keats and Shelley and surprised her with a recitation of "To Diana on her Sixth Birthday" by Michael Strange. He apparently had his own copy; Diana had a reputation for handing out copies of her mother's poetry books to suitors. She closed her eyes, rapt, and opened them to find him standing there, a twinkle in his eye and pajamas in his hands. She blushed, and he relented. "All right my dear, if you won't tonight, you will later."

Diana wrote later that Michael didn't approve of Bram, but surviving letters show a congenial relationship between the two. It was more the *idea* of Bram that Michael protested. Actors were an unrefined breed, she said. "I can never forget the eggs on your father's robe at breakfast," she told Diana, who scoffed. She adored everything about Bram, from his prowess at badminton to grumbling at her favorite horror movies, and had "reached the state of premeditated marriage," their only obstacle Bram's pending divorce from Helen Chandler. He and the *Dracula* (1931) actress wed in 1935 but collapsed under the weight of Helen's alcoholism. "He's a very fine man much too good for me," she wrote Fran, "but I'd like to try and make him happy." In Canada to play in Noël Coward's *Tonight at 8:30*, they met Ann Andrews, the outspoken actress who played the Ethel-inspired Julie Cavendish in the George S. Kaufman/Edna Ferber Barrymore satire *The Royal Family*. She quickly became one of Diana's best friends. Diana didn't have a lot of female friends: "They're bitches. A woman always has an excuse or a reason or something—something snide." The ones she had, she held close, cherishing their support as her career moved forward.

The Romantic Mr. Dickens opened at the Playhouse Theater on December 2, 1940, and closed five days later, a mere blip on Broadway but for one thing: Diana's debut on the Great White Way.

The show attempted to make a three-act play out of Charles Dickens during a contentious point in his marriage. Robert Keith played Dickens, and Diana was Caroline Bronson, the author's "fourth and final love" and the object of his "middle-aged philanderings." Michael offered to coach her daughter as she had done her husband. "Would [Robert] mind coming up and working with you and me? All your scenes are with him. After all, I worked with your father on *Hamlet* and other plays, and he said I was helpful."

"We worked like dogs for two weeks, Robert Keith, Mother, and myself," Diana recalled. "She was absolutely magnificent and helped us both." The morning of the show's debut the maid woke her with tea. She asked if Michael was up yet, and yes—actually, she hadn't slept a wink. The two took their tea together, had a long talk. Michael advised her not to be discouraged by bad notices. "Anything can happen," she said. Diana went to 11 a.m. rehearsal, got back at 4 p.m., had more tea and cinnamon toast, and tried not to panic. Michael arrived home to a nervous, nauseated Diana, and what emerged next was a Michael too rarely seen:

"I was like a child, and she gave me a bath at 5:30—the first she'd given me since I was seven." At 6 p.m., she had the butler fix two soft-boiled eggs and a pot of tea, "the only thing your father would have before an opening." At 7:30 p.m., she called a cab and made the driver promise to ring her when Diana got to the theater; Michael arrived separately, with friends Elsa Maxwell and George Jean Nathan, but sat with her daughter in her dressing room for around fifteen minutes while Diana held her rosary and prayer book. After a few moments, she began making up, and Michael left to take her seat.

"I took a swift look at myself in the mirror and decided that under bastard amber and surprise pink lights I might get by. Calling the maid, the dressing began. Three petticoats were zipped into place before the pale blue flannel skirt managed to rest securely. . . . I didn't put on my bonnet for a definite reason. There was something I wanted to do—look out front and see who was in the house. Every actor knows that it is bad luck to look at the audience before the curtain goes up, but in spite of superstition, curiosity won out." She saw Michael in that sea of faces, wearing her customary black velvet and a white mink, then stepped back and read the one telegram she grabbed from the stack piled on her dressing table:

DARLING ALL THE LUCK IN THE WORLD TO YOU TONIGHT.
WISH I WERE THERE.
      DADDY.

"I had my entrance—I walked in front of a window and called out, 'Mr. Dickens, Mr. Dickens.' I was out of sight of the audience. At the second 'Mr. Dickens,' before I even came on stage, the whole house started to applaud. And when I appeared in view, there was such an ovation! I've never had it since." Diana smiled recalling the night. "[After curtain] Mother came backstage in tears. She had cried through the whole performance. . . . [t]hey couldn't get all my flowers in the dressing room. It looked like a funeral. (Next morning when we read the notices we saw that it was.) Mother and Harry and I went home in a cab. He said, 'Very good, old top, very fine.' From him, that was equivalent to saying, 'You are Duse.' Mother just said, 'Catkin!' Just 'Catkin!' She didn't have to say more. She threw her arms around me and cried. When we got back she made me a glass of hot Ovaltine." Diana smirked. "In later years, my after dinner drinks were different."

Critic Alvin Goldstein thought it tedious and made Dickens into "a bit of a boob," but Diana surprised and delighted everyone with her poise and polish. Celebrated critic Brooks Atkinson, writing for the *New York Times*, proclaimed her "a vibrant young lady with an excellent speaking voice . . . a romantic performance that is surprisingly accomplished and that lifts the play out of the doldrums. This is the best Barrymore debut for some time, one bit of meat which made that turkey worth sitting down to." Diana wrote Mr. Atkinson to thank him, and he encouraged her in his reply: "What you make of acting will depend on how much you put into it . . . [t]he difference between and interesting actress and a great actress is a matter of mind and spirit."

She arrived for the second night's showing radiant over her notices, but quickly realized the only cheerful thing in the theater was her. "There was a deathly hush as I walked in. The play had been panned mercilessly . . . that night the authors put up the closing notices."

Her next Broadway play, *The Happy Days*, fared only slightly better. Zoe Akins adapted the French comedy about two sisters (played by Diana and British actress Barbara Kent Greene) in love with the same aviator. Plagued by a weak script, it ran at the Henry Miller Theatre from May 13 to May 31, 1941. "Klepfer" at *Variety* said the "[r]eal surprise of the cast is John Barrymore's daughter Diana. Showing good stage presence, she recites her lines effortlessly." Edgar Price of the *Brooklyn Citizen* called her "a chip off the old block. Miss Barrymore is going places . . . she gives an excellent performance." In August, she was Madame Trentoni in a revival of *Captain Jinks of the Horse Marines*, a bit of a faux pas; playing her aunt's (erroneously called her mother by critic Burns Mantle) first starring role broke a bit of "unwritten Royal Family law." Adelaide Keir sat down with her for the Associated Press and marveled at the "spirited girl of 20 with the voice and manner of a woman of 30." Also in the cast at the Ridgeway Theater in White Plains, New York: a young Gregory Peck.

In October, she returned to Broadway in George S. Kaufman and Edna Ferber's *The Land is Bright*, a three-act epic of the Kincaid family and their morally questionable rise from the nineteenth century to "present day" 1941. The autumn before, Kaufman and Ferber asked her to come read for the role of Linda Kincaid, the "thrill-seeking flapper" who matures into a proper matron by the third act.

"I felt I knew what this woman was, exactly what was expected of the performance. I read it. They made no comment, but thanked me and said they'd let me know within a few hours. I thought, *well, you've fluffed it.*" She gave them Bram's number and they waited at his house, sipping iced tea (Bram's favorite) and willing the phone to ring. Finally, it did. "'Well, honey, you're hired.' I nearly dropped dead. It was the most beautiful way to be hired.... I raced home to tell Mother that I had got a job in a Broadway play. I'd already had two but this was Kaufman and Ferber, this was important. I wasn't going to let that night go by without telling Mother that I'd gotten my first damned, really beautiful Broadway play.

"My eyes must have shown it because she exclaimed at once, 'You've got it!' . . . 'Oh darling, the two other things you did didn't mean anything particular but now—this will.'"

The Billboard thought she "overplay[ed]" her second-act role of gangster's moll "just enough to turn [it] into a near-burlesque," but Kaufman biographer Malcolm Goldstein disagreed. "If anything lifted the last two acts above the mundane, it was her artful performance." The show only lasted a mediocre seventy-nine performances at the Music Box, closing after New Year's 1942.

As her visibility increased, so did interview requests, introducing America to this fourth-generation Barrymore *wunderkind.* "The last of the Barrymores is a 21-year-old brunet [*sic*] with curls and the same sort of a flare [*sic*] for wisecracks that has kept Daddy John Barrymore in the news," wrote one syndicated article. "Movie acting is nothing but not doing anything," she said, but hinted about playing Ivy Peterson in the Spencer Tracy *Jekyll and Hyde* remake. The screen test turned out to be for novelty's sake—"[t]hey weren't thinking of me for the part" that went to Ingrid Bergman, "they just wanted a test." It didn't go well; "I nearly threw up." Still, she'd make any movie if the money were right: "I don't need it at present—but you never can tell about the future." She'd need it for her expensive tastes—"I'm simply mad about jewelry, can't pass a shop without going in and spending every cent I own"—not that she could manage her own finances: "I stopped even trying to learn arithmetic after I was 11. I still can't make a checkbook balance." She sported a shiner for one fan magazine interview, explaining, "my father, John, beat me." He was one of the ten greatest men in the world (the other nine were, of course, the Brooklyn Dodgers) but just because he lived in a "department store window" didn't mean she had to. "Don't be dull" and "oh, how idiotic" were default responses. (To call anything "dull" was the "most devastating" insult in café society "if you wanted to ruin or crush anybody.") Asked about her time at "finishing school," she cracked "they are aptly named; when and if you do go the full fifteen rounds, you're finished all right, mentally anyway, and you're ready for your first three hurdles, your debut, your marriage, and your divorce, in precisely that order."

Her mother was her best friend, and as for her two brothers, Leonard was "married and dabbles in writing," Robin "ummarried and dabbles." Her dresses were either barely there or frumpy, her home formal inside and "a primitive wilderness" out. She slept on baby blue sheets in tailored pajamas. No, girly pink nightgowns. No, she slept nude. She bared her "irregular teeth" to *Collier's* reporter Nord Riley and said she loved raw meat, leaving him—and everyone—bewildered at the "strange assortment of gifts" she inherited from her parents. She agreed. "Two parents like mine would discourage anybody." Occasionally, she was reflective. "What I want most of all to do right now is to play *A Bill of Divorcement* . . . and I'd like to do it with father. Wouldn't that be fine?" In films, she thought *Beau Brummel* (1924) her father's greatest role, his "great physical beauty allied to a magnificent talent in acting." When talk turned to the transience of fame, she replied, "I'm just going along on my own. If I succeed, all right. If I don't, I won't have anybody to blame but myself." A few minutes later, she was back to Diana again. "[I]f I ever get blue, I know a swell cure. You see Daddy's got a totem pole up at his house. You just look at the thing for a few minutes and you begin laughing yourself silly." John Decker described the sculpture looming over Tower Road as having "a raven nesting in the hollow head of the top figure and the croaking would have put Poe to shame." (Vincent Price bought it after Jack's death; it was returned in 2015 to the Tlingit people of Prince of Wales Island, Alaska, eighty-four years after Jack stole it during a yachting trip.)

Diana's love life was as uninhibited as her comments. One memorable encounter was with "Richie Merino," whom she met backstage in late autumn 1941 during the run of the short-lived Broadway play *Walk into My Parlor*. His "hint of violence" excited her, and they wasted no time getting back to his dingy flat near Madison Square Garden. She reveled in the "animal vitality" missing from her lovemaking with Bram. "I'm living. This is Life!"

"Richie Merino" was summer stock actor Nick Conte, discovered by director Elia Kazan and actor John Garfield while waiting tables at a Connecticut resort the summer of 1935. He impressed them enough to earn a scholarship to New York's Neighborhood Playhouse. "The Sardi's set is all a-twitter over Diana's current chest-pounder," wrote Walter Winchell. "Nick Conte of *Walk into My Parlor*, who walked right into her man-trap." 20th Century Fox signed him in 1943, and as Richard Conte he enjoyed a long career, most often in crime dramas and film noir. Modern audiences know him best as Don Barzini in *The Godfather* (1972), and he was a frontrunner for Don Corleone before losing to the equally intense Marlon Brando.

CHAPTER 5

THE BARRYMORE BRAT

PRODUCER WALTER WANGER MET WITH DIANA IN HER DRESSING ROOM AFTER the show. He was greatly impressed with her in *The Land is Bright* and wanted to bring her to Hollywood. Michael, who still blamed the movies for her ex-husband's downfall, suggested a temporary six-month contract. Ridiculous, said her agent, Louis Shurr. With her talent and name power a standard contract could pull $1,000 a week! Well, said a bold Diana, if they want me, they'll agree to both—and Universal did. Michael countered with "contracts" she drew up with Harry and close friend, children's author Margaret Wise Brown. First: Diana would live with Mademoiselle at the Hotel Beverly Wilshire until her twenty-first birthday and *under no circumstances* stay with her father while in Hollywood. Next: Mademoiselle would accompany Diana to all social functions, have her home by midnight, never leave her alone with a man, and provide weekly progress reports. Lastly: Mr. Wanger signed a letter swearing any mentions of Michael would be only in a "dignified manner consonant with [her] position as an artist." Her mother placated, Diana headed to Hollywood in January with Mademoiselle, Moka, her Great Dane Cleo, and an amethyst engagement ring from Bram. "I remember I was terribly disappointed in it. It was probably quite expensive. It was some horrible purple stone—for an old lady—it wasn't for somebody young. He knew we'd be apart and he felt he'd better come up with the proposal in case something else happened . . . it was hardly romantic."

Jack and a gaggle of press welcomed them at Union Station. "It's wonderful to have a daughter who looks like Hedy Lamarr," he crowed to reporters as they maneuvered to Jack's car. He frowned at Michael's rules but took her to Tower Road, from the outside a "divine house," she wrote Fran, "with a huge swimming pool" refilled for the first time in years. Her heart broke seeing the present state of his "castle out of fairyland" as they descended the hewn redwood stairs to the miniscule library.

"He went right across the room [to the] wing-back armchair—done in chintz—room very dark, a pannelled [sic] room—he let himself down in the chair and sighed. When he did, there was a sort of hoarse cough, a wheeze . . . 'Well, this is the room we live in.'" A "lonely room," said Diana. Her father's brow wrinkled. "There isn't anywhere in this whole god damn house— everything is a shell. This is the room I live in. This is the room I remember things in. . . . I'm so sorry this isn't the way it used to be. [In the margin of this story, a note, most likely Gerold Frank's: "very touching—I cried over this, somebody else should."] 'Darling,' [Jack] said, 'there's no way to begin a tour of this. I don't know where to let you know where anything began.'"

They went to his game room (think safari, not table tennis), cavernously empty save for a mildewing "old tired moose" and "a snake, dry, too dry, curled upon itself six times." Diana went up a few steps and gasped. "He said, 'Ah! My heads?' There were two heads [displayed] in this glass case. . . . I have a sense of the macabre, as he does [and] he said, 'Diana, look, if you ever want anything, one thing I leave to you are the heads.'

'That would be absolutely divine, Daddy. What would I do with them?'

'Why, put them in the middle of a table at a very chic party!'"

Another room, "the size of a yacht," was almost entirely glass, with a beautiful mosaic and fountain in the middle. Before Johnnie and Dede came along, it was Jack's aviary; afterwards, it became their playroom. "[W]hen they were tiny enough, they played in that pool," Jack said.

While showing her the freshly redone guest room, Jack paled and grew short of breath. Vermouth was the only thing that helped him, he said, and an alarmed Diana decided she would personally care for him, "renew[ing] a father-daughter relationship that had almost died from disuse."

At dinner, Jack introduced her to his dear friend, John Carradine. "Jack's been talking of nothing but you," said the actor, smiling. The men caught up on all news Barrymore until Diana confessed she didn't really know her aunt or uncle. In a flash, Barrymore and Carradine loaded her into the latter's ancient jalopy and sped to Lionel's place. Lionel was delighted to see his niece and the two chatted amiably despite his being stuck in bed with a bad arthritis flare. Eventually the small talk trailed off and Carradine broke into some of their favorite bawdy poetry. Diana pondered the generic visit on the way home. "He'd always been a stranger. He still was."

Shortly after she and Mademoiselle moved out of the Wilshire and into the Grosvenor Apartments in Los Angeles, the Wangers threw her a second debutante ball of sorts at their home and invited the biggest names in the business. The guest of honor cocked an eyebrow at the partygoers while the lovely Mrs. Wanger, actress Joan Bennett, floated impeccably among them.

These are the important people? she thought. They seemed so vapid, laughing at everything. She congratulated herself for being above it all, then noticed one merrymaker noticeably lacking in merriment. The actress—Diana's favorite since childhood—sat alone, shot-gunning cocktails. Diana stumbled upon her later in the guest powder room, weeping.

"I'm love with a man I can't have," said the actress. He was Clark Gable. "It's no secret, so don't be shocked."

Diana listened, dazed. Her marriages, her drinking—all attempts to dull the ache of unrequired love. "Sweetie, don't let Hollywood kill you as it's killed me." Tears dripped onto her gown, and Diana wanted to stay with her, comfort her. No, said the woman. "I have to pull myself together," she said, dabbing at her ruined eye makeup with a handkerchief. "I'm so ashamed!"

Diana never names the actress in her memoir, but there's little doubt she's talking about Joan Crawford. Sparks flew between her and Gable from their first meeting, and it was on the set of *Possession* (1931) that they began meeting discreetly—or so they thought—in Crawford's luxury dressing room trailer, a gift then-husband Douglas Fairbanks Jr. was still paying off. Gable was also married at the time, to Ria Langham, and the open secret irritated Louis B. Mayer enough to issue an ultimatum: knock it off or lose your contracts.

Both stars obtained divorces but Gable went straight into the arms of Carole Lombard, not Crawford, whose jealous remarks on set drove a wedge between the former lovers. It was Crawford, however, who nursed Gable back from the agony of losing the love of his life in a January 1942 plane crash. It was rumored that later that same year Crawford proposed marriage, but Gable enlisted in the army instead. While they never paired romantically offscreen, the two remained friends, and possibly more so, until Gable's death in 1960.

Diana said her goodbyes a little after midnight. She had an early call in the morning and accepted a ride home from "Mr. Lawrence," a "major producer" who walked her to her door, waited until she opened it, and pushed his way inside. She offered him a drink, every inch the sophisticate. He wanted something else.

In one swift move, she was on the carpet, his face inches from hers, holding her down with one hand while tugging at her clothes with the other. Diana knew about the casting couch. She also knew to choose her next words carefully.

Movie executives trading sex for stardom was "common sense," according to actress Veronica Lake. Things were different in the 1940s, she wrote in her autobiography *Veronica*. "Getting into movies was a big deal for girls those days," and "putting out for a role" was valuable currency. Lake recalled one producer proudly displaying what God gave him on his desk like a depraved hors d'oeuvre. "Most natural thing in the world," he said. "Let's have fun and then we'll talk about silly things like making movies." Lake's response, to her credit, was to flatten his genitals with a dictionary and run like hell as he screamed (and his secretary doubled over in hysterics). Diana chose a gentler route.

"Look," she said. "I'm not under contract to you. I'm under contract to Mr. Wanger. If he wants to do this, okay. But for you—no. You're not in this deal at all, sir." She paused. "Will you please get up and go home?"

The producer climbed off Diana and got to his feet, ruddy and breathless. He smiled at the unkempt Diana, now seated on the sofa. "You're quite a girl, Miss Barrymore. . . . I think you're miscast though." He strode to the door. "You belong in the script department. Good night."

Neither woman ever named their perpetrators, but there's a good argument for it being the same man: Academy Award-nominated film producer Arthur Hornblow Jr. Of course, Diana did write later of Wanger: "[He] was very fond of me—despite all the passes he made and all that—he couldn't help that. He liked me and I liked him. We both respected each other."

Diana went and got her driver's license, something she never needed in New York, and Wanger took her to buy her first car: a pea-green convertible Buick, paid for with a $2,700 advance on her salary. She made the rounds, from dinner parties at producer David O. Selznick's to lunch with stars like Mary Astor, Roland Young, even Louella Parsons. "I'd sort of look around at people and I knew most of them and I thought, *this is incredible!* Here I was, sitting round talking to all these people as though you've known them for years and you're completely socially accepted as part of the world." Thus ushered into Hollywood, Diana got down to work on her first picture, *Eagle Squadron.*

Based on the C. S. Forester novella, *Eagle Squadron* chronicled the lives of three pilots in the all-American volunteer division of Britain's Royal Air Force. Robert Stack, fresh off of *To Be Or Not To Be* (1942), was Chuck Brewer, a cocky flyer who thought Brits were soft until he and his buddies Johnny (Leif Erickson) and Wadislaw (Edgar Barrier) fought alongside them. Chuck also bonds with Anne Partridge (Diana), a young WAAF in his transport struggling with trauma of her own. Screenwriter Norman Reilly Raine built a rousing introduction from scrapped documentary footage of real Eagle Squadron pilots, many already killed in action, narrated by war correspondent Quentin Reynolds. The story was inspired by RAF Fighter Command No. 71 "Eagle" Squadron, Americans who responded to Britain's call for aid after the 1940 Battle of Britain. Two more squadrons added a year later were eventually absorbed into the newly stationed US Army Air Force in September 1942 (later the USAAF's Fourth Fighter Group).

Universal boasted that their film would be the first celebrating Eagle Squadron. 20th Century Fox cancelled the Don Ameche/Henry Fonda picture *The Eagle Flies Again*, but actually bested Universal a year before with the Tyrone Power/Betty Grable film *A Yank in the R.A.F.*, also containing actual aerial footage. Arthur Lubin helmed the drama as a reward for his directorial success with the Abbott and Costello films, and Flying Officer/Squadron member John M. Hill was technical advisor. Gladys Cooper, Jon Hall, Evelyn Ankers, Alan Hale Jr., John Loder, and Mary Carr made up the supporting cast, and the hundreds of extras included stars Jill Esmond and son Simon Tarquin Olivier, Peter Lawford, members of the Elwes acting family, and a brave tabby kitten named Li'l Blitz. "The First Great Picture of the Second World War!" received one of the largest exploitation units in Universal's history. Billboards. Newspaper articles and ads. Radio spots costing between $2,500 and $5,000 every two weeks. Disney even created an insignia for merchandising: an eagle in boxing gloves.

Pilots were on every screen in 1942: John Wayne in Republic's *Flying Tigers*, about American volunteers in Myanmar; James Cagney in Warner Bros.' *Captains of the Clouds*, about the Royal Canadian Air Force; Powell and Pressburger's *One of Our Aircraft is Missing* over at United Artists; and *The First of the Few* (released in the US as *Spitfire*), the last film of Leslie Howard, who also produced and directed. The US government needed Hollywood to bolster support of American war involvement in response to the numerous "America First" groups springing up across the country. Charles Lindbergh was a member, as was Michael, who felt "[w]e concentrate on Europe because we do not want to meet the problems of poverty and unemployment in our own country. We don't want to be bothered with these things. But we've got to be bothered very soon . . . [i]t is better to be managed by native ideals than by the ideals of foreign countries." Her comments like this and those praising Mussolini and Stalin annoyed Diana, who worried about Bram serving in the army overseas. Bram was deeply insulted: "Here is Britain bleeding and dying—their [*sic*] on the barricades—and people like your mother and Lindbergh aren't helping much." Nelson Poynter, assistant coordinator for Government Films, suggested only motion pictures could bring the "intangible factors of war" to the masses, answering the national question of "what are we fighting for?"

Diana's first day on set began with a list: heavy chin, small mouth, and— despite her nickname of "Profile Jr."—no trace of her father's. "They didn't allow me to see any of [the makeup tests] . . . I asked to see them—I wanted to know what I looked like but they wouldn't let me." Shooting was delayed ten days while her crooked teeth were filed and capped, something Diana called "extremely painful." Cinematographer Stanley Cortez noticed no difference. "An extraordinary face," he said. "One side has absolutely nothing to do with the other." The makeup department got to work while the cameramen fretted over angles. "This doll isn't even good-looking," Lubin told Wanger, who agreed: "I didn't buy a pretty face. I bought an actress."

Movies were nothing like the stage. She recalled freezing in fear during one love scene with "Bobby" Stack when the "huge inhuman eye" of a camera rose from the Thames. Lubin laughed, she said, and promised as many takes as necessary for her to be comfortable.

Lubin remembered it differently. Diana was "a brat" for whom "spitting in a director's eye was a hobby." Her other pastime was bullying Robert Stack, wondering aloud how anyone as "lousy" as him could photograph so well, or whispering during their love scenes, "As an actor, you really stink!" "I didn't really dislike Diana," Stack said. He pitied the girl who sported "many of the outer trappings of being a Barrymore" without the experience to back it up. Stack was no stranger to society life: he loved polo, boat racing, and dating lots of sub-debs, including Cobina Jr. He was also a champion skeet shooter who went often with his father figures, actors Clark Gable and Spencer Tracy (Stack's parents were divorced and his father died when he was nine). He was a minor heartthrob after giving Deanna Durbin her first screen kiss in *First Love* (1939), and his own crush, Carole Lombard, mentored him until her untimely death in January 1942. "Bobby" Stack was wholesome and mannerly, but not above a veiled jab at Diana. "The public has a new awareness of good work," he told *Photoplay*. "No more 'personality' boys and girls." He detested girls who drank, flirted—Lubin recalled her "on the make for every man on the set"—or made "scenes," and felt anyone could break into movies; true success was being liked by the public. Stack laughed remembering their publicity stunt "bowling date" for *Modern Screen*: "If Diana and I had ever gone near a bowling ball, one of us would probably have been tempted to throw it at the other."

She left the Grosvenor and rented Basil and Ouida Rathbone's home, made for entertaining with indoor pool and a 500-person ballroom that doubled as a private movie theater. She vanished during her own housewarming party, and Bram found her listening to records in her bedroom with actor Van Heflin. Diana said nothing happened but again met up with Heflin after the party to stargaze at the beach. It took hours to convince Bram of her fidelity, though she claimed Heflin proposed marriage multiple times that evening. Shortly after she rejected him, Heflin married actress Frances Neal.

The New York preview for *Eagle Squadron* was on May 29, 1942, but Diana's thoughts that night were of her gravely ill father. He'd recognized her briefly during her last visit, then lapsed back into semiconsciousness, calling for Mummum. The lights lowered. Diana cringed at what she saw on the screen: dumpy, stiff. Wanger promised she was fine. They were exiting to polite applause when an usher stopped Diana: she needed to get to Hollywood Hospital right away. She and Bram sped through the streets with a police escort, but Jack was gone before they arrived. A nurse escorted Diana to her father's room for a moment alone. Michael once told her daughter how "divinely beautiful" Jack was in his youth, like an "archangel." Lying peacefully, his pain and weariness erased by death, Diana witnessed traces of it, and wept.

It seemed there was never a time when one of the Barrymore siblings wasn't on the stage or screen, and both critics and fans acutely felt the death of this youngest and most colorful of the three. "He was so young," remarked Gene Fowler's son Will. The future journalist was as close with Jack as his father, despite the forty-year age difference. "He never seemed old, never at any time, and that was a wonderful thing." He was "a witty and willful playboy, a joker, an *enfant terrible*, who never grew up," wrote the *New York Times* in 1941. "Barrymore showed—battered and ravaged as he looked after seventeen years of revelry—that he was no broken-down hack . . . he was still a superb actor, who could dominate the theatre again if he wanted to." Thomas Mitchell agreed. "He had a most meticulous regard for the art of acting and for the staging of a play," said the actor and friend who worked with Jack on *Redemption*. "No matter how careless he may have been with his life, he was a martinet on stage."

Film and theater producer/director Oliver Morosco and his wife were the first to arrive at Pierce Bros. Mortuary, where Jack lay in state, the signature "Barrymore collar" of his white shirt crisp against the lapel of his dark blue suit. A red and blue foulard[10] tie and white pocket square completed the ensemble, and his neatly folded hands held a large mystery gardenia from Diana. Lionel's selective guest list annoyed former colleagues who wanted to pay respects. "I don't think John would like that," complained one elderly man denied entry, and after learning he worked with Jack on his first film, Lionel relented: "By all means," he said, "admit John's old friends."

One friend not mentioned in any documentation was Robin. "He and Daddy adored each other," Diana said. "When Robin went to the coast he saw a great deal of Daddy." The two men shared a love of art, literature, and

---

10. Silk or rayon with a printed design.

an unquenchable flair for the dramatic. Jack was in awe of Robin's "cyclonic vitality" and "often reiterated that there had never been a child like dear Robin—he was something extraordinary, absolutely unique." Robin said Jack was "so divine" and always asked him for photos of his Treepee, of whom he spoke proudly.

Errol Flynn's account of staring into the "puffed, white, bloodless" face of John Barrymore's corpse, stolen and propped up in Flynn's house by director Raoul Walsh as a gag, sounds too incredible to be true, and despite decades of confirmation—most recently by Drew Barrymore herself in 2020[11]—it probably isn't.

Gene and Will Fowler sat vigil with Jack through the night. Jane Jones, the Sunset Strip nightclub (and brothel) proprietor, stopped by after hours to kneel and pray by her friend. "Jack was a great patron of prostitutes," wrote Margot Adler in *The House of Barrymore*. "He would have appreciated one praying over him."

Over a thousand gawkers—mostly women and girls with cameras, "like Valentino's funeral," said Diana—surrounded the Little Chapel at Calvary Cemetery on June 2nd in hopes of glimpsing the Hollywood power players invited by Lionel, Gene Fowler, and Barrymore family attorney Gordon Levoy. Wilting slightly in the sultry late morning were Spencer Tracy and Katharine Hepburn; "Vanities" impresario Earl Carroll; Rudy Vallee, in whose arms Jack collapsed only days earlier; bigwigs David O. Selznick, Raoul Walsh, and Louis B. Mayer, accompanied by "the woman who ran M-G-M," his executive secretary Ida Koverman. Jack La Rue was there, as were most of the Bundy Drive Boys. Michael Strange was traveling and could not attend; serious illness felled Mark Nishimura, Jack's beloved "houseboy" removed to the Manzanar Japanese American internment camp.

Arthur Hopkins sent a telegram:

NO, JACK COULD NEVER BEAR A PART AFTER HE GREW TIRED OF IT. AM SURE HE HAS BEEN WEARY OF THE LAST ONE FOR A LONG TIME. AM GLAD HE HAS FOUND A NEW ONE.

A visibly grieving Clark Gable concealed himself behind a pillar. Only four short months earlier, this had all been for Carole. She loved Jack, and the feeling was mutual: "the finest girl I ever met," he told columnist (and later variety show legend) Ed Sullivan. "No hypocrisy, no smugness." After *Twentieth Century* wrapped, he gave her an autographed publicity shot of the

11. *Hot Ones*, season 12, episode 9, "Drew Barrymore Has a Hard Time Processing While Eating Spicy Wings," aired August 20, 2020, Youtube.com

two of them, made out to "a grand actress and a grand person—with the affectionate good wishes of John Barrymore." Her tragic death was said to have "shocked him to the core."

Maurice Costello, accompanied by Helene Costello LeBlanc, represented Dolores, allegedly too ill to attend. Dede recalled her mother being inconsolable the entire day; why she and her brother Johnnie weren't at their father's funeral is a mystery. Lionel comforted a distraught Ethel, touring with *The Corn is Green* and unable to get a flight in time.

Three tall candles stood on either side of Jack's silver-plated copper casket, the metal aglow in the late-morning light. Flowers suffused the chapel—the first arrangement sent by actress Billie Burke—flanked by three enormous white floral crosses. A veiled Diana and slumped Lionel arrived together and joined Bram in the first row, silent except for Diana's "honest tears as large as the pearls she wore." A strained-looking Elaine stood sniffling several rows back. Diana was aghast. "How could she be here?" Uncle Lionel shrugged. "You can't stop her." Her mother, Edna, provided moral support, and Elaine's figure-hugging widow's weeds provided gossip column material. Elaine never remarried, and, until her death in 2003, asserted her short time with Jack was "worth more than 50 years with anyone else."

Father John O'Donnell of Immaculate Heart Church presided over the commitment ceremony. He and Jack were friends for the past sixteen years, and it was he who performed extreme unction—anointing of the sick, colloquially known as "last rites"—for Jack on his deathbed. It was a wise choice to omit the requiem Mass and eulogy; even with the shorter, approximately fifteen-minute service, so many fans asked to use the restrooms perilously close to the chapel door that Calvary locked and declared them off-limits. Afterwards, Diana and Lionel had a few moments alone with Jack, then John Decker, W. C. Fields, Gene Fowler, M-G-M fixer Eddie Mannix, and makeup men C. J. Rudin and Stanley Campbell bore the fern- and orchid-covered casket to Lionel's crypt.

Jack asked to be cremated and the ashes buried next to Mummum at the Drew family plot in Philadelphia, but the Catholic Church at that time did not approve of cremation. Lionel instead interred him in his own crypt, beneath the Last Supper window, below and to the right of his first wife, Irene Fenwick. Though Jack's wishes were honored in 1980 by his son and grandson—who singlehandedly disinterred, cremated, and reinterred him in Philadelphia—the marble plaque, engraved with "Good Night Sweet Prince," remains. Lionel whispered a prayer for his baby brother, biting his lip to hold back tears. Fans cheered as stars filed out, prompting one unnamed actor to remark, "What a vulgar display!" Fields, who abhorred autograph hounds, doused them with enough venom for them to loudly swear off his movies for life.

Vulgar. Some described Jack this way, deep into "the prostitution of his dignity," reduced to a fool. "John Barrymore is dead at sixty," wrote critic Burns Mantle. "Twenty of his years were devoted to a groping youth; twenty were fruitful; twenty were waste." But death, as it often does, burned away the sardonic and bizarre, leaving only the "Crown Prince of the Royal Family." Frank Gill of the *Detroit Free Press* remembered "the last of the bravura performers." Ed Sullivan recalled Jack as "quick-witted, literate, articulate . . . a grand subject to interview." Actor and director Donald Crisp, who knew him for forty years, called him "the greatest Hamlet the world has ever known . . . a magnificent artist." Even Burns Mantle admitted the silver lining of the *My Dear Children* years: "Thousands who saw him in that circus would have missed him altogether otherwise; missed the genial warmth of him, and the bad-boy quality that made a kind of hero of him; missed, too his last reading of the *Hamlet* soliloquy, through which there flashed a touch of the person he was underneath and in his finer being." The last of the condolences came from Lord Barrymore, of County Carlow, Ireland, who cabled "[t]here were none before him like him and there shall be none after him."

Michael, in the days after Jack's death, brought out his old love letters to share with friends. They had "a pain and eloquence which no one could have imagined," she said.

> Do you remember you once told me a sculptor had told you I seemed unreal—as if everything had been burnt out of me inside? It wasn't that—it was only that the mainspring of everything that was real in me was fighting its way into the light . . .
>
> O my dear one, please, for the love of Heaven, believe that your future is strewn with little pieces of my heart for your poor little feet to walk on, that for months and months they need not touch the earth.

In almost all the news pieces reflecting on Jack's passing was mention of the comfort and happiness he found reconnecting with Diana, his pride at her continuing the family theatrical and cinematic legacy. Not mentioned was their estrangement, which haunted her now. "I think back night after night what I could have meant to that man. . . . I could have made that man's life happier."

In the beginning (and against Mummy's "contract"), she stayed frequently at Tower Road, cracking the mystery of her father. He was irascible, especially if someone watered his vermouth, but certainly not the priapic villain of her mother's former warnings. Michael wouldn't admit it, wrote Diana, but "I think she figured [I] was pretty safe because she knew by that time he was pretty gone." She was rewarded with a little surprise party on her twenty-first birthday at John Decker's house. Decker was a gifted artist, a deft forger, and one of Jack's rowdy group of friends nicknamed the "Bundy Drive Boys" after their meeting house, Decker's Tudor-style cottage on Bundy Drive in Brentwood, California. They were a raucous and varied group of enablers who loved each other deeply but "believed 100% in a man's God-given right to destroy himself": Decker, actor John Carradine, comedian W. C. Fields, writer/journalist Gene Fowler, and indefinable bohemian Sadakichi Hartmann were among its members. Jack arranged the entire thing himself, including the cake. Two days later, Uncle Lionel joined them for *Julius Caesar* on Rudy Vallee's radio program, requested by listeners after February's astounding *Romeo and Juliet*. "For five minutes, 35 seconds," reported *Time* magazine, "seated at his special mike, leaning his tired head on his fingers and forgetting to ham it, he played Romeo to his blooming daughter Diana's Juliet. He had coached her for a week and she was good." Jack sent an exuberant cable to Michael:

> DEAR MICHAEL,
> THIS IS MERELY TO TELL YOU THAT DIANA HAS TAKEN THIS FLATULENT CAVE OF THE WINDS KNOWN AS HOLLYWOOD BY STORM. EVERYBODY SEEMS TO ADORE HER. I MUST SAY SHE IN EVERY WAY JUSITIFES OUR SLIGHTLY CYCLONIC COLLABORATION. ALL THE BEST TO YOU.
> FIG

Buoyed by their radio success, she sought a producer for *The Light of Heart*, a play about a washed-up star working as a department store Santa to support his disabled daughter. She was certain it would rekindle public respect for her father and "take [him] out of the kind of roles he ha[d] been doing lately" but no studio wanted the risk of a drunken skirt-chasing has-been. Jack hugged his daughter. "You are going on to great things," he told her. "I am already dead." He expressed the same to Gene Fowler. "I am doing the work of a whore . . . [t]here is nothing as sad in all the world as an *old* prostitute."

Shortly after, as Diana told it, her father requested she phone a "call girl" for him. She refused, they shouted, he demanded. She angrily made the call and moved out. After two weeks' silence, John Decker called her to come fetch Jack off his sofa. She dragged him away from two blondes and back to Tower Road, Jack mocking her as "Miss Newport" the whole way. His eyes narrowed as they reached the door. "Aren't you going to check up?" he slurred. "Maybe your old Daddy's hidden himself a young lady to diddle with." She called him "disgusting" and left; it would be the last interaction they ever had. "That god damned boarding school *bitch*! I should have thrown my arms around that man and said, 'Daddy, there are five rooms here and you've done this for me and I'm going to stay—I don't give a shit.' I should have done it. And I'll never forgive myself."

There is another, more disturbing version of that night, where Jack, inebriated beyond comprehension, tried to seduce his own daughter. It wasn't only Michael that thought such a thing possible. Gene Fowler claimed to have discussed it with Diana, and she herself once wrote cryptically of the *Infanta* trip: "What happened on his yacht is something I'm saving for a book I'll someday write." Several news puff pieces circa Diana's arrival in Hollywood recounted Jack's attraction to and/or propositioning of Diana before learning her identity, and in a letter to writer Evelyn Waugh, British socialite Ann Fleming—wife of James Bond writer Ian Fleming—described an alleged conversation between Jack and Errol Flynn, where both men watch Diana walk by. "Ever f—d her?" Jack asked Errol. "Don't miss it. She's terrific."

Diana first met Dolores (now Mrs. John Vruwink) and her half-siblings John Jr. and Dolores Ethel Mae (Dede) in 1942. Diana adored Dolores and called her "Mommie," which Dede said delighted her to no end: "My mother loved the fact that Michael Strange's daughter would call her that!" Diana called Johnnie a "little monster" and loved roughhousing with the ten-year-old. "We wrestled a lot," he said in an interview. "Diana always won." Dede recalled one such match where Diana's robe opened, "exposing her breasts."

If Diana called her younger self "a prime brat" who "broke [rules] on general principles," Johnnie as a teenager bordered on degeneracy. He swiped cash from his mother, ignored his stepfather's rules, took the family car for joyrides, and tormented people, especially little sister Dede. "He could be really frightening," she recalled. "Think Jack Nicholson in *The Shining*." Diana claimed she caught him "slipping some of the family silver into his pocket at the dining table to he could hock it to buy a baseball mitt." As a grown man, he was sensitive, restless. Actor Jeffrey Weissman[12] met Johnnie in the early 1980s through a mutual friend, artist John Bowman Parker, aka "Buddha." He remembered his jealousy over daughter Drew's fame while harboring a "glimmer of hope" for his own, and how the bedroom in Johnnie's West Hollywood flat was wall-to-wall Jack, packed so tightly with his father's memorabilia that he slept on the sofa.

---

12. Jeffrey Weissman, phone conversation with author, March 2021.

Years later, Johnnie shocked his cousin with a confession: his first sexual experience had been with Diana, probably during one of her visits in 1946. He was fourteen, about the same age as Jack when he was seduced by his stepmother, and as with his father, shame and confusion turned him sullen, distrustful of women, and unpredictable. Actors' Equity eventually suspended him over his violent outbursts and substance abuse. His ex-wife, actress Cara Williams, called the Barrymores "one of the strangest families in the world. . . . I just couldn't understand nobody helping Johnnie, just as I couldn't see why nobody ever helped poor Diana." In an interview during their marriage, Williams referred to Johnnie as a "boy . . . he's never grown up, really." He remained that way until his death in 2004, daughter Drew lovingly referring to him as a "man-child." Dede felt he needed the love of his parents, but "neither were available to really show him they cared about him." Williams agreed: "he had never had real love in his childhood."

Some advance critics called *Eagle Squadron* "brilliant entertainment" and praised its authenticity—*Modern Screen* said that "the camera rides the sky with its pilots"—but military brass and Eagle Squadron members at the New York July 4th premiere disagreed and walked out in protest. Universal's conciliatory $10,000 check to the RAF Benevolent Association didn't change their minds, and Wanger later blamed any of the film's shortcomings on the military's uncooperative attitude.

Though, as Ida Belle Hicks wrote for the *Kansas City Star*, "it can hardly be said that 'Eagle Squadron' is a picture for the hall of fame," the "spectacular action" helped it survive against heavy hitters *The Magnificent Ambersons* and *Mrs. Miniver*. Many theaters reported good advance sales. The Orpheum in San Francisco did a tie-in with war bonds, raising $200,000, and houses in Pennsylvania, Ohio, Maryland, and Texas all reported holdovers.

The aerial scenes still impress even in the existing muddy print, as does a tense and ultimately heartbreaking scene of a nighttime raid behind enemy lines. "Diana Barrymore does not photograph to advantage, but gives a sincere and solid performance," wrote *Variety*. She excels in a lovely scene comforting frightened children during a shelling attack but overacts painfully over her father's deathbed, prompting the usual harsh assessment from the *New York Times'* Bosley Crowther: "Diana Barrymore as the girl friend [*sic*] is entirely inadequate and extremely affected to boot." Universal rereleased it in 1948 on a double bill with *Gung Ho!* (1943), then several more times in the 1950s, before selling it for "late show" television rotation through the late 1970s. Howard Hawks reportedly liked *Eagle Squadron* so much he wanted most of the cast for *Corvette K-225*, a war picture about the Royal Canadian Navy, but the film featured a completely different cast when released in 1943.

Universal announced *Boy Meets Baby* in January 1942, a reworking of the French comedy *Le fruit vert*. Stage actress Caroline Bishop, whom we meet during her closing night as Queen Victoria, goes home to visit her mother Chris between gigs. Chris is head over heels for Steven and admits to fudging her age; he thinks Caroline is a child, and Chris worries he'll leave if he learns the truth. Caroline covers by becoming "Carrie," a twelve-year-old home from boarding school. When Steven's friend Jimmy surprises Caroline out of her middy blouse, rehearsing for Sadie Thompson in *Rain*, she pretends to be her own Aunt Jennifer. The rest is a lot of Jim stumbling into and out of silliness with Caroline as Carrie, or Jennifer, or both. The family maid, Gallagher, honest to a fault, refuses to play along and spends most of the movie stuffed into a closet to keep her quiet. Eventually the whole mess is ironed out, Chris and Steven marry, and Jim sneaks on stage at Caroline's latest play—in a suit of armor, since *Rain* was changed to *Joan of Arc*—to confess his love for her.

Previously filmed by their German subsidiary as *A Precocious Girl* (1934), *Baby* was meant for director Henry Koster and producer Joe Pasternak's golden girl, Deanna Durbin, whose star turn in *Three Smart Girls* (1936) saved the studio from bankruptcy. Robert Cummings was already cast as Jimmy when Durbin unexpectedly declined, so Universal requested "America's Little Sister," actress/singer Mary Lee, from Republic. After studio negotiations fell through, other names entered the mix: Katharine Hepburn, Ginger Rogers, Diana Barrymore, Olivia de Havilland. Diana aced her screen test and was ultimately chosen, though execs secretly thought de Havilland would have been more convincing as a preteen. Kay Francis as Chris, John Boles as Steve, and Ethel Griffies as Gallagher completed the main cast, and shooting began in April on what was now called *Love and Kisses, Caroline*.

Scenes showing Caroline in action as Queen Victoria, Joan of Arc, and Sadie Thompson from *Rain* were added to showcase Diana's versatility. Jack Pierce, the genius behind *Frankenstein*, made her up as the octogenarian queen, and "British royalty expert" Madame Hilda Grenier taught her proper royal composure. Much of the film (now titled *Between Us Girls*) was shot at Malibou Lake in the Santa Monica mountains, a popular location used for *Frankenstein* (1931), *Gone with the Wind* (1939), *M*A*S*H* (1970), and *The Ring* (2002). "The film I'm now doing is the top," she wrote Fran. "The parts I play are really something—wait until you see me as a freckled child of 12."

Between Us Girls strongly divided critics upon its September release. *Film Daily* liked the "[c]lever comedy with excellent cast" and thought that Diana gave "an amazingly good account of herself. She goes through her role, which makes considerable demand on acting ability, with all the self-assurance of a performer of vaster experience than she possesses. In 'Between Us Girls' she reveals herself as a fine comedienne and establishes herself as star material." *Harrison's Reports*, another industry paper, agreed: "It is the excellent performance of Diana Barrymore that makes this comedy a highly amusing entertainment. Unlike her part in 'Eagle Squadron,' this time she has been given ample opportunity to display her talent . . . her portrayal of the child is outstanding." Columnist Jimmie Fidler thought she proved "her right for a crown," and Walter Winchell found her "first-rate funny." Louella Parsons thought the people "not too kind" to her about *Eagle Squadron* would "eat their words," and Ray Laning of the *Cincinnati Enquirer* agreed, saying "directors and producers failed completely" to use Diana to advantage on her previous film. *Between Us Girls* proved "the mistake was theirs and not Miss Barrymore's." *Motion Picture Herald* pushed things a bit: "Diana Barrymore is tops and just as good, if not better, than any of the other Barrymores."

Others found little to praise. "The picture is as futile as Miss Barrymore's performance is high school class playish," said Karl Krug of the *Pittsburgh Sun-Telegraph*, pointing out Deanna Durbin's superior work with Koster and Pasternak. "Even her late and illustrious sire [would] shudder and yell for retakes." The *New York Times* didn't sugarcoat things: "No doubt even the offspring of royal families must be allowed their little indiscretions, but why display them? . . . [i]f she has talent she should not conceal it in such a frenzied and labored exhibition . . . its only excuse for existence is as a showcase for a talented comedienne, and, as of the moment, Miss Barrymore hardly qualifies. She does not assume a role, she wrestles with it. She has not learned in comedy that the ribs should be tickled, not poked." *Variety* critic "Hobe" thought that "[t]he picture should help establish the late John Barrymore's daughter, one way or the other . . . [t]he film not only keeps Miss Barrymore, a comparative unknown, before the camera almost constantly, but it gives her every variety of things to do. The result is occasionally uproarious, but generally laborious, noisy and exhausting. . . . some of it is outright Keystone Cops [*sic*] stuff. Her performance shows confidence, occasionally even a glimmer of force, but she hasn't the ability and the poise to sustain such a big part, nor the necessary skill to give it shading."

Enough theaters rented it to make *Variety's* "Golden List" of films that pass $1 million in sales, but most of that was curiosity based on the Barrymore name. *Eagle Squadron* also made the list, which *Variety* attributed to current events. The prize for most perplexing synopsis goes to the *San Francisco Examiner*: "[A] young she-wolf who goes hunting for men in the guise of a starry-eyed 12-year-old."

Between Us Girls is an ambitious film. Yes, the gags are overlong, Cummings falling in love with underage Carrie is creepy, and both Francis and

Boles are wasted—Michael O'Hanlon, film historian, says Francis is "trashed" in her "last real Hollywood movie . . . in an attempt to build the career of Diana Barrymore"—but Diana is good and her physical comedy fantastic. There's an extended roller-skating sequence that seems straight out of *I Love Lucy,* and her pratfalls in the ice cream parlor with Guinn "Big Boy" Williams are effortless. Jack occasionally reminded the public that he started as a slapstick comedian. and Diana clearly inherited some of that affinity. She is passable as Sadie Thompson and Joan of Arc, better as Queen Victoria, lovely as the glamorous Caroline, and hoydenish as Carrie; with a different last name or gentler expectations, she would've been a hit. Instead, her insecurities, combined with the over-promotion of the "brand-new brilliant Barrymore," sabotaged the entire project.

"I think she had some of the mental difficulties her father had," recalled Koster. "I don't think she had any of the Barrymore talent but she had the *Madam Sans-Gene* attitude." (*Madam Sans-Gene,* the play about outspoken laundress turned Napoleonic duchess Catherine Hübscher, had its most famous adaptation with Gloria Swanson in 1925.) Diana's delays and retakes kept Cummings from the set of his other film, *Princess O'Rourke,* shooting simultaneously over at Warner Bros. The frequent production breakdowns made costar Olivia de Havilland sick from stress and led to her successful lawsuit over contract rights, resulting in the "de Havilland Law," updated California Labor Code Sect. 2855, allowing actors greater rights over contractual obligations. Diana and Cummings, if studio gossip is to be believed, were at each other's throats. Diana slapped Bob, hit him with a stick. Bob shoved Diana, went after her with a "lead pipe," and spanked her, to the delight of the crew. "I'll never walk on a set where that — is again," he said. Diana expressed similar feelings, kicking him in the shins during one scene. Koster, at wit's end, forged apology notes to/from them both in order to finish the film. After Diana ordered a visiting Deanna Durbin off the set (she made her "nervous"), Hedda Hopper fumed. "Diana as yet has no slightest grasp of real acting . . . she's starring in a picture in which she might much better be playing a bit." She warned the "headstrong" girl to "change her tone—and quickly."

The reviewer for the Office of War Information disliked the film and had a hell of a grudge with Diana:

ACTING: satisfactory except on part of Diana Barrymore
DIRECTION: good save for the latitude allowed Diana Barrymore
CAMERA: good but not sufficiently expert to conceal Diana Barrymore's facial defects.

Time magazine was the most objective, acknowledging Diana's hard work—she "took her lickings" during the roller-skating scenes and had the bruised coccyx to prove it—but also the weakness of the film that she was "supposed to ride to stardom." It was voted one of the worst films of 1942, and Hedda Hopper reveled in it. "[Critics] hard put to it to say nice things . . . boy! Did they let her have it!"

Michael and Robin flew in two months earlier for Diana and Bram's wedding on July 30th. "I would marry him right now," she told the *Salt Lake Tribune* back in March, "but I am making a picture. We want to do it right, with a honeymoon." The studio again wanted them to postpone but Diana refused to wait any longer. Universal costume designer Vera West made her gown, and a Lutheran pastor married them in their new home, the former Jack Dempsey-Estelle Taylor estate. Robin gave her away, and Uncle Lionel took a short break from the set of *Tennessee Johnson* to come kiss the bride. "I only wish Jack were here to see you now," he said. People strained at the gates for a glimpse of stars sipping champagne around the swimming pool—boxer/actor Max Baer allegedly fell in.

About a month after the wedding, Diana started shooting her third film, the noirish spy thriller *Nightmare* starring B-movie tough guy and former Leyendecker model Brian Donlevy. Dwight Taylor (Laurette's son), whose previous credits included the musicals *The Gay Divorcee* (1934), *Top Hat* (1935), and *Long Lost Father* (1934), with Helen Chandler and John Barrymore, produced the film and adapted the script from a Philip MacDonald story. Tim Whelan directed, and the supporting cast included Gavin Muir, Hans Conreid, and Henry Daniell.

Broke gambler Dan Shane (Donlevy) resorts to squatting in what he thinks is a vacant London house until he runs into Leslie Stafford (Diana). Rather than call the police, she offers him money for a return trip to the US. One catch: he must first help her get rid of her husband (Daniell), dead at his desk with a dagger in his back. He manages to pull it off but sticks around, intrigued by Stafford, who pushes him away—until hubby's body mysteriously reappears. The police are tipped off but the pair escape to Scotland (exteriors shot on location), where they land in a Nazi plot involving her husband's cryptic last words, her German-born cousin, bugged cars, secret codes, and explosive whiskey bottles. "Brian and I had many love scenes," Diana said. Donlevy had sent a telegram to her the night *Between Us Girls* premiered:

HOPE EVERYTHING YOU'VE WORKED FOR AND DREAMED OF COMES THROUGH TONIGHT BUT DON'T GET TOO

EMOTIONAL OR STAY UP LATE BECAUSE WE'VE GOT TO
MAKE LOVE TOMORROW.

"I hardly knew him but he had been kind and considerate enough to send
me this word of encouragement," she told columnist Harry Evans. Soon they
were spending long lunch breaks alone in his bungalow, and Bram bristled
when Donlevy began sending her little gifts. She made dinner for both men
to clear the air and while they got along beautifully, she was struck by the
difference between Bram, her husband of nine weeks, and the "full of vitality" Donlevy. Diana's stomach dropped. They'd only been married for *nine
weeks*. "[O]f course I was married to Bram but was still rather intrigued with
Donlevy," she admitted, "thinking probably of better things to come."

Available for viewing, *Nightmare* starts briskly, then crawls until regaining
its pulse at the end. There's clear chemistry between Donlevy and Diana—no
wonder Bram was suspicious. *Film Daily* called it a "taut and suspenseful
melodrama" and *Hollywood* said it was "fairly entertaining," but most of
the trades and newspaper columns thought it too tepid and "draggy" for a
first-run house. Dan Shane was one of Donlevy's favorite roles and he drew
heavily on him for Special Agent Steve Mitchell on the hugely popular radio
drama *Dangerous Assignment* (NBC, 1949–53). A television version financed by
Donlevy flopped. As for the leading lady, "Diana's performance, while good,
might have been better if she had been less wooden," wrote *Screenland*. "In
spite of her efforts," agreed Wanda Hale for the *Daily News*, "the picture is
better when she is not around." In an interview with columnist John Todd,
Whelan predicted Diana could be "as great as Bette Davis" someday. He
might have been the only one who thought so.

Several columnists, whether out of allegiance to Jack or by request from
the studio, attempted to turn the tide of public opinion. Louella Parsons
asserted both *Nightmare* and *Between Us Girls* were "cleaning up" at the box
office. Frederick Othman called her a "whiz-ding" in *Between Us Girls*, and
when she first came to Hollywood, admitted Erskine Johnson, she "wooed
and won a lot of enemies" but learned her mistake and was now the alleged
"darling of the [Universal] lot." Jimmie Fidler also suggested the "changed
girl" conquered her internal Barrymore and apologized, something "no other
Barrymore has done within the memory of living man."

The Barrymore wunderkind failed to materialize, like Donlevy's request
for her to appear in Fritz Lang's *Hangmen Also Die* (United Artists, 1943) or
the plays she swore were written for her by her friends, Wimbledon tennis
champion Bill Tilden and writer Sinclair Lewis—who knew her mother
and "always had a soft spot in his heart for me." By 1945, Diana's projects

reflected a studio burning off what remained of her contract. They dusted off *Fired Wife*, a shelved sequel to the Rosalind Russell/Brian Aherne romantic comedy *Hired Wife* (1940). Robert Cummings, five years into his contract and hot after Hitchcock's *Saboteur* (1942), was offered a reboot with Teresa Wright, Charles Coburn, and Eddie "Rochester" Anderson, and a director "comparable to the talent of Leo McCarey or Frank Borzage." After he signed, Universal pulled a classic bait-and-switch, yanking the A-list cast and crew. Cummings refused to make the "cheapened" film, adding "the fact that you offer Diana Barrymore is still no inducement." He was suspended five weeks and, when the studio refused to pay his $1,500 weekly salary, he considered himself no longer under contract. The studio retaliated by forcing him into minor parts, over which he sued and won $10,700 in withheld wages. *Fired Wife* was reinvented as a vehicle for Robert Paige and Louise Allbritton, Universal's attempt at cinematic super-couple William Powell and Myrna Loy.

Hank (Paige), an advertising executive, elopes with Tig (Allbritton), the personal assistant of eccentric theatrical producer Chris (Walter Abel), who will not work with married people. They strive to keep their marriage secret, are discovered, argue, and reconcile, all while Hank is forced to babysit Eve Starr (Diana), children's radio personality and professional man-eater. Eve tries to vamp Hank while Chris insists Tig marry his new foreign leading man to avoid deportation. Eve convinces Tig that she and Hank are a couple, Tig gets a Reno divorce, and everything culminates in—you guessed it—a race against time. Hank learns the truth from his butler and rushes to prevent Tig from marrying the leading man; Chris and Eve rush to prevent Hank and Tig; and audiences rush for the exits after Hank and Tig reconcile, remarry, and celebrate (surprise!) the news of Tig's pregnancy.

Available for viewing, it's a lame attempt at screwball, with weary gags and stale dialogue. The climactic end chase is interminable and suspense-less. Paige and Allbritton are visually appealing, and Paige does his best Cary Grant impression, but there is little chemistry between them and even less between Paige and Diana, who is noticeably heavier and delivers her lines through her nose. Apart from one very funny scene involving a sound effects machine, there's isn't much to recommend. The critics' response can best be summed up by Harold V. Cohen for the *Pittsburgh Post*: "[A]ll the airy freshness of a three-day smog, and the performances are pitiful." Mildred Martin of the *Philadelphia Inquirer* concurred. "Not very funny . . . [cast] wasted in such frazzled nonsense . . . on the strength of her current role and the unflattering camera treatment she received, it's no wonder Diana's bent on getting back to the stage as soon as possible."

On the heels of *Fired Wife*, Paige and Diana jumped directly into *Frontier Badmen*, a Wild West story of honest ranchers fighting to break a criminal syndicate's hold over the cattle market in Abilene, Texas. Paige and Noah Beery Jr. are ranchers Steve and Jim, Lon Chaney Jr. is syndicate henchman Chango, Anne Gwynne is Chris, the ranch boss who Jim falls for but who secretly loves Steve, and Diana is Claire, the gold-hearted saloon girl who wins Steve's heart. Comic relief comes courtesy of Slim (Andy Devine), Chinito (Leo Carillo), and Cherokee (Frank Lackteen). As with all good cowboy stories, the good guys win, Jim gets Chris, Steve gets Claire, and the bad guys meet their maker. William Farnum—supposedly wearing the same suit, boots, and hat he wore in *Riders of the Purple Sage* (1918)—has a small but key role. Shooting was interrupted for three weeks by a decidedly not nineteenth-century cacophony of overhead bombers and fighter planes. The cast and crew of 150—including Tex Ritter, Kermit Maynard, William Desmond and a host of other old-timers—retreated to Placerida Canyon, where Paige and Beery Jr. practiced roping steers, Gwynne went riding, and Diana hid somewhere with a book.

Available for viewing, this effort tied with *Between Us Girls* as the best of the bunch. Robert Paige's charisma demonstrates why he was so successful in B's for four separate studios. Beery Jr. is suitably heroic, while Gwynne is attractive and spunky. Diana cracks wise, looks terrific in her Vera West costumes, and slides Beery Jr. a gun to finish off a villain during the climactic gunfight. She gets shot but also gets her man, riding into the sunset with Steve during the denouement. Carillo and Lackteen's racial stereotypes mar what is otherwise very funny work, especially during their "weapons contest" with Devine. Released in August, a month before *Fired Wife*, critics praised it as a better-than-average "horse opera," formulaic but tightly paced and well-written with superior production values. "[A]ction compensates for the old familiar tunes," wrote Peggy Simmonds for the *Miami News*. Kate Cameron of the *New York Daily News* quipped that Diana "reverse[d] the usual order of Hollywood procedure by descending from the starting role of a grade A production to a secondary part in a western opus." The *Louisville Courier-Journal* noticed her "oozing out of her bodice, which well exposes the all-too-mortal Barrymore flesh" but liked her in the role: "[W]e at once applaud Miss Barrymore while hoping that she will, in the future, follow her bent for delectable comedy of the sort that she purveyed in 'Between Us Girls.'" Diana didn't address *Frontier Badmen* in her memoir, which is strange, since it offered hope she could shine with the right material. In fact, when *Motion Picture Herald* tallied ballots from the "entire exhibition branch of the industry" for their 1943 "Top Ten Stars of Tomorrow," she clocked in at number eight.

The complete list of whom they thought "most promising for development and elevation to stardom" appeared as follows:

1. William Bendix
2. Philip Dorn
3. Susan Peters
4. Donald O'Connor
5. Anne Baxter
6. Van Johnson
7. Gene Kelly
8. Diana Barrymore
9. Gig Young
10. Alexis Smith

The 1943 winners were "unusually versatile," and exhibitors thought Diana ably "carrie[d] on 'the Royal Family' tradition." Diana knew she "overact[ed] like mad" at times but hoped this meant better things ahead: "It's hard to tone down. But I'm trying to learn."

Back when *Nightmare* was released, Louella Parsons mentioned Wanger optioning war correspondent Virginia Cowles's 1941 memoir *Looking for Trouble* expressly for Diana. It was the basis for *When Ladies Fly*, a screenplay about the Women's Auxiliary Ferrying Squadron (WAFs) written by Norman Reilly Raine and Doris Gilbert with the full approval of the USAAF. Principal shooting began in August 1943, the pilots bearing their new name, WASPs (Women's Air Force Service Pilots).

Roberta Harper (Loretta Young), inspired by real life aviators Jacqueline Cochran and Nancy Harkness Love, leads the WASPs as they fly finished bombers from factory to final destination. The rest was soapy melodrama: recklessness, tragic accidents, sibling rivalry, romantic triangles. Diana originally costarred as Roberta's glory-hound sister Vergie, but the studio replaced her with better box-office bet Geraldine Fitzgerald. Her new role of Nadine was yet another vamp seducing a fellow flyer's husband. Anne Gwynne, Lois Collier, Philip Terry, and Evelyn Ankers made up the main cast, supported by June Vincent, Samuel S. Hinds, and Janet Shaw as the unfortunately named "Bee Jay."

The film, released in February 1944 as *Ladies Courageous*, was a stinker. Real WASPs dubbed the "flock of mascaraed glamor girls" "Ladies Outrageous." Almost every review was shocked the USAAF signed off on it. "Hysterics, bickering, and unladylike, nay unpatrotic conduct," chided one critic. "Judging by their actions," wrote another, "they cannot be trusted to pilot a perambulator, much less a B17." One or two, such as *Photoplay*, liked the movie, but the rest panned it. Modern critics agree; Leonard Maltin called it "hackneyed."

It's refreshing to see, even during a time where misogyny was rampant and accepted, that the Office of War Information bristled at the male officers' "patronizing" tone to the WAFs, depicted as joining "for the thrill of adventure rather than a desire to serve their country." Even after three script changes, reviewer Sandy Roth said *Ladies Courageous* gave "a misleading portrayal of American women in service [and] would contribute little to the War Information Program." As a recruitment tool it was useless. It was one of the first pictures to show women serving, and those women were "weak and irresponsible." Who would want to join an organization like that? "If the characters were shown to be really dependable and efficient," Roth continued, "the film would help to dispel rather than perpetuate the harmful prejudices that still exist regarding the capabilities of women."

Diana's character, Nadine, was singled out for criticism. "Nadine is an inconsiderate girl who puts fun first [and] weakens the general presentation." Among other lines, they strongly objected to Nadine's commentary that "we're just a mistake the War Department hasn't gotten around to mopping up."

Universal's ballyhoo included a "Lady Courageous" mail-in contest cosponsored by WLW Radio, where the winner in each of seventy cities received flowers and a scroll signed by Wanger for civilian service during wartime. The "Ladies Courageous" Aeronca bomber provided atmosphere during the ceremony, and all winners in the four-state radius of Indiana, Ohio, Kentucky, and West Virginia were announced on the radio. Trade paper *Harrison's Reports* scolded Universal for exploiting inferior product, "making the public believe that 'Ladies Courageous' is a good picture [when] no one who has seen it believes it is." Audiences looked to studios to produce good films, they argued, particularly about the military, and this would harm "the entire industry . . . the public will undoubtedly lose faith." Universal rereleased it in 1950 as *Fury in the Sky* but it still, well, bombed. It, along with *Frontier Badmen*, lingered in TV syndication for decades.

Diana knew she was finished and decided to pretend it was her idea. The studio only owned her for one more picture, she flippantly told the press, and then she was returning to Broadway. When her part in the musical comedy *She's for Me* (1943) fell through, and she was replaced by Susanna Foster in another musical comedy, *This Is the Life* (1944), the studio settled on Olsen and Johnson's murder farce *High Spirits* (released as 1944's *Ghost Catchers*), costarring Gloria Jean, Andy Devine, Lon Chaney Jr., and other studio regulars.

Absolutely not, she replied. She refused to sully her good name with it—or the Abbott and Costello film they offered instead. Universal cancelled the rest of Diana's contract and told her to go home.

She and Bram went to New York for the holidays, and she swore she'd never step foot in Hollywood again. "I was an ass . . . I made eight pictures. Seven were lousy." In her total she included her uncredited bit part in the George Raft-Marlene Dietrich-Edward G. Robinson drama *Manpower* (Warner Bros., 1941), and an appearance as a "junior hostess" in *Hollywood Canteen* (Warner Bros., 1944). The first thing on her list after coming home was seeing Robin, who had stopped acting and swapped his East Fifty-first Street garden duplex for a 165-acre estate in New Milford, Connecticut. He had sublet it to Garbo, but she backed out after press leaked the deal. There he lived the life of an "eccentric country squire," throwing lavish brunches from his bed, reclining on black silk sheets as butlers passed around champagne and caviar. His partner, William Lloyd Rambo, was a navy veteran who claimed to be a cousin of infamous "Queen of Hearts" Sandra Rambeau.

Robin and Billy stopped by to visit Diana on December 16th. She was under the weather, and Robin brought over one of his famous "goody baskets." He loved giving gifts, particularly of the finer things; it was Robin who bought Diana her first fur coat—"not a mink, but some old squirrel"—when she was sixteen. As she dug for the Cartier bauble that was always at the bottom, she noticed Billy was preoccupied, restless; when she asked what was wrong, he replied, "You'll know soon enough." That evening, Robin called Diana looking for Billy, who never came home.

Around 4 p.m. that afternoon Billy finished his cigarette and jumped off the eighty-sixth floor of the Empire State Building, landing somehow on his feet amidst Christmas shoppers on Third Street and Fifth Avenue. The draft card in his wallet named Robin as next of kin, and Michael officially identified the body, pristine from the waist up. A note arrived for Diana in the next morning's mail: "I'm sorry to do this to Robin, but I just can't take life." He was only twenty-four.

Robin showed up at Diana's later that day, "looking like what Mother used to say he looked like when he was ill—so pale that he looked like he was dying." He couldn't go to Michael, he said. "Robin loved Mother deeply, as I did too . . . absolutely adored her but he could not live with her." Michael's jealousy marred any conversations about Billy, especially since he was the first partner about whom Robin was ever serious. "You understand about Billy and myself completely," he told Diana. "I suppose I was difficult to live with. . . . I used to fight with him." All people in love fight, she replied. She and Bram were fighting right now, in fact. She didn't tell Robin why.

"Bram came back and I told him [what happened] and he said, 'Now *really*, are we going to go through this [with] your fairy brother?' [H]e couldn't understand how one man could feel that way about another. I said, yes, indeed we are . . . if you don't understand after being in the theatre as long as you have, then it's just too bad."

Diana made up the sofa bed and got Robin settled. She heard crying during the night and found him curled up, sobbing, trembling. A photo of Billy was on the floor; Robin fell asleep holding it, then awoke to cruel reality. "I got on my knees because the sofa bed was small and he was a big boy," Diana said. She cradled her 6'2" brother. "I said, 'Baby, quiet, shh . . . ' He said, 'Don't leave me, don't leave me Diana.' I said, 'You know we're catkins and always have been.'" She told him he could stay forever. Bramwell, repulsed by what he called Robin's "depraved" and "disgusting" lifestyle, sent him packing after three days. "Bramwell drove him out," remembered Diana. She stayed with him at his East Fifty-first Street apartment for a few days, until he was ready to go back to Connecticut. A friend, playwright/screenwriter John Colton (*Rain*, *The Shanghai Gesture*) lived with him for a short while, followed by Marjorie Colt, wife of Diana's cousin Jackie Colt.

After Robin went back to Connecticut, Diana and Bram plotted their next steps in New York. They were leaning towards doing something together, perhaps emulating Alfred Lunt and Lynn Fontanne, the sophisticated married actors of Broadway and the West End, when something interesting emerged: Victor Payne-Jennings, the producer responsible for successes such as Aunt Ethel's *Whiteoaks*, was mounting a Broadway edition of his successful London stage version of Hitchcock's moody, atmospheric thriller *Rebecca* (1940). Daphne du Maurier, who wrote the bestselling gothic novel on which the movie was based, adapted it, and actor and Actors' Equity president Clarence Derwent would direct the American premiere. Diana and Bram signed on as Mr. and Mrs. Maxim de Winter, the great Florence Reed played the mad Mrs. Danvers, and rehearsals started at the end of March.

There was an emergency phone call the night of their Cincinnati premiere, April 13, 1944. Michael was hysterical, almost incoherent. Robin was dead, "the result of a nervous breakdown." He had passed away three days earlier, in bed, where he'd spent weeks binge-eating and drinking cases of whiskey. When the alcohol stopped numbing his pain, he wrote letters to his loved ones—including one to Margaret apologizing for treating her poorly—and took a handful of sleeping pills. Marjorie Colt found him. Michael refused to believe it and had an independent autopsy performed, which concluded he died of pneumonia, but Diana knew "he died of a broken heart." Robin's last wishes, in a letter to Billy's sister Mildred, were to be buried alongside his love at the East Germantown Lutheran Cemetery in Indianapolis, Indiana.

Michael accompanied Robin's body on the train trip to Indiana, staying the night with Diana during a stopover in Cincinnati. This time it was her anguished mother whom she cradled. "They've taken the one thing I love!" Michael screamed, and Diana agreed. She too would never fill the emptiness losing Robin left in her heart. Diana was grateful for the distraction of *Rebecca* as they toured through September, with record bookings in Baltimore, Pittsburgh, and Boston. It was rumored the show would hit Broadway around Christmas, then San Francisco in the spring.

It took until January 18, 1945, for *Rebecca* to open on Broadway. Unfortunately, without the evocative cinematography of the Hitchcock film, *Time* thought the limits of the stage turned a "long, dusky, atmospheric tunnel" into a "dry and uphill path." Critic Lewis Nichols thought it "tedious" and "mainly talk," and Diana's role especially "lifeless." Bob Francis of *The Billboard* said it was "curiously disappointing" and "woefully contrived," but Diana was "a much improved young actress . . . she gives a sensitive and appealing portrait of a shy and frightened girl." In his memoirs, Clarence Derwent indulged an I-told-you-so towards Diana and Florence Reed, from whom he "rarely received less cooperation from members of a company." He claimed *Rebecca*'s spell lay not in its script or cast but the novelty factor with people who loved the book and movie, and Diana's insistence on Broadway doomed their roadshow "gold mine." It limped along for twenty performances and closed on February 3, 1945. "It does not remain in my memory as one of my happiest experiences in the theatre [*sic*]," wrote Derwent.

After its Broadway run flopped, *Rebecca* went back on the road for west coast engagements. In early May, the *Jack Carson Show* reached out, offering $1,000 a week for "less than five hours' work" playing a burlesque of herself. "[Carson] was an affable, charming, big, tall, very attractive guy full of yaks . . . [he] was very, very brilliant [and] a hell of a good guy," Diana said. The actor's popular comedy wouldn't be her first time on radio; in 1940, she played spoiled debutante Mona Sheldon on the CBS drama *Big Sister* (1936–52). Ruth Chatterton, Dorothy McGuire, Mercedes McCambridge, and Orson Welles all appeared on *Big Sister*, as did Zasu Pitts, whose character spanked Diana's with a hairbrush. (Spankings seemed to follow the Barrymores; while Diana was getting hers on radio, Elaine was on stage getting them from Jack in *My Dear Children*.) She followed it with guest spots on everything from *Star-Spangled Theater* to *The Inner Sanctum*. She decided she couldn't let her aversion to Hollywood rob her of the chance to add the "old reliable

Barrymore touch" to the Carson cast. "I was sweet-talked by all the MCA people.... '[Y]ou're going to do for the Carson show what your father did for Rudy Vallee' which was, needless to say, not [said] in Mr. Carson's hearing." She played Mrs. de Winter in a series of California shows, "receiv[ing] the traditional blessing of the fabulous Barrymore clan" at one opening from Aunt Ethel. "Ethel Barrymore passed the apple across the footlights to the daughter of the late John Barrymore to continue a family custom which has launched the stage career of every member of the famous clan." British actress Pax Walker took over as Mrs. de Winter after they played Seattle in late October; Diana knew her from small parts in *Nightmare* and *Eagle Squadron*. Ethel Griffies, Diana's colleague from *Between Us Girls*, replaced Florence Reed as Mrs. Danvers. Jack Carson—or, rather, Carson's terribly proper English butler, played by her old summer stock colleague, Arthur Treacher—introduced Diana to audiences on October 24, 1945.

She rented playwright Clifford Odets's house and convinced old friend Johnny Galliher to move in with her. They'd known each other since the deb days, and Diana liked to say he was "well-bred and well ... everything else." His appealing mix of good looks, wit, and graciousness made him essential to every soiree and a favorite of Cole Porter, designer Elsa Schiaparelli, and even the reclusive Greta Garbo. Their house parties ran seven days a week and cost them thousands in food and liquor. The dark-haired, blue-eyed Galliher, who was gay, became one of Diana's surrogate Robins, and the two spent every spare moment together—except for their sex lives, which they dished over breakfast the next morning. Diana's conquests read like a motion picture directory: Rory Calhoun, George Brent, Jimmy Stewart, Henry Fonda, Jack La Rue, Victor Mature. She reinvented herself for each man, dungarees for the outdoorsy Calhoun, cocktail dresses for the urbane Brent. None of them ever saw the real Diana Barrymore—if *she* even knew who that was. "My time was my own. So I filled it with men and parties and everything ... I wasn't in love with any of these people. I was slightly attracted to some but not in love with anyone." She and Galliher were at John Decker's January 18th party when fists swung between La Rue, her cousin Sammy Colt, and bad boy actor Lawrence Tierney. Diana jumped into the fray, slapping Tierney several times while screaming, "Why don't you hit a woman?" She wore a big emerald ring she called a "knuckle duster" and knew it hurt. Galliher hustled her out, but photos made the morning papers, and Michael called as soon as she read them. "It's exactly what I thought would happen ... you're following the same disgusting pattern as Jack!" Michael remembered his days carousing with Decker and his ilk. Nothing good came of it. Diana tuned her out; her independence and freedom were too exhilarating. Then, one night, the phone rang. *Rebecca* was finished and Bram was coming to California.

She rarely answered Bram's letters and dreaded his phone calls. She no longer loved him; her skin crawled imagining sharing a bed again. "I started thinking the more I went out, for God sakes, I'm married to an old man who wants to go home after the theatre and have a couple of drinks up in the suite and play Parcheesi." She moved Johnny out and dutifully met Bram at the airport, then went back to the house and gave him the dollar tour, ending in the bedroom. Alcohol was the only way she could be intimate with him that night.

She rarely slept after their reunion, preferring to sit downstairs in the dark, alone. Once, bleary with exhaustion and scotch, she saw Robin before her, silent, expressionless. Oh, how she needed him! She cried out to "Robin-cat" to stay with her, but he vanished, never to return. "I lost something I could hold on to . . . [l]ike two people at sea together . . . no, you take the lifeboat—no, you do. You both grab it at once and if you both sink, fine."

Everyone noticed the growing distance between Diana and Bram—gossip columnist Danton Walker quipped the "chill" wasn't from "the coal shortage"—but their marriage truly broke the night of Luther Green's dinner party. They spent the evening in near silence until, on the way home, Bram asked if the rumors were true. Out of Diana's mouth streamed the litany of stallions who'd kept her bed warm, men who excited her, men she desired. She never wanted him that way, wasn't sure she ever had. Bram quivered with anger. "I wouldn't remain here if you were the last woman on earth," he growled. When they reached the house he packed a bag and stormed out to stay with friends. They separated at the end of March.

Diana's own words resonated shamefully through her head. One night in April, she ran upstairs and counted out a handful of pills, then called a friend and announced her intentions. She changed her mind by the time he got there but dramatically descended the staircase, unexpectedly blacking out at the bottom. She regained consciousness as family friend Dr. Hugo Weinberg pumped her stomach, later describing it "as though a live eel had been forced down my throat and into my very bowels." Weakly, Diana asked Dr. Weinberg to call Bram, who stayed on just long enough to confirm she was out of danger. Calming Michael down was a little harder. Diana assured her hysterical mother things were fine and would be kept private, but Michael insisted she come to New York while they figured out Diana's next steps. Michael was not unkind to her daughter about Bram, but wondered: after all the hoops Diana jumped through to marry him . . ? They talked for a long while, about sex and compatibility and the difference five years' experience can make. Michael had entertained her share of lovers. "We understood each other completely," Diana said. Both women agreed Diana needed a quickie divorce—how about going to Reno, as Harry had, or maybe Las Vegas? Vegas it was—she'd always wanted to go there. "I think [Bram] did definitely love me, there was no doubt about it.... I was the nearest he'd come to loving anything except himself."

Robin's will was probated on December 2nd in Philadelphia, and his estate was valued at close to $1 million. Cash bequests: $100,000 each to Mom, Diana, and niece Vivian, to whom he also left the New Milford house. (A Bible school bought the palatial 1840 colonial and attached fifteen-acre land parcel in 1947 to use as a summer retreat.) While there is no record of specific gifts he left to Diana, he left a $5,000 platinum and sapphire cigarette case and ruby cufflinks to Leonard; a carved ruby and diamond stud and cufflink set to Yvonne; and an 18-carat gold and ruby cigarette case with matching lighter—a little reticulated goldfish with sapphire and ruby eyes—by Schlumberger for Tiffany & Co. to his mother. Michael also inherited Robin's other worldly possessions, including his art collection, and adopted his dog. She made a little shrine of his furniture and antiques up at her house in Connecticut, and slept in his bed for the rest of her life.

Back at *The Jack Carson Show* they were dangerously close to firing Diana. She showed up hungover for the Monday broadcasts and refused to attend mandatory critique sessions after the Friday ones. Her part shrank drastically; one available 1946 program[13] barely gives her five lines. Her agent cautioned her against participating in the upcoming live broadcasts at the Strand in New York City. Did she really want to play her hometown like that? Diana stayed behind but absolved herself of responsibility, saying she declined to appear because the idea of being "second billing to a motion picture" was "humiliating." Actress Randy Stuart replaced her in New York.

On April 1, Jack's dear friend Ned Sheldon passed away. Michael introduced her to "Uncle Ned" as a child, just before she and Jack separated. "[I]'d go to see him as often as I could because he was the only person I could talk to about Daddy," she said. Ned loved a Jack Barrymore almost no one knew; he saw, as Sheldon's biographer Eric Wollencott Barnes wrote, that "[u]nderneath the mask of devil-may-care cynicism there was a tender dreamer, and behind the dreamer a lost child." Ned recognized that same lost child in Jack's daughter, and was one of the few people from whom the adult Diana received genuine love and guidance. "I was made to go to church

13. "The Search for the Mystery Lady Continues," *The Jack Carson Show*, no. 58, February 13, 1946.

every Sunday but going to Ned's was more like church than church, because I could tell him anything . . . [w]henever I left him, I felt as if my heart had wings to it. I felt as if I had been to confession." Hearing of his death was a "horrible, horrible blow" to her. "I felt as if I had lost contact with God."

CHAPTER 6

THE DIANA BARRYMORE SHOW

FLASHY, TITILLATING LAS VEGAS WAS A GOOD MATCH FOR DIANA, AS WAS new friend John Howard, a six-two, twenty-two-year-old former tennis pro "with a smile that could win a bobby-soxer away from Sinatra." After a perfunctory dinner invite, which Diana declined, he cut to the chase: "Then let's make love." (Compliments to the publisher for delicacy.) He was "the antithesis of Bramwell," their time together filled with "unabashed animal vigor." He and Diana traveled to El Paso for a tournament, where he introduced her to marijuana. For thirty-six hours, they giggled, played records, had sex, and Diana got the munchies for scrambled eggs. When the pot wore off, that was it—she swore she'd never touch it again. She returned to Vegas for six more weeks. John tagged along for the first three, emptying his savings and $5,000 of Diana's with his fondness for roulette. They stayed under the radar until May 15, when John got into a skirmish with actress Anne Sterling during Diana's "divorce party" at the Trocadero. He wanted to leave, Diana and Anne wanted to stay, and when Anne protested, John slapped her. "I guess I slapped him back," said Anne. John insisted they were old friends; "we are if John says so," Anne replied. By the end of June 1946, the press teased a serious romance, which Diana denied. "John isn't divorced yet," she protested. "How can anyone discuss marriage under these circumstances?" Her own divorce came through on June 27th, and Diana rushed to Boston in July immediately after John's divorce from first wife Ruth was finalized. He already leaked their "engagement" to the press, so there was no avoiding it: the time had come to break the news to her mother.

A professional athlete? Michael was intrigued. Was he a "gentleman tennis player" like the graceful "Big Bill" Tilden? No, said Diana. He wasn't a gentleman anything, really, but Michael would love him because he gave her lots and lots of "health." Ahem. Sexual satisfaction doesn't exactly inspire a mother's ardor, and neither did his behavior during their weekend together at Michael's Easton, Connecticut, home. John spent the time sprawled on

83

Michael's sofa, reading comic books and blaring the radio, and Michael's suggestion he do something productive—mow the lawn, perhaps—was declined with a smile and a "I'd use the wrong muscles." "Keep him as a lover if you must," Michael advised, "but for God's sake don't marry him!" Diana, as usual, didn't listen.

She and John married at the Park Avenue Central Presbyterian Church on January 15, 1947. Leonard convinced an uneasy Rev. Dr. Spears to perform the ceremony, something he rarely did for divorced people. She and her brother grew closer since Robin's death, and he gave the bride away. Diana wore a Henri Bendel printed day dress given by her mother and bought her own hat, which Robin—who once ran a millinery shop in Mexico City with his poodle, Bagatelle- would have hated. Diana also paid for the groom's dark striped suit and tie. Leonard and Yvonne gave the reception at their Park Avenue apartment, the guests primarily Michael's friends like Diana's godmother, Mrs. Cass Canfield, wife of the head of Harper & Bros. (now HarperCollins), and Mrs. Cole Porter. No one on John's side attended. They honeymooned for a month at a resort in St. Augustine, Florida, after John shrewdly traded the use of Diana's name in publicity for a free stay.

Shortly after the wedding, John and Diana were visiting a friend when she caught the two of them eyeing her tennis bracelet. The diamonds had been her mother's, a gift from Harry. The two men thought maybe she could "lose" it, file a claim, then the three would split the proceeds. Insurance fraud? She argued about it with John in private, which never got them anywhere except into bed. That was the crux of their relationship: "It was not love. It was lust."

John's new job as a resident tennis pro came with free room and board, so he, Diana, and their dog Minou moved to Kentucky in April. Club president Dale F. Linch greeted Diana with orchids and cajoled the newlyweds into a kiss over the net before showing them their home: a two-room shack thirty feet from the courts. Things soured quickly. She resented his playing pinball in between lessons instead of helping her with the housework. He sneered at her pampered background, called her soft. That's why he refused to introduce her to his family: "They live on the wrong street for you." Her crack about his mechanic father got her a split lip and an AWOL husband. She drank while he holed up with another woman in a cheap motel, returning after a week to restart the cycle of sex and violence. Each time, however, they slipped lower. They tussled with three police officers during a May traffic stop for drunk driving and spent the night in jail, where Diana's insults and John's accusation of petty theft led to a $60,000 slander suit by the officers involved. They settled later that year for $1,500, a bit more than Diana and John's original $10 fine for assault and disorderly conduct. An offer to play the lead in a summer stock production of *Joan of Lorraine* was the chance Diana needed to escape, arriving in Salem, Massachusetts, on June 17, 1947, almost six months to the day since her wedding.

One of the first people she met was rumpled, dark-eyed Robert Wilcox. He had just finished drying out at the Payne Whitney clinic, he explained, and took the train straight to Salem, polishing off a pint of whiskey on the way. His deep-voiced refinement immediately attracted Diana, and the two went to dinner that night. He was also a Universal alum, discovered during summer stock and signed in 1936. Bob was best known as Bob Wayne, secret identity of the Copperhead in Republic's 1940 serial *Mysterious Doctor Satan*. The studio invented the superhero after being denied the rights to Superman, but kept details meant for the Caped Crusader in their script, such as Lois (Ella Neal), the intrepid girl reporter. (In costume, the Copperhead was played by stuntman David Sharpe, stunt coordinator for Republic from 1939–42.) He attained the rank of captain in the army and organized special services shows for the troops after being wounded. His 1937 marriage to sportswriter Grantland Rice's daughter, actress Florence Rice, ended after two years. Bob left Hollywood and its "same damned cop-and-robbers" typecasting and was reinventing himself and his career. The longer he and Diana talked, the more they clicked.

Joan of Lorraine is Maxwell Anderson's play-within-a-play about the story of Joan of Arc and the actors who stage a play about her, especially star Mary Grey/Joan and director Jimmy Masters/the Inquisitor. Diana did *Joan* in summer stock, then agreed to a winter tour for $750 a week—as long as Bob stayed her costar. His salary was $250 per week.

Ingrid Bergman's Tony-winning performance in the 1946 Broadway original created a lissome template for Joan, and producers sent Diana to physiologist Harold J. Reilly to slim down before the tour. He was globally renowned for reshaping stars like Sonja Henie, Burgess Meredith, and Bob Hope. "Miss Barrymore set out to trim herself down to Joan's size," but not quickly enough for Reilly, who ordered her armor a size under, forcing Diana to diet more strenuously. There was understandable "fire and brimstone in the Barrymore eye" when Reilly confessed the ruse, yet even at her ideal weight, many of the reviews felt it necessary to point out Diana wasn't as delicate or petite as Bergman. They did appreciate her "finish and sincerity" as well as Bob's "natural and easy performance."

During the run she crossed paths with Jules Ziegler, once an assistant of her old agent Louis Shurr, now head of his own agency. "She looked beautiful—always looked good when she was on stage. She wasn't drunk." He and Diana talked about the old days and her current situation. "She said, 'This is not what I want—stock isn't what I want. I want to get back to Broadway. You know, you S.O.B., you're the only one that can do things for me . . . do you want to handle me?' I said, 'All right, my door is open to you at any time—you come in as soon as you are through with the tour.'" They parted with the usual well-meaning promises to keep in touch.

Michael met up with her daughter down south and had tickets to the Atlanta show on January 19, 1948. Diana was *nervous*. Nothing in the world meant as much to her mother as the Maid of Orleans, in Michael's opinion "the most sacredly enigmatic person in all history." Michael wrote books about her, recited lecture pieces in character, even shopped around her play about Joan titled "Forever Young." She adored George Bernard Shaw's *Saint Joan* so fervently that she forced the author to listen to her perform a monologue from it. Diana hoped she would do her almost-namesake justice.

They all acted their hearts out that night. "Miss Barrymore lives up to everything the famous Barrymore name stands for in the dramatic world," wrote critic Paul Jones for the *Atlanta Constitution*, her performance of a caliber "rarely displayed on the stage by a road performer." It was one of the greatest nights of Diana's life, with numerous curtain calls and hearty congratulations from her fellow castmates . . . until she noticed Michael wasn't there. Someone mentioned she'd returned to the hotel and Diana relaxed. She had a huge party planned in her own suite at the Tutwiler, and Michael was guest of honor; they'd meet there. But Michael didn't show at the party, either. Bob found her pacing in her own room, convinced Diana no longer needed or cared about her. He reassured her until she agreed to make an appearance. "She strode up to me. Her lips brushed my cheek. 'I won't hold you Diana, you're so busy.' Before I knew what to say, she had turned and left."

Michael forged jealousy and resentment into a passive-aggressive knife and boy, she knew how to twist it. A sitting with Spanish painter Ignacio Zuloaga during Jack's *Hamlet* run mysteriously became a portrait of her in *Hamlet*-esque costume, over which she feigned embarrassment: "no doubt [done by Zuloaga] for publicity reasons." She demeaned Margaret's work regularly in front of friends; now, she withheld love and approval from her own daughter.

In Missouri, two understudies lost control of the costume truck and crashed into a tree. The cast did their February 12th show in St. Joseph in regular clothing and wept backstage when they learned Francis Louis Abad and Alexander Polarevic did not survive. An upset Diana called Margaret, but instead of comparing Michael battle scars as usual, they discussed how off she looked the last three months. She blamed her collapse after a London performance in November 1947 on the rigors of touring, and at first ignored Margaret and Diana's suggestions to see the doctor. A second collapse changed her mind. Tests revealed leukemia as the cause of Michael's persistent exhaustion, and Diana guzzled a fifth of vodka after hearing the news. The next day, scared straight, she and Bob quit cold turkey, joined a gym, and began B1 shots. ("We both had lumps on our cans," wrote Bob.) Michael, on the other hand, went into complete denial. Who cared if her physicians recommended she cancel her tour and rest? Michael Strange did not listen to medical advice. Diana learned that in 1940 during Michael's spinal issues. "The problem is you have no faith in any of your doctors," she wrote her mother. "If you put yourself in Goldthwaite's [sic] hands," thought positively and did what he asked, she would be "completely well soon!" Dr. Joel Goldthwait founded the orthopedics program at Massachusetts General Hospital and was a pioneer in the field, but Michael was certain her illness had only one cause: Margaret.

While Michael always held an air of condescension in regard to Margaret, it was just before Robin's death that she graduated to scapegoat. Michael, exasperated by her children and her own stagnant literary career, "began to turn in bitterness against Miss Brown." The more Margaret tried to please her, the worse Michael treated her. Then, something horrible happened: while staying at a friend's house, Robin's dog was left unattended by a "scatterbrained" hostess and ingested some rat poison. "Michael was beside herself" at the dog's death, "the last relic remaining" of her boy; she blamed Margaret for the accident, since she suggested the dog-sitter, and after that the emotional abuse grew "utterly brutal." Michael now decreed they must cease all contact, kicked a devastated Margaret out of the house, and put her energy into making amends with God for His divine retribution.

She also turned to Bramwell. A year earlier, Diana noticed her mother and ex-husband spending time together, and Bob found a small gold Catholic medal, engraved, from Bram to Michael. "Mother has been seeing a lot of Bram," she wrote Kellogg in November 1947. "God knows what has gone on!" He now stepped in to fill the void, and the two began sharing everything from lunches to a villa in Italy. "[Michael] invited us up one week-end when he was there, hoping it would be a shock to Diana but it wasn't. Bramwell got me off to the side and said, 'Let's take a walk.' He said, 'Do you understand this girl?' And he tried to tell me about Diana. I never understood Diana, but Bramwell understood her less than I did."

The year 1949 opened with Michael doing six shows at Times Hall in New York City, January 6th through February 10th. Diana gasped audibly as she took the stage: her favorite Grecian robe with split sleeves and gold belt, the one Bob joked made her look like a "poor man's Aimee Semple MacPherson," hung on her wasted frame; only the "magnificent shock of black hair" and "dark and flashing eyes" identified the pallid woman as her mother. Every audience member felt the shadow of death that night. It would be Michael's final "Great Words with Great Music" recital. Diana's own year began with a terrible bout of food poisoning, but the Personality Deb was back a month later, performing a scene from *Joan* for a hospital fundraiser in Pennsylvania, then guesting on both *The Phil Silvers Show* and Ed Sullivan's *Toast of the Town*. She was still in demand with everyone from Savarin Coffee to the March of Dimes but was also quietly collecting unemployment and pawning jewelry—"hunks of ice," she told Earl Wilson—to satisfy debts. She'd somehow managed to keep the truth about her financial circumstances (and living arrangement) from her mother. An ailing Michael cancelled an April trip with Bram and went to her house in Connecticut, where Bram visited her and taught her to paint while Diana and Bob did a summer tour of the Moss Hart showbiz comedy *Light Up the Sky*. They were en route to Atlanta that September, after a short segue doing *Mr. & Mrs. North* at Long Island's Sea Cliff Theater, when CBS dropped a life-changing opportunity in Diana's lap: her own "disc jockey" television program for the still-untapped late-night market. A popular fixture in nightclubs, "disc jockeys" acted as emcees, chatting with patrons and providing color commentary of the evening's doings. Diana's televised version would be thirty minutes long, with room for ad-libbing and showing off that Barrymore wit; she accepted immediately. *The Diana Barrymore Show*, sponsored by Ansonia Shoes and with Earl Wilson and actress Nina Foch as guests, would premiere at 11 p.m. on October 17, 1949.

The day she was hired, she had "no reaction . . . like a clam that hasn't been open and eaten." Now, jitters consumed her the afternoon of her debut. She rubbed her ear; it got nicked three days earlier by a falling chunk of ceiling plaster. This was no small audience; what if she screwed up? Liquid relief beckoned from across the room. Maybe a nip to calm her nerves. A nip became a glass, became two glasses . . . she lost count of the refills. Bob came home to a wobbly, slurring Diana around 9:45 p.m. and pleaded with his Muzzy to feign illness, an accident, anything to keep away from the studio. She held firm, and he drove her to the CBS building. People whispered as she teetered to the studio set, which was surprisingly calm so close to broadcast. Earl and Nina were nowhere to be found, and when producer Hardie Freiberg sat her down gently, she knew. Opening-night butterflies, she told Freiberg. It happens to everyone! If they postponed to next week she'd be fine. Freiberg handed her back the cocktail dress she'd dropped off earlier that week, told her to go home and get some rest. They'd talk tomorrow, he said, smiling.

Bob changed the bar's television to CBS at 11 p.m. sharp, wincing at the "circumstances beyond our control" message. The next day, CBS announced that due to Diana's ceiling plaster "accident," newcomer Faye Emerson would take over the time slot starting October 24th. "For months everywhere I looked, stories and interviews and photographs of Faye Emerson leaped out at me," Diana later wrote. "You fool, you idiot [I thought]! It could have been you."

In December, everything fell apart. On December 14th, she went "wham down the stairs" and suffered two black eyes, a broken nose, missing teeth, and a concussion. (She later sued the property owner for $10,000, said the fall was due to weakness since the ceiling plaster incident. Her lawyers advised her to settle and avoid probable "very embarrassing" questions in court; she did and got $750.) As she recovered in Roosevelt Hospital, two "marihuana[sic]-happy gunmen" robbed Bob in a bizarre (and slightly fishy) incident at their East Fifty-second Street–Park Avenue apartment. Two men showed up at the door bearing long bouquets of gladioli for Diana, from which they extracted equally long shotguns. According to Bob, they identified themselves as "ex-GIs" who couldn't readjust to civilian life: "We are on the marihuana [sic] and get a kick out of doing this." They bound and gagged him with Diana's stockings and stole her silver fox, her mink, a camera, some costume jewelry, and Bob's jar of $50 in quarters. A neighbor, artist and illustrator Alex Orr, heard Bob "mumbling" after the men left and called the police. "Poor child," Bob said about Diana. "I guess this makes her the unluckiest girl of the year."

Michael was in Zurich, Switzerland, conferring with specialists who said their strength-building regimen would put Michael's leukemia into remission. She returned home more optimistic than she'd been in ages and was planning a lecture tour at the Vatican when she learned about the robbery—and Diana and Bob's living arrangements. This necessitated a lunch date, with Michael's surprise guest: Bob's brother, New York surgeon Dr. Ross Wilcox. Poor Dr. Wilcox thought he was at an intervention for his brother's drinking problem. Instead, he sat silently as Michael carried on about reputations. Didn't they care about the optics of living together, unmarried? It was downright immoral! The usually reticent Bob quietly reminded his mother-in-law how she "started taking up with John Barrymore" while still married to Leonard Thomas. He then took Diana's hand and left, leaving a spluttering Michael (and dazed Dr. Wilcox) behind. "No one had ever talked back to her like that," Diana wrote, calling Bob her "home run [after] two errors."

Radio writers Jack Carhartt and Nicholas Winter cast Diana as the lead in *Shadow of a Doubt,* their ultra-low-budget thriller for Film Classics. It was released in January 1950 as *Cry Murder*, starring Jack Lord and Carole Matthews, with all of Diana's footage (if there ever was any) scrapped. Michael went back to Switzerland a month later with Robin's friend, playboy/escort Ted Peckham (an opportunist, like Johnny Galliher, who had also traveled to Europe with Michael), who drained her bank account in exchange for long countryside walks in matching clothing a la the glory days with Jack. Back then, a perplexed Aunt Tessie asked, "In God's green earth what's the matter with you, baby?" She thought they resembled "a couple of equestrians" in their identical suits and hats "cocked at a similar devastating angle." In the spring, driving through Virginia on the way to Atlanta for *Light Up the Sky*, a driver sideswiped Diana and Bob's Oldsmobile, confining Diana to bed for three weeks with a badly wrenched back. Audrey Christie, who played in the original Broadway version, took Diana's place while Bob daubed some makeup on his black eye and went on as scheduled. Diana needed to stop drinking and rest, let her body heal from this latest injury as well as her earlier concussion, but as soon as she was able she flew to visit Michael in Europe. If she picked up a newspaper on the way she might have read about seventeen-year-old Johnnie's screen debut as a "trigger-happy Texan" in the Eagle-Lion Western *The Sundowners* (1950). Would *he* be the next big Barrymore?

Mother and daughter returned to the US in May, and Michael checked into Memorial Hospital in Manhattan for treatment. Diana, relieved at Michael's consent, headed to Albany, New York, for *Laura*. After four weeks of proper medical care, Michael improved enough to spend the summer in Maine, and Diana got her mother settled at Bar Harbor, then returned to upstate New York where she had a few irons in the fire besides *Laura*: fundraising for a play about "dipsomania" in which she hoped to star, finishing a biography of her father for possible publication by Doubleday, and more *Light* with Bob and her friend Anne Francine.

She was featured in *The Charming Woman*, one of those books you got with a coupon from the back of *Glamour* or *Modern Romances*, a finishing school in one volume by experts in their fields: Helena Rubenstein on skin care and makeup shades to suit your complexion; Charles Revson (Revlon) on achieving the perfect manicure; Clara Ogilvie on hair care and styling. Editor Helen Fraser called Diana into service for the "charming speech" section, helping "the ordinary girl in business and social life [to] acquire a well-modulated speaking voice and the ability to use it correctly." She acknowledged that being Jack and Michael's daughter gave her a "head start" but insisted her "delightful[ly] throaty" voice took "plenty of work" to maintain. Twelve lessons covered breathing, elocution, resonance, even advice on being a good conversationalist. Above all, she stressed, don't imitate others: "Be natural. Be yourself." Diana was previously in *Opportunities in Acting: Stage, Screen, Radio, Television*, a 1946 vocational manual for high school hopefuls. "Diana Barrymore has as trick of switching her eyes toward another player, especially with an upward lift. This is most effective in suggesting girlish impressionability," wrote Frank Vreeland under the heading of "Face Control."

John Howard resurfaced in May 1950, admitting during a hotel vice raid arrest he hadn't been "playing much tennis lately." After the divorce, he coached at the University of Maine but bailed after a year to shack up with Junior Karr, aka Betty Allen, a twenty-something "blonde model" and John's "call girl." Allen told police she made $8,000 in sixteen weeks; "I don't demand money from these women . . . they just give it to me," John replied. Charges were dropped due to lack of evidence, but the Louisville Boat Club permanently banned him over the bad publicity and by June he was in Mexico City working as a tennis instructor. The FBI began monitoring him a year earlier when, charges claimed, John persuaded a movie extra to become a high-class "prostitute" in 1948, moving her to New York and setting her up in a "lavishly furnished" Midtown apartment. In July, a month after he relocated to Mexico, a grand jury secretly indicted John Howard on violation of the Mann Act. John pleaded not guilty to the two-count indictment, still insisting that "women simply like[d] to support him." He was released on bail.

Jules Ziegler's office door buzzed one afternoon in April 1950. It was Robert Wilcox. "Jules, you talked to us," he said, then smiled. "Diana and I think you're great—would you like to handle us?" *Us?* thought Ziegler. "Where's Diana? Why do you come alone?"

"Well, you know Diana never leaves the house." Bob's features froze into a mask of geniality. Ziegler patted his desk and stood up. "[I]f you want to talk to me, come in tomorrow with Diana." He remembered the summer of 1947, how she still had "a lot of talent left in her" and a "great personality."

Bob and Diana showed up bright and early the next morning. Ziegler was prepared.

"You're going to cut out all your shenanigans, and you're going to cut out all the things that you have been blamed for, and I'll work my head off for you. The first time that you break any rules, I'll drop you like a hot coal." He looked pointedly at Diana. "You know I mean what I say because you and I have had it out before." She looked "terrible . . . like she had had a terrific night before." Her hair was uncombed, her eyes red-rimmed, bloodshot. "You've never lied to me, Diana. All I want is your word . . . [g]ive me your word and I'll go to hell for you."

"Anything you want I'll do," she replied. "You've got me—I'm with you 100 percent."

Ziegler sighed. "I can't stop you from drinking, I know that, but if you can just curtail your drinking, I'll be satisfied. I don't want you ever coming into a theater when you're drunk. I don't want you ever to give a performance while you're drunk." To Bob, sitting mutely, he said nothing . . . yet. "He was a worse drinker than she was. I was leading up to something . . . I had my method."

He phoned every summer stock theater operator in his files. They all declined. We don't need trouble—"[y]ou couldn't pay us to use her." Ziegler switched into sales mode. Funny you should say that, he said; I believe in Diana so much—she's got real drawing power, and you know there are fans who will always lay down their dollar for a Barrymore—I'm willing to work on a percentage. "I said, 'If she makes money for you she'll make money for herself—I want no salary!' Of course the producers have never been faced with a problem like that or a proposition like that."

After thinking it over, he had six theaters ready to take a chance . . . but only without Bob Wilcox. Privately, Ziegler agreed. "This guy is no good. This is the guy that's ruining Diana." But he promised it would be a package deal, and after a little massaging, got the six to accept. If Wilcox was coming, however, they wanted a $5,000 bond as "insurance against losses," in case she showed up drunk—or didn't show up at all. Of course, if Diana came alone, no bond was necessary; everyone felt "Wilcox was the instigator" and, as in the days of Rory Calhoun and dungarees, "Barrymore never thought these things up by herself—if she liked somebody she wanted to do what [everybody] else wanted to do."

Great, Ziegler thought. *How do I approach this?* "I didn't have nerve enough to say, 'Please leave your husband home [then] I can book you [and] I can do great things for you.'"

Instead, he invited Bob to his office. "I want to be honest with you," he said. "I am forced because of you to put up a bond if I want to book Diana. I have no faith in you, Wilcox. I don't give a darn if you are a success or not but I do believe in Diana and I think a lot of money can be made on Diana if you'll behave . . . I can't ask you for five thousand dollars—you haven't got it—but, I'm going to have somebody put up the five thousand dollars for me because I, as an agent, won't put it up."

The moment arrived: Ziegler activated his method.

"You come here tomorrow and I'll introduce you to the people who are putting up the bond for you . . . you are both a husband, a bodyguard, and a friend. You got to live up to it."

Leonard Thomas Sr. with Robin (left) and Leonard Jr. circa 1917. Diana Barrymore Papers, NYPL. Used with permission.

Blanche, circa 1916. Diana Barrymore Papers, NYPL. Used with permission.

Michael in *Vogue* magazine, 1917. Conde Nast Archives. Public domain.

Jack as Hamlet, 1922. Diana Barrymore Papers, NYPL. Used with permission.

Diana and Jack, frontispiece to *Confessions of an Actor*, 1926. Diana Barrymore Papers, NYPL. Used with permission.

Michael and Robin, circa 1923. Diana Barrymore Papers, NYPL. Used with permission.

Beach day, circa 1926. Diana Barrymore Papers, NYPL. Used with permission.

Diana note to Tibi, circa 1927. Diana Barrymore Papers, NYPL. Used with permission.

"I was the ugliest child I knew," circa 1928. Diana Barrymore Papers, NYPL. Used with permission.

Michael in *L'Aiglon*, 1927. Diana Barrymore Papers, NYPL. Used with permission.

Robin, circa 1931. Diana Barrymore Papers, NYPL. Used with permission.

Lovably awkward, circa 1930s. Diana Barrymore Papers, NYPL. Used with permission.

Michael in 1929. Author's collection.

"Robina" and Diana, circa 1930s. Diana Barrymore Papers, NYPL. Used with permission.

Diana letter to Michael, circa 1934. Diana Barrymore Papers, NYPL. Used with permission.

Diana and Michael, 1933. Author's collection.

The 3 Magi (left to right): Diana Barrymore, Jane Shaw, and Carol Case, 1935. Author's collection.

Diana, Leonard Jr., and Robin are catkins, circa 1936. Diana Barrymore Papers, NYPL. Used with permission.

Diana and Michael, circa 1937. Author's collection.

Diana sketches her day at school, circa 1937. Diana Barrymore Papers, NYPL. Used with permission.

Jack performing the Bard on NBC-Blue, 1937. Author's collection.

Life magazine, July 31, 1939. Author's collection.

The Princess of Theatre's Royal Family at eighteen, 1939. Author's collection.

Doing her best Barrymore scowl, 1940. Author's collection.

In her dressing room at Ogunquit, 1939. Author's collection.

Backstage at *My Dear Children*, before the storm. 1940. Author's collection.

Elaine Barrie and Jack in *Radio Mirror*, 1940. Media History Digital Library. Public domain.

Diana by Arnold Genthe, 1941. Library of Congress, Prints & Photographs Division, Arnold Genthe Collection, LC-DIG-agc-7a01247.

Jack, Diana, and Viola the Afghan hound, 1942.
Media History Digital Library. Public domain.

Universal promotional still for *Eagle Squadron*
(1942) with Robert Stack. Author's collection.

Uncle Lionel, Diana, and Daddy, 1942. Author's collection.

Diana and Robert Stack
at *Modern Screen*'s bowling date, 1942.

At Jack's funeral with Uncle Lionel, 1942.
Author's collection.

Universal promotional still for *Between Us Girls* (1942)
with Robert Cummings. Author's collection.

Universal Studios promo shot,
1942. Author's collection.

Universal promotional still for *Between Us Girls* (1942). Author's collection.

Glamour shot, 1942. Author's collection.

Bramwell and Diana on their wedding day. 1942. Author's collection.

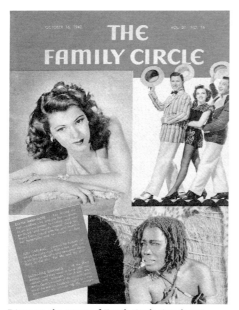

Diana on the cover of *Family Circle*, October 16, 1942. Author's collection.

The "ugly one." 1942. Media History Digital Library. Public domain.

Universal promotional still for *Nightmare* (1942) with Brian Donlevy. Author's collection.

Ad in *Radio Mirror*, 1945. Media History Digital Library. Public domain.

Promotional still for *Rebecca*, 1945. Author's collection.

John Howard and Diana, 1946. Author's collection.

Diana in Las Vegas, 1946.
Author's collection.

Diana looking coy, circa late 1940s.
Diana Barrymore Papers, NYPL.
Used with permission.

Actor Jack La Rue and Diana at
the Stork Club, late 1940s. Diana
Barrymore Papers, NYPL. Used
with permission.

Out on the water, circa late
1940s. Diana Barrymore
Papers, NYPL. Used with
permission.

A gathering of Joans of Arc (left to right): Ingrid Bergman, Luise Rainier, Diana, and Vera Zorina. *Radio Flash*, 1948. Media History Digital Library. Public domain.

Promotional still for *Joan of Lorraine*, 1948. Author's collection.

Back home from Australia, 1952. Author's collection.

Bob and Muzzy, circa 1953. Diana Barrymore Papers, NYPL. Used with permission.

With a twinkle in her eye, circa early 1950s. Diana Barrymore Papers, NYPL. Used with permission.

A Sunday painter, circa 1950s. Diana Barrymore Papers, NYPL. Used with permission.

Dungarees! Circa early 1950s. Diana Barrymore Papers, NYPL. Used with permission.

Always with the cigarette, 1955. Author's collection.

Telling her story, 1957. Author's collection.

Too Much, Too Soon ad, 1958. Newspapers.com. Public domain.

Maggie the Cat, 1958. Author's collection.

Diana and Tennessee Williams, circa 1959. Author's collection.

The Rev. Sidney Lanier presides at Diana's funeral. Media History Digital Library. Public domain.

The two men shook hands. "Nobody has ever confronted me with any-thing like this," Bob said. "I realize this is the last chance."

The following day Ziegler introduced "two of the roughest actors that he didn't know—one with a flat nose and one with a cauliflower ear . . . [t]his was an act I was putting up because I couldn't [do] it any other way . . . [t]hey had been rehearsed very thoroughly." These are the men putting up your bond, he told Bob. "I can't get anyone legitimate [because] your reputation is bad and I have to go to people on the outside—it's costing me a lot of money for this.

"He looked at these two fellows, and I'll never forget his words . . . 'I've got a lot at stake—I've got a reputation at stake—you fellows will never find me doing anything that's wrong and your money is safe.'"

The tour of *Light up the Sky* went so smoothly that every town they toured wanted to show off their real live Barrymore. Diana gave grand prize trophies for the "Diana Barrymore Trot," a harness racing event, in Ohio, Pennsyl-vania, Massachusetts, and other states on the tour. In Portland, Maine, she spoke at the Home Defender of Freedom meeting "to discourage hoarding and combat communism." Rotary Club speeches, local radio interviews—the summer of 1950 passed this way until Ridgefield, Connecticut, and a call from a worried theater owner.

"I think I'm going to have a lot of trouble . . . there seems to be a bunch of people here who don't want Diana in this town—that she had insulted a lot of people." Ridgefield wielded the torches and pitchforks of litigation since their last visit, when Hurricane Wilcox smashed dishes at a restaurant and broke the bed and cracked the paint in their room at the boarding house. Diana et al. spent Sunday at a hotel about twelves miles away, biding time until Monday and opening night. "Jules, everyone in this town is against me," she said. "I think we made a bad booking . . . we should not have come here." Any publicity is good publicity, he reassured her—"as long as they spell your name right." Monday night is historically the "worst house," and Diana thought business would be extra terrible, but Ziegler was right: "all it did was make people come that wanted to see the Diana that was so-and-so. There was a long line waiting for tickets." They played to a full house, did excellent business the entire week. After the last show on Saturday night, instead of picking up their check, Diana and Bob rushed to the hotel bar and ordered twelve double scotches. In Connecticut, they explained, you couldn't order drinks after midnight, but you could finish the ones on your table. "I promised you that I wouldn't go into the theatre drunk—I didn't promise you that I wasn't going to drink," she said. "Have you had any complaints about me?"

Ziegler frowned. "No . . . [but] one of these days you'll take one too many and you won't show up, and where will I be?" Saratoga Springs, New York, as it turned out.

"Nobody knew where Diana was—nobody could find her—nobody knew where she was eating or drinking. I went to the theatre at eight and no Diana and no Wilcox. Ten after eight—the curtain goes up at half past eight [and] nobody has seen them all day." At 8:15 p.m., Diana walked in wearing two different shoes, her hair a tangled mess. Bob staggered behind her. "I could think of only one thing," Ziegler said.

"She had a terrycloth bathrobe—I soaked the entire bathrobe in ice water, and I was so mad that I took the soaking robe [and] put the two of them under it." Anne Francine "felt sorry for them" and tried to block him but he tightly wrapped them, "yelling blue murder to get out," and said they weren't going anywhere for ten minutes. Afterwards, Ziegler saw the "miracle of miracles":

"My wife and I—if we hadn't been in the dressing room—we never would have believed that there could be that great a conversion. She was still making up when the curtain went up. A person without talent could never have done this. She went on and gave the greatest performance she ever gave in her life. The applause was deafening . . . my wife said, 'Look, why don't you tell her how great she was?' I said, 'Diana, I would like to say that I am proud of you. If you'd given me this performance without the performance you gave me in the dressing room . . . as an actress, nobody can top you. You're absolutely wonderful.'"

With autumn came somber news of Michael's move to Massachusetts Memorial Hospital and their cutting-edge leukemia program. Forty thousand dollars' worth of Swiss therapies did little, and Memorial in Manhattan could do nothing more. At this stage, everyone feared, Boston would only provide hospice care.

She entertained from bed as Robin once had, surrounded by fresh flowers and her favorite books and records. Leonard or Ted served as doorman, while her maid Ethel Malcolm ran errands or arranged for meals to be brought in. Diana flew to Boston and sat with Michael, reading her favorite poetry aloud or talking. They never really talked before, and Michael had plenty of time to think. "I failed Robin," she told Diana. "I should have been more of a mother to him in later years and less of a mother before." Michael's eyes welled. "I failed you too. I gave him too much affection and you not enough."

The previous Christmas, Michael wrote Margaret asking her to settle her estate, stating anything not allotted should be split equally between her and Diana. She didn't trust Diana to do it and thought Leonard's wife Yvonne too sentimental. Margaret made sure her wishes would be honored, down to disinterring Robin and moving him to the family plot in New York.

October brought bedsores, internal bleeding, pleurisy, and pain against which even morphine was useless. Somehow, Michael held on through all of it, bolstered only by transfusions and Margaret, who rented a hotel room close to the hospital and spent day and night at her side. She brought Michael her favorite primroses and held her hand as they talked of the Great Mystery: her parents, her son, everyone she had loved and lost waited to embrace her again. Diana and Bob wanted to cancel their week-long Miami run of *Light* but doctors assured them death was not imminent. Troubled, but in dire need of the money, they went. Diana never told Michael she married Bob on October 17th; it was a simple affair in a Newark, New Jersey, lawyer's office, with reception at their apartment and no honeymoon, and the news would have only further upset her mother. Bob was convinced Michael knew anyway, as "there were 97 photographers there . . . Diana keeps a secret like a sieve." As for husband no. 2, he was now officially in the custody of the FBI, arrested at the US-Mexico border for "white slavery."

Margaret thought hypnosis might help relax Michael, who was delirious with pain and lack of sleep. Doctors rejected her idea and instead banned all visitors from seeing Michael. Margaret didn't protest, especially after the rumors swirling about Michael's reassignment to the psychiatric ward, but Michael's wails during a 1 a.m. phone call were too much to bear. The head nurse refused at first but, haunted by Margaret's pleas, called back with approval a few hours later. As soon as Michael saw Margaret she managed a little of the old General Strange, demanding *her* orders be followed after the doctors bungled her medication. The head nurse found another doctor to administer painkillers, and Michael's breathing told Margaret time was short. She stayed in the room until she was again escorted out, left to stand in the hall while Michael sobbed. The cries grew weaker, then stopped, and a different nurse opened the door. Margaret could come in now. Michael was gone. Margaret longed to embrace her, but the presence of medical personnel held her back. Margaret closed Michael's eyes, quickly kissed them, took her hand and—shockingly—Michael squeezed it back. Though Michael passed only moments later, Margaret fulfilled her promise to hold her love's hand as she went into the next adventure. Michael wanted her prized pearls to go to her eldest son, and Ethel Malcolm suggested they remove them "before someone else does." Afterwards, Margaret cradled the older woman's head and covered her with her favorite grey robe.

News of Michael's death broke nationally with almost identical headlines: "BARRYMORE EX DEAD AT 60." The *New York Times* remembered her as "the tall actress with the Byronic hairbob." Others called her a poet, a suffragette, a "socialistic socialite," recalling Garbo being so interested in filming her life story that she allegedly offered $100,000 for the rights. Michael asked for Leonard in those last days, but he refused to see her; Margaret, "an extraordinary girl [who] showed every devotion and attachment possible," lied that a head cold prohibited him from visiting. Some obituaries erroneously claimed Leonard was at his mother's side when she died. All the obituaries left Margaret out entirely.

"Michael was a flamboyant, bombastic, most unusual person," said Yvonne Thomas, and nowhere was this as apparent as in Michael's arrangements for her funeral: she was to lay in state at her home in Easton, Connecticut, surrounded by flowers, with Wagner's *Parsifal* playing softly on a loop. Leonard and Diana reviewed the details and shared a drink without judgment. "I've had a few myself," Leonard said, pouring two whiskeys. "This is not going to be a very amusing day." He had called Diana and Bob in Miami; "everyone I've ever loved died while I was working," she later wrote. When they arrived at the funeral home, she was dressed as requested in her white recital robe, wearing her wedding band, but Diana frowned and called for the cosmetician. Michael's makeup was all wrong, and she would do it herself. She tenderly drew on her mother's signature "swallow's-wing eyebrows," then she and Leonard brought her home for the last time. For three days, people lined up to pay their respects, Diana as set designer, Bob minding the record player. "I've never seen such a beautiful thing in my life," wrote Bob. "A Catholic priest came to her home and read the services and mass right in her home which [was] practically unheard of." Every night, after everyone left, Diana pulled a prie-dieu next to the casket, knelt in prayer, then kissed her mother goodnight.

At Woodlawn Cemetery, on a breezy, unseasonably warm November day, the mythic Michael Strange was laid to rest next to her beloved boy. Twin headstones with verses from the Song of Songs marked their graves:

Robin: My beloved spake and said unto me / rise up, my love, my fair one, and come away
    Michael: For lo, the winter is past / the rain is over and gone

She may have "reeked of Newport and good breeding," according to Bob, but she also "could let down her hair and be a lot of fun." In spite of everything, he would miss her. Diana stood at the graveside, picked up a handful of dirt and tossed it onto her mother's casket. "[S]omething of my own life, my own faith in myself, died with the sound." Bob said Diana "collapsed, actually

. . . watching that hole swallow her mother . . . it made a marked change in Diana's whole venue [*sic*], her life. She became less disciplined, less sensitive, less everything. When her mother died it was like throwing off chains."

The family gathered for Michael's will on December 3, 1950. It was dated only nine days before her death, and Michael's estate was valued between $30,000 and $50,000, with Leonard and Diana principal beneficiaries. There were several specific bequests to family and friends, such as Mr. and Mrs. David Noonan, friends in Southampton on Long Island, to whom she left her dogs Banani and Percis, along with a $500 stipend and the wish that they never be separated. Leonard and Diana deeded the house in Maine back to Margaret and gave her some of Michael's furniture. Margaret was also made Michael's literary executor, and after Margaret's untimely death in 1952 the steamer trunk stuffed with manuscripts, poems, notes, and letters reverted to Diana. "[Mother] thought she was successful. She said, 'When I die . . . all geniuses, all great people are never recognized till they die.'" Diana kept the love letters between Michael and her father, some of her own childhood notes to her mother, and the sheet music Michael once called "more valuable to her than life itself," then ordered the rest to the incinerator.

CHAPTER 7

BOB AND MUZZY

MARCH 23, 1951: DIANA'S EVENING GOWN RUSTLED AS SHE WALKED TO THE microphone. "Hello, children," she said, flashing a smile. "I'm absolutely green and untried . . . and I'm a little nervous, too." The audience at the Somerset Hotel's Balinese Room welcomed her warmly, and Diana thought back to her conversation with agent Jerry Rosen a month earlier. The Palace—the most famous vaudeville house in the world—was putting together a nostalgia show headlined by old-time superstars Smith and Dale. Rosen thought it would be the perfect chance for her to reinvent herself, and the two of them, along with agent Alan Corcelli, worked up an act.

She opened with impressions of actresses Tallulah Bankhead, Katharine Hepburn, Judy Holliday, and her aunt Ethel, loosely stitched into a "Diana calls for advice" skit. A final impression of Ethel Merman segued into "There's No Business Like Show Business" and "You Can't Get a Man with a Gun." Next, "Waterloo Station," a dramatic monologue pinched from comedienne Sheila Barrett, and then, after a little patter, the closer: the potion scene from *Romeo and Juliet*.

She had the "back-breaking assignment" of following Smith and Dale, and her nerves bested her the first couple of shows, but after a mild sedative (and concerted effort to stop "hitching up" her off-the-shoulder gown) she found her groove. Critics and the public fawned over the potion scene; her "dubious vocalizing," not so much. "I'm not very good," she admitted, possibly thinking about her cousin, professional singer Ethel Barrymore Colt. The Palace show pulled in $19,000, around $5,000 more than the previous week, and she took her act on the road. "This is the first time a Barrymore has played in a night club [sic], I believe," she told reporters. Diana Barrymore, "satirist and singer," was born.

This new Diana, however, remained "every bit as volatile as her famous father," barking during rehearsals, "Let's get going, I can't be here all day!" Once, when a singer's practice session ran into hers, she plopped a chair directly in front and glowered at him until he stopped. "He sounds like he needs a lot of rehearsing," she sniped as he and his band packed to leave. She also stopped in the middle of her act to scold waiters "if they so much as rattled a single dish."

Her weekly paycheck of $1,000 dwindled in the face of mounting debts, including the bills for her "lengthy long-distance calls" with Bob. She wasn't left with a lot, but between the act and endorsements like "Blackberry Julep Cordial," at least money was coming in. "Daddy told me, 'They say I'm a buffoon. I probably am, but it's paying the rent and I'm paying back what I owe.' I thought, it's the same with me." Diana wasn't immune from buffoonery of her own. An appearance on *The Steve Allen Show* on June 10th resulted in "nauseating ad-libs" and some uncomfortable moments when she affected the country bumpkin style of comedienne Judy Canova and "tried to sing a hillbilly number, with very little success."

She and Bob returned to the stage that summer with *A Streetcar Named Desire*. It started promisingly but quality suffered the longer they toured. Clare Boothe Luce and Philip Kenneally were rushed to take over the July shows at New Jersey's Grist Mill Playhouse after she left due to "laryngitis." In reality, the theater didn't want to risk her "off-script remarks," which "resemble[d] B.S. Pully" as of late." (Pully, best known as "Big Jule" in both the Broadway and film version of *Guys and Dolls*, worked "blue" in his nightclub act.) That same week in Hinsdale, Illinois, her brother Johnnie pulled out of *The Hasty Heart* at the Salt Creek Theater due to cold feet, horrifying Aunt Ethel. "John let the family down, the first time in 300 years a Barrymore failed to comply with a billing," she told Dorothy Kilgallen. "I am deathly sick about it."

The Celebrity Club in Sydney, Australia, heard the good buzz about Diana's act and offered her a month's booking at $750 a week, including airfare. Leaving without Bob wasn't an option, so she exchanged the round-trip ticket for two going one-way and they escaped like "suddenly freed prisoners."

Her first two weeks at the end of September impressed Melbourne's Princess Theatre into offering her a "legitimate theatre" booking. Bob flew there to negotiate, and Diana dealt with her loneliness by getting so sloshed Celebrity Club manager Joe Taylor cancelled her run. He released a statement blaming "a series of laryngitis attacks," but Diana began hallucinating a disgusted Michael, glaring and calling her a "cheap spectacle." She scared the hell out of Bob one night screaming at the emptiness at the foot of their bed. "I said, 'Diana, you're letting this thing prey on your mind.' [S]he felt she had let her mother down."

A flurry of well-wishing telegrams greeted them in Melbourne. Bob's "brilliant characterization" of "exasperated" backer Sydney Black and Diana's "brash personality" as his wife Frances made *Light Up the Sky* a sold-out hit. After playing to capacity for almost a month, they abruptly switched to Noël Coward's *Fallen Angels*. Bob recorded some of the events over the next few weeks in his diary:

> Dec. 26, 1951
> [Australian actress] Daphne Winslow came over Xmas Eve and we made our starting effort to run lines . . . [w]e had been rehearsing Coward's The Marquise but the management suddenly discovered that they didn't have the rights so now we are doing Fallen Angels by Coward and only three days to get it into shape.

It was uncertain whether the play would even open due to a lack of funding—Diana even "offered to put up a $1,500 bond"—but in the end they opened on Saturday, December 29th. Bob said it was a "personal triumph" for Diana, but several reviews noted unprepared players "star[ing] blankly at each other until the obliging prompter said his piece." Like *My Dear Children*, Diana's "superb drunken clowning" with costar Daphne Winslow amused audiences but, just as with Jack, signaled her boredom. "[S]he becomes bored very quickly with a show [or] anything if it goes on too long . . . so on the stage she began to do strange things; she'd ad lib, and swear, [then] tries to justify her own stupidity by becoming arrogant. . . . Diana does not like regimentation of any sort." This infuriated their by-the-book director, Eric Reiman.

"[T]he 'director,' and I use that word with a great deal of care," Bob wrote, "is not what he would like to think he is . . . he has been given a small amount of authority and it goes to his head." After a heated argument, Bob and Diana walked, forcing Reiman to cancel the rest of the run.

Bookings dwindled after this most recent of "temperamental outbursts." Brisbane's Theatre Royal sandwiched them between risqué stripteases, but Diana proved too much even for a burlesque house: manager Laurie Smith fired them after her "salty" language and songs "offended the audience" so badly "many walked out of the show." She and Bob sulked for several weeks in Tasmania.

> Friday, Jan 4, 1952
> On Thursday we went to the local courts for some tennis and Diana hit herself in the mouth knocking out $750.00 worth of dental work . . .

I've never known any one [sic] to get so many bad breaks as she's had in [the] past two years!

Saturday, Jan 5, 1952
    Diana had gin and got loaded as is usually the case these days. I don't know what to do about her. It breaks me in half to watch her behaving this way . . . [s]he is now on the bed—cursing me with all her capabilities and that is very capable believe me.

    Bob's entry for January 7, 1952, hurts to read:

This has been a day to end all days. Diana is on the rampage again. There is no telling why it happens so often and there is no underlying cause unless it's a sense of weakness and frustration which she covers by an attitude of arrogance—which is almost frightening. She has abused me thousands of times but today was the worst . . . I'm a "very bad actor and wouldn't be anywhere if it weren't for her name Barrymore"—"I'm a Goddamned lousy F—ing Shit Son-of-a-Bitch." Where this all will lead to—I've no idea.
    I am trying now to decide what to do. I have—in spite of what she says to me—a little self-respect left. I had a great deal when I first knew her but she has killed all that . . . I've loved her too long to see her come to any harm and yet I am seeing myself in "Skid Row" unless I take a drastic step.

Bob usually cooked eggs in their room, or warmed a can of stew on the wood stove, but one night they splurged on the hotel's meatloaf, which Diana raved about. When she liked a dish, Bob said, "Diana gets the great idea she wants to go to the kitchen and see the chef and find out how he made it. And mostly she is successful. She's always done that, which is a very likeable trait in her. It's almost childish again but it's wonderful, because she gets so enthusiastic." She went down into the kitchen, all smiles, and was met by the snide hotel owner. "I know all about you," he jeered. "I've read in the papers what you've done." Bob wasn't surprised when she stomped into their room and said they were thrown out. An insulted Diana doesn't get upset; "she turns around and says, 'That dirty S.O.B., I'll tell him.' And she becomes the person they have said she is."
    Reporters caught up with them. "All I want to do is sleep and then I wanna go home," Diana said. The Wilcoxes consoled themselves with a three-day belated honeymoon at the Royal Hawaiian in Honolulu—a trip costing $500

of the $700 they had left. "We spent wildly," wrote Diana. "We knew the ship was sinking."

She was all smiles on March 13, 1952, the day they returned to San Francisco. Australia hadn't kicked them out; they chose to leave and were "never going back." According to her and Bob, the whole country was antiquated: Sydney removed her from a beach for skimpy swimwear, hotel accommodations were "fifty years behind the times," and as for her scandalous on-stage behavior? "It's all right for a night club [sic] master of ceremonies to tell off-color jokes, but let a woman get up and sing songs like that and they're offended." All they had left was $100 in travelers' checks, $25 in cash, and their battered pride.

Life sank to new lows. They stayed with Dr. Wilcox for a couple of weeks, then rented a room in a cheap Sunset Strip hotel. Her mother's tennis bracelet, Robin's gifts from Cartier, the gold-and-crystal cross Jack personally designed for Michael—all now property of the pawn shop. Bob's two severe attacks of pancreatitis considerably weakened him, and doctors felt a third might kill him. The sedate job Francis Kellogg had set up in the Wanamaker's shoe department depressed him so badly he didn't last the day. Diana's offers were scarce on the heels of the Australian debacle. "Why are people so mean to me?" she asked Marjory Adams for the Boston Globe. "If I acted as badly as they say, how did it happen that an engagement of three weeks stretched into six months of work?"

She jotted notes for an autobiographic article which can only be called Diana unfiltered:

Let me say honestly, I use the name [Barrymore] to open every door I can, because fundamentally I am damnably impatient, and it has always proved an Open Sesame.

I was born of two Royal families. One social, the other theatrical. But both these worlds have one thing in common. They nourish and thrive on sham and make-believe.

I am not nor have I ever been subject to neuroses. No more than my share, that is. At least I have never been couched, and I use the term professionally, with any psychologist, psychoanalyst, or psychiatrist.

During the telling [of my story], there will be many big and small names dropped. Let them drop where they may. Any similarity to personal living or dead is strictly intentional.

She submitted chunks to American Weekly magazine, pleading for "discipline, guidance, [and] encouragement . . . I'm tired of playing for kicks. I want to play for real. Other people have done it. Why can't I?" The response from longtime movie magazine writer/editor Adele Whiteley Fletcher, a year into her tenure as *American Weekly's* women's feature editor was as follows: "As I explained, the editors found much of the material in your manuscript interesting but are agreed that it did not follow the story line discussed . . . [p]erhaps we can get together later on and plan a story that will be right both from our point of view and yours."

She ended, perhaps thinking of all the Barrymore articles that crossed her desk over the years: "Kindest personal regards."

Diana thumbed through her Rolodex looking for willing donors. A&P supermarket heir Huntington Hartford begrudgingly sent $100, as did Tyrone Power, insulting Diana—she thought being Robin's sister was worth at least $1,000. Harry Crocker of the *Los Angeles Examiner* invited them to Romanoff's for dinner and wound up paying their overdue rent. Gifts, a remittance from Michael's estate, and regular checks from Leonard kept the wolf from the door. Set designer Tom Oliphant saved them from imminent eviction with $150 and an apartment. It wasn't fancy, but they could use it for free until his mother, who owned the building, rented it. They detested the stark white "hospital operating room" walls from the moment they moved in, and after too many beers painted the ceiling bright red. They were readying to paint the walls dark green when Oliphant's mother popped by unannounced, saw the mess, and booted them out.

Diana's highly public struggles inspired the character of Georgia Lorrison in *The Bad and the Beautiful* (1952). Lana Turner played the love-starved alcoholic actress with a "pinned up shrine to [her] dashing, dead, John Barrymore-like actor-prick of a father" easily exploited by producer Jonathan Shields (Kirk Douglas) in this harsh expose of "Hollywood mores and backlot intrigue." People no longer thought of her as an actress or socialite: Diana Barrymore was merely a has-been, "an unhappy hangover of family fame" who "irritated and sometimes disgusted" everyone around her.

One of the few people who stuck by her was Dolores Costello. She was Mrs. John Vruwink now, happily married to her former gynecologist, Dede a "radiant" twenty-two-year-old with children of her own and Johnnie, a "vital [and] electrifying" twenty-year-old hungry for stories about Jack. When talk inevitably turned to Diana's financial situation, Dolores suggested she call Ethel, who sent a limo for her the next afternoon. Aunt Ethel's world was pink, from the stucco of her home to the frilly bedjacket in which she received her niece (like Lionel, she was in bed). Diana privately smirked at the set design. It reminded her of the last time she spent an afternoon with Aunt Ethel, when she received her from a chair by a big French window overlooking the East River. Diana patted her purse then, filled with news-paper clippings of good notices. "You know, I did Juliet."

"'Really,' she said. And went on to another subject. I tried three times to get around to what had happened and each time she'd run on to another subject . . . then Aunt Ethel said, 'Give my love to Blanche,' and that was that. . . . I never got around to my clippings or myself."

This time, they had tea, made small talk, and Ethel read to her from her memoirs-in-progress until Diana timidly mentioned the reason for her visit. She immediately wrote a check for $300 and handed it over with a kiss. The kindness surprised and moved Diana; why couldn't the Barrymores always be like this?

The settling of Michael's estate in November satisfied Diana's debts and left her with $8,000[14]. She and Bob reconnected with old friend Ann Andrews and Jack's former costar, silent film vamp Nita Naldi, until Michael's estate lawyer Winfield Huppuch reined in their spending, forcing them to exchange their apartment at the Hotel Madison for a modest flat on Sutton Terrace. They began 1953 chastened and looking for work. Armando's, the East Sixty-first Street café popular with the society set, wanted a "lady disc-jockey" to interview clientele on WABC Radio. They hired her on the spot, and on broadcast night she showed up promptly at 8 p.m., bright and bubbly. By the 10 o'clock airtime, she'd downed one too many complementary drinks. "Good evening, ladies and gentlemen. This is Diana Barrymore. I hope you'll like me. If you do, fine. If you don't—who gives a damn?" Her first guest was socialite/cabaret singer Beverly Paterno. "Now, tell me, Miss Paterno, just what makes you think *you're* a singer?" The insult to Paterno, as known for fighting with showgirl (and princess) "Honeychile" Wilder as for romantic involvement with mafioso "Lucky" Luciano, ensured Diana never reached the airwaves.

Jack, in later years, endured lousy scripts to pay the bills. Diana rejected all that came her way, and now received nothing. They spent the days on a "seesaw in hell," taking turns drinking, passing out, waking up, downers to sleep, uppers to stay alert. Bob remembered Diana as "skin and bones, [she] weighed less than 100 pounds . . . I used to get up and feed her six to eight times a day, soup and omelet. She would wake up not knowing day or night." Though it's unclear whose decision it was, they both agreed it was time to try Alcoholics Anonymous.

She and Bob sat in the Lenox Hill Hospital auditorium and stole a glance around the room. Bob said she was too recognizable to slip out early, so they settled in for what felt like an eternity of talk about God and positivity. She

---

14. After Lily's insolvent estate cleared in 1965, Michael's estate ballooned to $530,000.

tried listening, but these people didn't share her upbringing or lifestyle—how could she relate? The minute it ended they fled to the York Inn, the bar on the ground floor of their apartment building. Their pre-meeting buzz badly needed refreshing.

The York Inn was where Bob introduced Diana to his drinking buddy, "Tom Farrell," a rather strange guy who recognized Bob from the movies and always bought him shots. Diana's own drinking buddy was a young East Fifty-first Street patrolman, anonymous since he had "a wife, two children and a Buick." Tom Farrell was dark-haired, rugged, built much like her most recent lover, actor Steve Cochran. "One night I hadn't come home. . . . I'd been with Steve and his dog. It was always a good idea to say I'd been walking the dog with Steve a few times." When Farrell called later that night looking for Bob, she invited him up. The attraction was mutual.

"Tom Farrell" was John Patrick McNeill, age twenty-six, an unemployed self-described "professional vagabond." Diana described him as "John Howard with a Bramwell Fletcher technique." He quoted Whitman, talked philosophy, gave her his rosary. He wrote poetry and watched the water dreamily, like Tony had. He also slapped her around, which Diana found erotic. Violence turned her on, always had. Her favorite lovers were aggressive, often professional boxers or street toughs, and she once remarked, "Noël Coward said women should be struck regularly like a gong and he's right. Women are no damn good." Professional middleweight Nenos "King" Solomon, who dated Diana in the 1950s, called her a "sexual pervert." Whether from watching her parents or her quest to feel something genuine, she was incapable of experiencing pleasure without pain.

McNeill brought things out of the bedroom, showed her off in restaurants and nightclubs of which she couldn't afford to speak, much less visit. He didn't work but never lacked for money, the origin of which he never disclosed— along with his address or phone number. Maybe he was involved in organized crime; he told her he was once married to the cousin of a mafia kingpin. Later she found out he "peddled heroin." Red flags didn't exist for Diana, only sex that was sufficiently mind-blowing to send her sneaking out of the house at midnight to meet McNeill under the East River (now FDR) Drive.

Bob vacillated between verbally lashing out or drinking himself unconscious. Once, he slapped Diana so hard she stumbled and hit her head on a table, necessitating stitches. Despite it all, he never considered leaving; there was a comforting predictability in their dysfunction. Bob called it love, and eventually convinced Diana to break things off with a dubious McNeill. "The whole plot of my life is now twisting and turning," Bob wrote, "and I'm the hero and she's the heavy—then I realized that we are both the heavies."

Elsewhere in Manhattan, Assistant U.S. Attorney Louis Kaplan had close to fifteen young actresses-turned-call girls taking the stand in late March against John Howard. "There are big names involved," said Kaplan. The girls charged $500 per night and $1,000 for "special vice exhibitions." One "red-headed starlet from the Coast" netted him $10,000. The star witness was actress Sandy English, real name Shirley Edgecomb, whom Dorothy Kilgallen once called "one of the screen's hottest young musical comedy stars." She and John had been "dating" while he was still married to Diana. In 1950, Diana told reporters she wasn't surprised by John's activities and this time spoke to the feds for an hour, refusing any comments to the press. His defense attorneys were Martin Benjamin and Sam Segal, known for representing Mickey Jelke in his sensational vice trial. Benjamin quit the case after tussling with John in the men's room but later returned to deliver his client's guilty plea, due to "human weakness," not ill intent. The court charged him as a "transcontinental vice procurer" and sentenced him to a year and a day in prison. It also labeled John Howard a "psychopath," noting his army rejection for "schizophrenic tendencies."

One night in early June, Diana and her "boys" from the precinct met up at the York Inn for booze and pinball. She got home at 3 a.m., twenty dollars richer, wondering if the girl she called to entertain Bob was still there. She opened the door gently. Bob sat on the sofa, Caruso played in the background, and John McNeill was next to him. Broken glass littered the floor, and Bob gestured to the window. "Your lover boy just came through it," he said pleasantly. He patted the sofa, and the three—the girl wisely bailed hours before—chatted, drank, and drank some more. Talking turned to shouting, and then . . .

"The big fight started over three simple lines," she told the *Daily News* over "eight martinis and two gin-ginger ales." "Bob said, 'You've taken my wife away.' Johnny said, 'I haven't taken your wife away, she's right there if you want her.' I said, 'But I don't want him.'" The men yelled and shoved each other, and Diana glibly requested they not kill each other because "it would be awfully messy." Bob hurled a kitchen knife at McNeill as Diana ran down the hall to call the police, returning to McNeill sprawled on the floor face down in a puddle of blood. The knife missed, but the heavy silver cigarette box lying near him didn't. She lugged him down the hall to her bedroom and stuffed a pillow under his head to stop the bleeding until paramedics arrived. Two dozen photos of her father watched in "rare confusion" as police swarmed the apartment and took McNeill out on a stretcher, Diana following closely behind. Two exhausting hours later a reporter drove her home. "I suppose Bob was in the right; the defiled nest and all that sort of thing," she told him as they climbed the stairs. "I was tired of the man I was living with and I wanted something new."

"Isn't that dreadful!" she said, staring at the "large dark oval" marking the parquet floor. "[L]ook at Johnny's lovely blood!" Bob, shrugged and swigged his beer. "That man broke up my home—as far as our marriage is concerned, we're through." He swore, softly, under his breath. "She keeps me. I have no money and I haven't been able to get a job. . . . I am an honest, decent guy and I've never done any harm." Morning arrived, and with it, their usual reconciliation. Bob cheerfully greeted the newest relay of reporters with news that their impending divorce would be "amicable and decent." Diana smiled, nodded. "After all, darling, after six years you just can't kick somebody out." She was done with McNeill, whom she called a "very cagey guy." She asked her boys at the Seventeenth Precinct to keep an eye on things; they obliged.

Acquaintances and fair-weather friends called laughing over her latest incident, but those who loved her saw no humor in it. Leonard's wife, Yvonne, called it "like the Grand Guignol." Ann Andrews said Bob should have "horsewhipped" them both. "That man will do you in one of these nights," Nita Naldi told Diana, remembering one impromptu visit when he'd stuffed her into a cab "[b]efore she could remove her coat." Nita worried about her so much Diana called her "Mother Moonbeam," after Nita's nickname, "Moonbeam McSwine," the raven-haired beauty in Al Capp's *L'il Abner* comic strip. In return, she called Diana "Vesuvius," echoing Jack's description of Michael as a "live volcano" on the verge of erupting.

Bob could relate. He joked he was married to two Dianas, never knowing when Jekyll would become Hyde. He really deserved better, thought Diana. "He's the kind of man who will get up at two in the morning and go out to buy me a cheeseburger if I complain I'm hungry," she told the *Boston Globe*, emphatic about his "great kindness." She worked hard at being a better wife and partner, and for a few weeks their marriage improved. Then one night while watching TV—Bob said their happiest times were watching boxing together, him "hold[ing] the aerial so [the picture] wouldn't wobble"—the phone rang, and Bob deduced the caller by the dazed way Diana hung up the phone and went to the door. He looked at his Muzzy with pain-filled eyes as she kissed him on the cheek and went to meet McNeill. "Poor darling, every time anything happened he went absolutely white . . . [h]is whole face sunk like a child who lets his balloon out when it's grown large." The next morning, Bob left for Rochester.

McNeill nearly killed her the first week of August 1953. He broke into and ransacked her apartment over an imagined discretion, then lay in wait for her return. Only days before he'd beaten and threatened her with a broken bottle for lying. Diana recalled the terror of coming home and finding him, intoxicated and blind with rage: "his fist crashed into my face. I actually felt the small bones of my nose crumble." He beat her into unconsciousness. Nita stayed several days with her as she recovered from "lacerations, a shiner . . . left hand [*sic*] in a sling," a broken nose and multiple contusions, what columnist Earl Wilson called "love tokens from ardent admirer John McNeill." Ann brought soup and broth, the only foods Diana could eat. Contrary to her memoir, it didn't dampen her romance with McNeill. "Don't be silly, darling," she told Wilson. "He's coming over tonight and was here last night." Bob stopped in to retrieve his belongings en route to employment in Los Angeles. Diana confessed she hadn't really wanted Bob to leave; it was just her habit of saying things she didn't mean. Diana often spoke without thinking. A neighbor, Captain Nicholas Psaroudis, filed a disorderly conduct charge against her for calling him an "illiterate foreign peasant" and his wife "vile and indecent things." (The case was eventually dismissed.)

Bob worked as a day laborer in a Pennsylvania steel mill for as long as his weak heart allowed. The letter he wrote Diana suggests he knew he was on borrowed time:

> You seem to think that I am unaware of my failures as a husband— especially in the money department. Not for a moment. If you decide on a divorce—you can be sure I will do nothing to stand in your way . . . [g]et back your self-confidence—your self-respect—and be happy.
>
> Now I've got to start exorcising a few ghosts. The ghosts of our life together and the ghost of a wonderful—kind—sweet—loveable woman. When I can get all this in proper perspective—I'm sure I'll be a stronger—better man.
>
> Goodnight, darling. Try to think of some of the good things about me.

Leonard rented Diana a Park Avenue apartment after her landlord refused to renew her lease. She moved and didn't leave for weeks, subsisting on a Robin-like stream of pills and booze. "Was I trying to hurt myself? I think it was my own way of killing myself. Somebody needed to do it for me, and I thought the only person who could was me. . . . I absolutely went off my rocker." Nita, Ann, and her many "gentlemen callers" attempted to spoon feed her like a sick kitten; "[they] would order food from the Casserole Kitchen and literally put the fork in my mouth and say, 'Please, Diana, will you eat?'" She lost over forty pounds and developed neuritis,[15] a condition

---

15. Painful nerve inflammation caused by injury or infection.

that plagued her the rest of her life. Leonard and Yvonne offered to pay for rehab but the thought terrified Diana, and a gin-blurred visit to a priest only confused her.

Yvonne washed her hands of her sister-in-law. "I used to love Diana. Now I dismiss her. I no longer think about it because it upsets me, it upsets me the way one gets indigestion or doesn't want to hear about the war . . . she is a very, very warm—passionate human being and when those forces are not guided just right they can play havoc . . . [n]ow the point is whether Diana wants to live or wants to die. That is the only issue that is left. If I were right now in her place I would give up everything—do that, and see what I could salvage of myself."

Theatrical producer Anna Wiman called the night before she left for Bermuda and invited Diana along. Wiman owned a house there and would cover all expenses for her friend, including daily trips to the doctor for vitamin shots. She happily accepted. The swimming did wonders for her neuritis, but she sabotaged further progress by sneaking gin into her orange juice. By the trip's end, she was screaming lines louder than Charlton Heston from her seat at the opening of *Macbeth*, "minus lingerie and not caring who knew it." She hadn't worn a bra most of her adult life. "Years earlier," she wrote, "my doctor had warned me: 'Don't ever wear a brassiere, it's fatal, like putting your arm in a sling. It destroys muscle tone. Take it off and they'll fall down to your knees.' Well, sweeties, I've followed his advice, and things are holding their own." Back home, neighbors alerted the landlord of her revolving door of men, and she was evicted on suspicion of prostitution. From her new walkup apartment on East Eightieth Street, she called the only person she thought could help: Bob. He was the only man for her, she lied, and would pay for his plane ticket home. Bob's love, patience, and cooking got Diana back on her feet, but it wasn't only depression she battled; along with chronic migraines, the doctor confirmed the early stages of cirrhosis. "She had absolutely no self-respect; she flaunted herself . . . [i]t was a crazy phase," he said. "I'd say, 'Diana, Diana, you're going to wind up in the street, wind up in the gutter.'"

She and Bob started over, existing only by the grace of God and Leonard's checks. They shoplifted food, saving their extra pennies for their mutual poison. Their electricity was turned off and they lied to friends about a dinner party to borrow candles. "It happens to be urgent," Diana griped to Len in a summer 1954 letter about finances. "[I]sn't it always?"

The Litchfield Summer Theater reached out to Bob and Diana about *The Fourposter*, a melodrama about 35 years in the life of a married couple, as seen solely from their bedroom. The play often starred real-life husband/wife actors, and starred Hume Cronyn and Jessica Tandy in the original 1951

Tony Award-winning Broadway production. They met with managing director Leonard Altobell and some of the cast and crew at Altobell's home, including a young actor named Bob Jorge. Jorge, best known today as Goodman in *Coven*, the low-budget horror film at the heart of the 1999 documentary *American Movie*, remembered Diana's first appearance, "simply dressed [in] slacks":

"Of course, darlings, I shan't remember any of your names until the end of the week, so don't feel embarrassed if I call out, 'Hey you!'"

Altobell was kind but frank: any missed performances or on-stage intoxication and they'd shred the contract, including any accrued salary. "This was enough to stop her from going beyond the danger point," said Jorge. Diana's performance as Agnes, who ages from eighteen to sixty by play's end, was "instinctive" and "excellent."

She and Bob always joined the company at the bar after shows, and Diana made sure all eyes were on her, whether through her high decibel laugh or Hawaiian print dresses. One night the group packed into a small coupe and Diana rode home in the back seat, on Jorge's lap. Bob said Diana liked Jorge a lot because he reminded her of Robin; when she heard he was straight, she scoffed. "Oh, this is impossible, because I have never in my life made a mistake about a [gay man]." "Impossible" might've been a little strong; the two necked all the way home. "I've tried to express my feelings for the girl; people have said she's nothing but a drunk. This isn't true," said Jorge. "[I]t's very easy to fall in love with that girl. Despite all her bad things, they seem infinitesimal in comparison with her charm and sweetness and other qualities."

Two weeks later, the producers talked about *Laura*, but what she really wanted was *Moulin Rouge*. The production hinged on finding a properly sized "name" for Toulouse-Lautrec, now that Hume Cronyn and Burgess Meredith declined due to previous engagements. "I do need a Broadway show desperately, it's been a long time," she wrote. Her last Broadway play was the 1946 debacle *Hidden Horizon*, called "the damndest, longest, dullest" adaptation of Agatha Christie ever staged. It closed after twelve performances, and critic Jack O'Brian openly wondered if Diana's involvement in this version of *Death on the Nile* was because she "lost a bet." She still played the nightclub circuit and just "audition[ed] for General Artists . . . you know I hate it but a buck's a buck. . . . frankly I don't like asking you for dough," she told Leonard, "but I'm rather trapped—and it ain't no lie about the two shows." She prayed by the time his check cleared she would be in *Moulin Rouge*, *Laura*, or "some strange Club de Nuit."

Moulin Rouge came through in July with a "Stage '54" production at the New Strand Theatre in Wilmington, Delaware. Producer Day Tuttle hired her as "spitfire prostitute" Marie Charlet and found Toulouse-Lautrec in twenty-one-year-old Karl Schanzer. Diana intimidated him, so she slept with him "and kept it up through the end of the play." She poured the rest of her energy into a marvelous performance, "explod[ing] upon the stage [with] a vitality that shock[ed]" critics, and returned home in August with a "protégé." Schanzer crashed on their sofa for a week, after which Bob stormed out, preferring to sleep on a park bench. First thing Diana did was invite Schanzer right back to party, along with Nita Naldi and a few other friends. Word spread, and around 3 a.m., John McNeill strolled in, refusing to leave until police escorted him out. Cops at Diana's place were such a regular occurrence that the *New York Daily News* called her career "more like a police blotter than a playbill." Later that day she held a presser, clad in her mother's nightmare: a "deeply cut flaming red evening gown." She and Bob were again divorcing but it was "up to him to get the wheels rolling to Reno," and as for McNeill, she was "probably an idiot for not pressing charges." Bob merely mumbled "no gentleman sticks around when he's not wanted." Diana called Jorge and asked if he would stay with her if she and Bob separated. "I said, 'You know I would.' She asked, 'Would you be upset if I brought a friend home?' I said no . . . I would be her secretary." But, as usual, the Wilcoxes were back together by September 5th, taking daily walks with Fini, the little black poodle McNeill gave Diana as a parting gift.

In November 1954, they started a special two-for-one ticket tour of *Pajama Tops*, a comedy based on the French sex farce *Moumou* "as delicate and subdued as a circus calliope." They opened in Bob's hometown of Rochester, New York, and Diana hated Bob's friends thinking the scantily clad brunette on the poster was her. Producer H. Clay Blaney held back half their salary to ensure they didn't bail on the play, and a contract clause forfeited any salary if Diana was ever too drunk to perform. The broad humor and quadruple-entendres missed the mark—"definitely not Broadway," said critics. While the *Hartford Courant* admitted that "Diana has one thing her father bequeathed her, a great sense of timing [and] great ability at slapstick," Claudia Cassidy, writing for the *Chicago Tribune*, felt "more than a twinge" of sorrow seeing a Barrymore playing in such "leering trash."

Reporters in Cincinnati broke the news to her of Uncle Lionel's death. They requested she pose for them, gazing tenderly at his photo, but it was just more acting. "I thought, my uncle is dead, and it means absolutely nothing to me." Chicago patrons complained they were tricked into buying seats for what they thought was the hit Broadway play *The Pajama Game*. "Nobody's trying to fool anybody," Diana told the press, rolling her eyes. The publicity machine went into high gear: guests of honor at the Saddle & Cycle Club Ball benefit for the Wilmette Little Theater, a toy drive for needy kids via the *Chicago Tribune*'s "Good Fellows Fund." December 1st was particularly "rough," Bob wrote in his diary. A visit to a TV talent show didn't wrap until 2 a.m. (surprise—they were the judges), and after very little sleep, they dragged themselves to a rehearsal without another cast member. Felix Deebank left the show after one too many insults from Diana, and now Brook Byron quit. Bob thought her a "snob" because she couldn't tolerate "little hardships" on tour, the kind he and Diana leaned on whiskey to endure. At home for Christmas, Diana did what she could to make the place festive—"a small Christmas tree, greeting cards up, a wonderful little spirit," said Jorge. "Regardless of the bitch she may tend to be from time to time, this is a wonderful person."

Tallulah Bankhead came to Detroit in late February with a special six-day run of *Dear Charles* at the Shubert. It overlapped with the "embarrassingly bawdy" *Pajama Tops*, giving Diana a chance to meet with her father's old friend. "I was mad about that fascinating woman," she told the *Boston Globe*. Bankhead tactfully mentioned how haggard Diana looked. "[S]he started telling me how to make up better . . . she threw my green eye pencils out of the window!" She also advised her to nurture her inner beauty, "because you have spent so many years trying to destroy it." After that, said Diana, "we decided to be friends no matter what we read about each other." Bob liked that she was "entirely different" than he expected, "kind, gentle yet hard at the same time." It was a watershed moment for someone who patterned herself after Bankhead so closely that she was known as "the poor man's Tallulah." Bankhead told Diana not to imitate her, "but Diana doesn't want to be Diana."

In Philly, she went on stage visibly intoxicated, with all the "general restraint of a Jerry Lewis." "I wasn't tight but I wasn't sober . . . another paper said Martha Raye. I got practically the worst notices I ever got in Philadelphia."

Get your act together, yelled producer H. Clay Blaney, while she wept and blamed Bob for worsening her drinking, herself for "sell[ing] the Barrymore name so cheap." Blaney flew to the April 18th opening in Boston to personally deliver an ultimatum two hours before curtain: screw this up and there'd be charges with Actors' Equity. He went backstage again around 9:30 p.m. and Diana faked sobriety, convinced it worked until she ducked into her dressing room for a "refresher" at intermission. On the table sat the whiskey-filled cough syrup bottle normally in her makeup case, empty, a farewell note from Blaney under it.

The next morning, after her usual first drink-vomit-second drink routine, she swallowed a fistful of sedatives ("blue jackets and yellow jackets," brilliantly described by Gerold Frank as "a succotash to oblivion") and washed them down with "a double shot of Four Roses." Bob discovered her, rushed her to City Hospital. "I only tried to calm my nerves," she insisted later. She couldn't sleep due to a cold and the doctor prescribed them—she just took too many, that was all. Bob, on the other hand, suggested depression over her fight with Blaney and missing Michael. She reprised her role on April 28, 1955, "breathing heavily [and] lean[ing] on a chair for support three times in the first three minutes." She thanked her Barrymore constitution for her recovery: "Anyone else probably would have died." As with so many other shows, ticket sales were brisk due to rubberneckers. The tour wrapped in Connecticut in May.

CHAPTER 8

TOO MUCH, TOO LOUDLY

DIANA AND BOB WERE IN COLUMBUS, OHIO, DOING *SEPARATE ROOMS*, A "stock farce" critic Harold Cohen said played "like commuters hurrying for the last local" and the *Pittsburgh Press* called "limited in scope and intelligence," when Bob's pancreatitis struck again. He was hospitalized for four days and went right back to booze as soon as he left. In the spring of 1955, when Canal Fulton offered Diana the lead in *Glad Tidings*, she and Bob lived in a hotel "where even the obscenities on the walls of the men's room were misspelled." The hit comedy about a journalist who discovers he has a grown daughter with the actress he left some twenty years earlier had much in common with Tallulah Bankhead's illegitimacy comedy *Dear Charles* and her father's *My Dear Children*. It was a great fit for Diana, and she accepted even without Bob being offered a role. She flew to Ohio for the summer season, and on her first night there met leading man "Dan Freeman," a young and "rather personable" Broadway veteran with whom she began an emotional affair. Freeman, real name Roy Shuman,[16] focused his energy on fixing her: pep talks, long walks during downtime, and absolutely no alcohol. "His directness and enthusiasm excited me. I felt nineteen again, Diana Blyth(e) with the world before her." The result was a rejuvenated Diana that delighted critics with "many of the mannerisms" of her father. "[A]l eyes were on her. The other players were as puppets on which she was pulling the strings."

Diana avoided Bob until his call from New York Hospital, where he'd been for a week after a binge triggered pancreatitis attack no. 4. He missed her, he said, and had turned to the bottle for comfort. She coldly repeated Shuman's advice: change or risk death "in an alcoholic ward." She sent the $200 he needed for the hospital bill, then moved her wedding ring to her right hand and herself into Shuman's bed.

---

16. Shuman later acted on soap operas *As the World Turns* and *Search for Tomorrow*.

A week later, Bob called Diana again, proud he'd gone seven days without alcohol. She was on the wagon too, she replied indifferently, all thanks to Shuman. Bob should go to Rochester and maybe stay with his mother for a while. Bob goaded her until she admitted the affair, adding she would never again be tied down to such a sick, sad man like him. "Does she really enjoy the men?" Bob once wondered aloud. "I don't think so . . . [s]he said it was something physical . . . just a new experience for her." Diana admitted as much. "When I slept with men, I didn't do it to be promiscuous. I did it because I wanted to, because I do everything in my life I want to do."

That night he packed a bag, gathered up Fini, and took the train to Rochester. As they pulled into the station, a porter heard barking and discovered Fini pawing at Bob's body. An enlarged heart and "liver ailment" caused by excessive drinking took the forty-five-year-old's life on June 11, 1955. Diana collapsed at the news of Bob's death but managed the evening's performances, honored by both audiences with standing ovations.

Walking with Shuman the next day, Diana reflected on her complicated marriage. Bob was the only man she ever truly loved, she said, while breaking down in Shuman's arms. Sleep came fitfully that night; every time she closed her eyes, she saw Bob's pained face searching for her. She was unable or unwilling to attend the funeral but sent yellow roses, his birthday gift to her every year, and requested they be placed by his head.

H. Clay Blaney's latest crisis involved his production of *The Little Hut* and its star, Veronica Lake, an actress whose life paralleled with Diana's. *Variety* attributed Lake's collapse in her Detroit hotel room to a "breakdown," others to a "suspected heart attack." Blaney remembered how improved Diana was in *Pajama Tops* the year before and called in a favor. *Variety* said Diana was "ready to go" for that fall, the play renamed *The Bamboo Bed*. "How does one explain such things?" she later wrote. "I was drunk when I presented myself at the theater in Detroit." Diana still wasn't ready a week later in Rochester, so Veronica Lake's understudy Marie Corbett went on yet again. Diana protested daily that she'd be ready the next day, but she never went on. Some reports said she checked out on November 4th and flew back to New York, others that she stayed in Rochester a bit longer. The play was labeled a "fiasco" and closed November 5th. *Variety*'s quip "The Last Straw" wasn't merely wordplay; "there will probably be no more two for one legits in this town for several years, not until the impression of 'Little Hut' wears off." Corbett gave a great performance, but no big names meant no ticket sales. Auditorium manager Robert Corris held up approximately $3,800 in receipts, saying Blaney violated their contract. Blaney cried foul; he himself was still owed money, including $180 in baggage fees and taxi runs from

Diana. "Miss Barrymore's cancellation of her contract cost this management over Five Thousand Dollars ($5000.00)," they wrote. "This is the first time in this management's thirty years of producing that a member of Equity has caused such an occurrence." They turned to Actors' Equity for help, the correspondence from which Diana ignored, violating prohibitions and acting in the pre-Broadway preview of *Indoor Sport* (on Broadway that September as *How Happy I Could Be*, starring Sloan Stevens).

Neither Bob's death nor Shuman's influence was enough to keep Diana sober. She called Bob Jorge and begged him to stay with her; the days were all right, she said, but the nights were unbearable. "My immediate thought was that I was in the wrong room," he said. It was a "shambles." Michael was "monstrously untidy, which I inherited," Diana said. "It takes a minute to hang up a blouse or skirt . . . Mother never did. [She] left money all over the apartment. I used to steal it and get candy [for] about three or four years, knew she wouldn't miss it because she never counted it." In the middle of the mess stood "pathetic, absolutely beat" Diana, wearing an ill-fitting sundress. She'd gone from 125 pounds to 100 in the last two weeks, drinking and obsessing over her last phone call with Bob. Jorge would tuck her into bed after she inevitably passed out. Her agent received a request in late June for her to play Blanche DuBois in *Streetcar* with the Kenley Players, and Jorge convinced her two weeks in Bristol, Pennsylvania, were just the thing to break the monotony of grief.

Diana stayed focused and sober through a week's worth of rehearsals. The local establishments refused to serve her alcohol, and she spent a lot of time with clean-cut leading man Philip Kenneally and his wife, Jerri. The devoutly religious Kenneally, who filled in for Bob as Stanley back at the Grist Mill in 1951, was a former Golden Glove champion who gave up a Notre Dame scholarship for acting. On July 3rd, she went to Sunday services with the couple, and during Mass, her façade cracked. She didn't know who she was without Bob, she said. "I saw myself already on the skids just like Blanche [Dubois] . . . what in the name of God was I going to do when I was alone?" She broke down and had to be led out of the church. How could she open tomorrow?

Later, she sat in on final rehearsals and watched her understudy, a protégé of Tennessee Williams named Maria Brit-Neva. Out of the theater, she was Maria St. Just. St. Just met Williams a decade earlier and, instantly smitten, became his confidante and protector. It was she on whom he based Maggie the Cat in *Cat on a Hot Tin Roof*. When rehearsal wrapped Diana stood up. No, she said. This woman isn't Blanche. The people came to see Barrymore, and they are *going* to see Barrymore! She and the Kenneallys went back to the hotel and worked until dawn. "She went on Monday, July 4, opening night, and missed no cue . . . [she] did beautifully," recalled Jorge. She gave "an outstanding performance."

Back in New York and with nothing on the horizon, she went back to drinking and ruminating. Jorge stocked the fridge for Diana's daily routine: wake around 11 a.m., make a Bloody Mary, then grab her phone book. "[She] starts from A and works through Z," said Jorge, pausing only for bourbon or vodka. "She has a schedule—Ann Andrews daily. A must. Then Mother Moonbeam. She has to talk to someone."

"Either I am talking or telephoning or drinking or moving, or if nothing's happening I've got to pick up a telephone and say hi," Diana admitted. "I can't relax." She fell off a friend's yacht in mid-July, breaking a rib, and cut herself badly with a paring knife attempting to open a bottle. Part of it was the city itself. Returning to Manhattan "click[ed]" something in her, she told Jorge, "and she almost goes berserk." Relief came in the form of another engagement of *Glad Tidings*, and the two left on July 24th for Maine.

Lodging in Kennebunkport was with the show's producer, Robert Currier. Diana talked incessantly at lunch the first day and ate her lobster roll in the car; privately she told Jorge she planned it so Currier wouldn't see how much her hands shook. Maine was a dry state, and Currier was in Alcoholics Anonymous. She brought no liquor with her and was in agony. Somehow they persuaded Currier to take a sightseeing drive by the state line, where Jorge picked up enough vodka to stash until the end of the show—always one bottle open and one waiting.

The first couple of days Diana commandeered Currier's hi-fi and spent hours in his den, playing records and daydreaming as they waited for her leading man to arrive. "What do records do to me? . . . the actress [comes] out." When she heard it was once again Kenneally, she stopped dreaming and started planning.

July passed, each day like the next. Rehearsal started at 10 a.m. Jorge woke Diana at 9:15 a.m. with a shot of vodka to stave off shakes—she especially dreaded vocal tremors—and a cup of lukewarm coffee (she hated it hot). As she sipped, she told Jorge her plan: she was going to get Kenneally into bed. "I said don't do it, the boy is very Catholic, he's married," Jorge remembered. "Well, some morning when he gets up, if he says, 'Which way is the church?' you'll know," she replied. The morning of July 27th, Jorge noticed Diana's wedding band on her nightstand when he left her coffee. Around lunchtime— Diana never ate a thing until dinner at 10 p.m.—he ran into a "perfectly guilty" Kenneally, who asked where the nearest Catholic church was.

That evening Diana filled in the details: in order for a man and woman to have authentic onstage chemistry, she insisted, the two of them must sleep

together. Kenneally thought it would be all right as long as they acknowledged their sin first. He asked Diana to kneel by the bed, and they recited
the rosary together and prayed for forgiveness. "There was a difference in
Phil thereafter," remembered Jorge. "[H]e slowly disintegrated."

Currier's displeasure unnerved the cast into blowing their lines the next
night. Everyone but Diana, who remained calm, unfazed, and in control. On
August 3rd, she (along with Kenneally and costar Eleanor Phelps) smiled her
way through visitors' tea at the Portland Museum of Art, then performed
"earnestly, seriously and well" as actress and assistant director the following night. She had "talent, spirit and dignity," wrote critic Harold L. Cail.
Although Kenneally's "commanding personality" lapsed at times into "tumult
and shouting," he liked the ensemble, including the "capable" Jorge. "[O]nly
in the love-making scene," he noted, did things get "farcical."

On August 8th, back at home, neuropathy sent her to the hospital. The
last time, it partially paralyzed her: "I couldn't sit up, I had to lie on my back
the entire day. My legs wouldn't function [and] a couple of times I nearly
fell down." She rehearsed that week with Kenneally at her bedside, but the
theater manager cancelled, spooked by gossip of Kenneally's faltering and
Diana wearing her bathing suit to shows. She came home on August 16th,
resumed partying August 17th. Jorge remembered her phoning everyone
she was "cured" from drinking "while she had [a] drink in [her] other hand."

A revival of Thornton Wilder's *Skin of our Teeth* was playing at the Anta
Theatre and Jorge got tickets for August 22nd. Diana really wanted to see
the Pulitzer Prize-winning black comedy, and Jorge thought she should go
backstage, schmooze a little, prove to everyone she was ready to work again.
She liked the idea and walked into the Anta Theatre that Saturday night
sober. During the Act I intermission she sneaked a double vodka; during the
Act II intermission, another one. She guffawed and stage-whispered through
Act III, and by backstage time, she was plastered. She tripped down a few
steps while exiting and fell onto her knees, cackling as Jorge and an attendant
helped her up. She burst into lead actor George Abbott's dressing room and
startled him in his boxer shorts. Next, saccharine fawning over Mary Martin—*so* much better than Tallulah was—and a hug that lasted a bit too long
for Martin's husband, Richard Halliday. She praised their daughter Heller,
also in the play, about whom she audibly complained only twenty minutes
before: "That thing can't act her way out of a phone booth."

A man stationed at lead actress Helen Hayes's dressing room door said
no one was being admitted. Nonsense, said Diana. Tell her who's here. She's
feeling a bit ill, he said, not even seeing her closest friends. This continued a
few moments until Diana exploded: "The *least* you can tell her is *who I am!*"

Jorge pried her away from Hayes's door. "[I]f Diana had not been drinking, she would have been the soul of discretion," he said. He suggested they cancel dinner plans with Nita Naldi and Felix Munseau and go home. Get them on the phone, said Diana—we're going to Sardi's! Jorge sagged at the suggestion of the historic Broadway eatery. "Of all the places—why didn't she stand nude in Times Square?"

Sardi's buzzed with clientele at every available table. "You can't challenge Diana," said Jorge. "She takes them all." She scanned past the maître d and saw actress (and friend) Patsy Kelly. She sailed across the room, "darling!" all the way, then jostled a space for the four of them at Kelly's table. Naldi took Jorge aside. "Well, this is nothing new.

"When I did my show 'In Any Language' [spring of 1952] with Uta Hagen, I asked Diana to see me, naturally. She arrived, happily pickled, and during the entire first act told whoever was with her, plus six rows in front and in back, the goings on of Miss Hagen and Mr. Paul Robeson, elucidating all of the lurid details, much to Miss Hagen's furious mortification. Miss Hagen would come off the stage and rage, 'Throw that woman out!' She just couldn't go on, she was all jitters, all nerves, all tears. She didn't want to make another entrance. At the end of the first act the management asked Diana to leave, and she left with her party." The next day, Munseau told Jorge "it was now all over the entire profession—not a person on Shubert Alley who doesn't know how Diana made an ass of herself." Said ass remembered nothing, "amazed" by her own behavior.

"There are two Diana Barrymores. I'd like to know why there are," she once wrote. "[T]here is one who goes about losing her head . . . [a]nd there's a second, who's outraged at all this, who doesn't believe it when she sees it in the papers . . . on some occasions I behave like a tramp, and on others, like the lady I was brought up to be."

NBC dangled possible TV work and reached out to set up a late August meeting. DO NOT DRINK, begged Jorge. Please, for the love of God, don't blow this. "Oh please," she replied. "I can take one or two." She went to NBC buzzed and returned swaggering. They "flipped" over her, she crowed, cancelled long-distance calls and appointments just to speak with her. Jorge rejoiced. When did her project start? Well, they didn't have anything right now. Nothing personal, Miss Barrymore, they said. They'd keep in touch, they said.

Around Labor Day, she went to lunch with a friend and met Billy Flinn, the grandson of Senator William Flinn, whose construction firm of Booth and Flinn shaped much of Pennsylvania. "[H]e said, 'I met you when you were sixteen years old when you were in Southampton and I met you again in Hollywood.' I said, 'Darling, I'm terribly sorry, I don't remember you, but you're charming.'" The fair-haired, grey-eyed young man "reminded [her] of Robin . . . a very good-looking boy and a very sweet boy, [in] an erudite way." Flinn was also gay.

Four days later he "delighted" her with a dinner invite. "I was very lonely . . . I got myself all done up and he arrived looking extremely handsome." Cocktails at the Hotel Madison, then off to his favorite place, The Five Five. The East Fifty-fifth Street restaurant was a gay men's hot spot, and it tickled Diana being "the only woman in the place." Scads of friends—Diana knew many of them from her summers at Fire Island on Long Island—sent a steady stream of "champagne, then stingers and God knows what else" to their table.

The phone rang back at Diana'a apartment, sometime after 11 p.m. Jorge answered. "[Diana] said she was going to be married." They discussed it sometimes, though never as an option with each other. She would do it again, but "to hell with love"—this time it would be for money. "I had been told he had all these millions coming," Diana said. "I thought, why not? I've had the great love of my life, I'll never be in love again. This time marry for money [or] marry a gentleman—and Billy was both."

Did Billy propose? "[O]ddly enough none of my husbands ever proposed to me. They never said, 'Will you be my wife' or 'Will you marry me' or whatever men say, I don't know . . . [h]e was lost, as I was lost." Marriage struck them as a way for "two strange wandering children" to navigate a confusing existence. They called all the papers about their engagement, "drunk on happiness and love."

Jorge moved out and Flinn moved in, going home only for clean shirts and a shave. "He was the first man in the world I was ever able to sleep next to," Diana said. "Had we anything to do with each other as man and woman? No, nothing." She claimed she no longer cared about "that aspect" of a relationship. "I don't know why, because I'm a hell of a physical dame. . . . I don't know how two people can be so apart in the way of sex." In the six weeks they lived together, she later wrote, they only attempted intimacy three times. "I had to be the man to get him at all to be a man himself. I'm sure you understand what I mean by that."

Diana traded her usual sexual fixation for a spiritual one. "This telepathy thing . . . [h]e and I say the same things at the same times and think the same thought at the same moment . . . it must have something to do with astrology. The incredible thing is that we're both Pisces—he's March 15th, I'm March 3rd—and there must be some extraordinary affinity." It "frightened" the skittish, needy Flinn. "[T]hat's why he gravitated towards me, he want[ed] somebody strong to protect him and love him," Diana said. "God knows I did."

She loved him fiercely, as Diana-cat protecting Robina, as Michael clutching her beloved boy from the arms of death. "I said, darling, we are going to be friends as long as we live, I hope, because I adore you. . . . I'd wake up in the morning and that little pixie face would look at me [with] the sweetest face that ever was."

Leonard supported the marriage, mostly because she'd stop asking for handouts, with the added benefit of a caretaker for Diana's next health crisis, which came later that month:

> What woke me up was a spasm . . . I woke up in a cold sweat. It was pouring off and I was shivering . . . I got a terrible pain as though someone had hit me right by my heart. Every so often my arms, shoulders, legs, everything twitched. I kept getting up to throw up . . . [e]ach time I got up I could hardly walk to get to the bathroom to be sick. I never had anything like this before and it scared me.

On Columbus Day, the bubble popped. "[H]e said this morning, 'I still love you—I'm not in love with you, I never was' . . . I just pulled myself together and said, 'Look, Billy, let's face it . . . you're not even in a position to be in love with a woman.'" They agreed to let the ersatz romance "fade away decently, with good taste," and move on.

Good taste stayed out of reach that month. "Ann Andrews called me yesterday afternoon and said, 'Well, you've done it again,'" Diana said. She made the cover of one of the gossip rags, with a full recount of the McNeill drama inside. "I knew I had rather good billing—it's the second story," she quipped. Andrews wasn't amused. "Maybe through reading it you can take some cognizance of yourself." It took Diana a couple of days, but she read the article. "I just said, 'My God, what have I done to deserve this . . . what they said about the one man I loved—I could kill them for it. . . . I was weeping over it today for what they said about Bob.'"

Back to barbiturates for sleep, stimulants to counter the sleeping pills, booze in between, and barely eating. Around Christmas, she showed up at a party with a black eye, the result (she said) of a mugging while barhopping with friends in Greenwich Village. Shortly after, what should've been a minor infection sent her to Doctors Hospital with a high fever and convulsions. Dr. Joseph Criscuolo ("Dr. Martin Hemmings" in her book) took one look at her chart and warned her: "[What] took your father sixty years to do . . . you'll manage in a much shorter time." Eight days later, she walked out of the hospital and into the arms of a double vodka. Martinis, stingers, brandy, gin—still barely eating, sleeping all day, waking only to vomit, wash off the cold sweat, and gulp down whatever she found in the icebox. She gazed at her bloated, mottled reflection in the mirror and finally acknowledged she could no longer care for herself. She picked up the phone and called Leonard, her "rock to cling to." It took some searching but he finally found a slot for her at Towns Hospital, the same place where Jack once recovered. "[H]e can afford to put his little sister away for a while," she told Earl Wilson, shortly after Leonard paid for a six-month stay. "I'd be very delighted if you write that baby—that's me—said she can't do it by herself because she thinks it's psychiatric."

Diana spent the first two months of 1956 in group therapy, a new diet and exercise regimen, and a monitored alcohol withdrawal program. By the time of her departure in March, she drank only ginger ale with bitters—her favorite—and "never want[ed] to see a sleeping pill again." She was vastly improved, even if she hadn't "licked alcoholism," as the papers claimed. "I spent January and February in a sanitarium and I'm on the wagon," she said. "This so-called comeback of mine isn't from Skid Row." Her agent suggested going back to writing her memoirs (working title *So Far, So Good*). Back in early 1954, after an initial deal with playwright William Berney fizzled at Simon & Schuster, they contacted Henry Holt & Co. editor Howard Cady about securing Gerold Frank. Diana's story might just be another *I'll Cry Tomorrow*, the tawdry, triumphant memoir he cowrote with actress (and recovering alcoholic) Lillian Roth.

After several visits with the "limp-haired, unsteady, disheveled" Diana at her and Bob's "shabby Hell's Kitchen hotel," Cady asked Frank for preliminary ideas:

"As I see it now: Working title, 'Too Much, Too Soon,' subtitle, 'An Intimate Autobiography' . . . the following to appear on the page opposite title page:

"'And to me it is clear that Shakespere [*sic*] sought to depict a great deed laid upon a soul unequal to the performance of it.'—From the Preface of the Temple Edition of Hamlet.

"The book could close on this line: 'As I write this, I am lost'—or something to that effect. For between quotation and closing line, we shall have 350 pages of Diana's story, told as candidly and honestly as one human being can tell others . . . the account of a life which has been, until now, a slow, relentless fall from grace.

"She was to appear on the Hi [*sic*] Gardner TV show two weeks ago, but took a drink and then a second and a third to bolster herself: she was drunk when she showed up . . . [w]hen she broods about this—how cheaply and humiliatingly they now buy the name Barrymore—she turns to drink . . . [i]t was this—plus money difficulties—that led her in Boston last month to take an overdose of sleeping pills. 'I didn't want to die," she says. 'But I didn't want not to die.'"

"People seem to think I'm trying to write for *Confidential*," Frank said. He drew sweetness and honesty from Lillian Roth for *I'll Cry Tomorrow*, eventually did the same with Diana (with whole stories and chunks of dialogue borrowed from news clippings), and planned the same with Zsa Zsa Gabor. "Why must he do Zsa Zsa?" Diana said, almost possessively. "You'll see, he won't get anything out of *her*." But he did—living up to *Life*'s summation as "the world's most eminent—and unusual—ghost writer."

Diana's interviews resembled her father's, "rich with incident and utterly lacking in respect for chronology." She also resorted to her childhood fibbing. "I lied to him and I am a brilliant liar," she told *Life*. "But he'd know. Or he'd find out." Frank fact-checked everything though interviews with everyone from husbands (except for Bramwell Fletcher, who declined to be interviewed) to servants to doctors to neighborhood transients, weaving a visceral, vulnerable story powerful enough to make its subject cry. "Oh, you son of a bitch," she said, dabbing her eyes as he read the first chapters aloud. "Read me some more."

He didn't shy away from the hard questions. "[I]t is apparent that if you didn't drink and remained sober for a long period of time . . . any door would be open to you as an actress. Why is it that you keep on when you know there is a door?" Diana pondered. "For someone who had everything to begin with who has now ended up with nothing. What do I think are the causes? One thing, liquor . . . it's an insidious monster and I don't know . . . it's the easiest way out—I can't face it. I never thought I was a coward but I think I must be. . . ."

Diana didn't like Frank's proposed ending, which he amended to: "I am lost. Help me."

"If I say 'help me' people will say, 'Oh, well, she wants another job or oh, well, she wants something.' It would be half and half as a matter of fact. Half will say, 'I'm glad she had the guts to say what she said in the book.'" The ending was nixed.

On May 25, 1956, she returned to the stage with the Provincetown Players in *The Ivory Branch*, the play Black theater critic Miles Jefferson called an "atrocity." Diana "stumble[d] badly" in choosing the tale of a Black child born to white parents in the "deep South" as her comeback vehicle, and *Variety* agreed, calling it "deplorable." Critic William Hawkins disliked the play but felt "Miss Diana Barrymore certainly succeeded in proving something . . . she should by no means be relegated to the second-rate, sleazy comedies she has recently toted around the country." She earned $30 per week until it closed on June 19th, and when someone asked if she felt Jack's presence watching over the production, she smirked. "Darling . . . Daddy's ghost wouldn't go off-Broadway."

Henry Holt & Co. prepared to release *Too Much, Too Soon* in April 1957 with an oil portrait of Diana by Spurgeon Tucker on the back. Memoirs and autobiographies, including those of her father, Uncle Lionel, and Aunt Ethel, were lovely things, full of resiliency and hope. Diana's book wallowed in unpleasant details and proffered no valor of its subject, a "strikingly modern" approach.

Look magazine paid $50,000 to run exclusive prepublication excerpts, and clearing those excerpts required finesse. "You will observe that a cut was made in the end of the installment removing the call girl episode," wrote *Look* book editor Margery Darrell in a letter to Gerold Frank. "The cut was made by Mr. Gardner Cowles, owner of the magazine, and although I still feel that there are many reasons why this episode should remain in the story, I have nothing to say about it at this point . . . I trust you're having a ball."

"I am sorry, too, that the call girl episode was deleted, for it had a flavor and a connotation necessary to Diana's story," Frank replied. "I am having a ball, but I am not always sure whether I am the ball and who is the tennis racket. Ungrammatical, but exciting."

Another letter to Frank, this time from Henry Holt & Co. publicity agent Betty Ringler, brings up "the possibility of Diana's appearance on radio and television programs to tie-in with the first *LOOK* issue. . . . Diana's psychiatrist advises against any interviews at this time." Ringler suggested Frank go easy on appearances, especially with "top network shows": "We do want to save you for *Too Much, Too Soon*, itself." Ringler adds a cute but pointed postscript: "I'm sure you'll remember, in any interviews you do, to mention that the book will be published April 8 by Henry Holt and Company!"

The book's release was met with, well . . . people were not ready for that modern approach. "There must be a lot of cringing going on right now in certain social and entertainment circles," smirked Luther Nichols at the *San Francisco Examiner*. "For Diana, bless her heart, slavers over her romances with prominent males like a writer for *Confidential*." "Hollywood doesn't like *Too Much, Too Soon*, the Diana Barrymore confessional . . . perhaps it's all because it's too much, too close to home," preferred *Photoplay*. Gene Fowler called it "Too Much, Too Late—Too Bad." Frances Neal burned over the Van Heflin story. Hedda Hopper renamed it "Long Day's Journey into Oblivion" but admitted Diana had "much to tell . . . more than any other member of the Barrymore clan." Louella Parsons was succinct in summing up the book as "too much, too loudly." Walter Winchell thought it "cost her the few friends she had left."

Johnnie didn't bother to read it: "Diana's a total stranger to me." Critic Pete Arthur found it hard to stomach. "The book is full of sex, but none of it is pretty . . . why should all this dirty linen be washed in public?" John Barkham's review praised Frank's writing as "dramatic rehabilitation" for its subject, not that she deserved it: "Diana Barrymore had neither the moral fiber to resist the temptations nor—let's face it—the acting talent to match her name." Another confessed it was "the sort of lurid book which may keep you up late, only to make you hate yourself for your vulgar curiosity in the morning." Day Tuttle wished she'd not pinned so much on her mother and father "because it isn't until we take the full responsibility for our own acts—and stop blaming others—that we begin to have a chance for content and patient humility." Nancy Barr Mavity, writing for the *Oakland Tribune*, felt that "the 'fatal flaw' in this fizzling, sizzling shooting star is a complete lack of any sense of responsibility," It was "a cheap, cruel piece of exhibitionism," dancing to the "tune of jingling cash registers." It had its fans; John Chapman of the *Daily News* "admire[d] her guts" and praised Gerold Frank as "an admirable collaborator" with a "compelling" style. Mel Heimer at the *Cleveland Plain Dealer* recommended the "shocker" of how "a thoughtless genius of a father and a self-centered mother let a sensitive girl grow up the wrong way," Most, though, sided with Missouri's *St. Joseph News-Press*: "a detestable book we do not recommend to any human being . . . stay away from it. It stinks."

Entertainer and striptease artist Gypsy Rose Lee once called the genre of autobiography "setting yourself up as a clay pigeon." Drama critic William F. McDermott worried about Diana's ability to withstand being "spiritually naked for the world's scrutiny." He'd spoken to her once on the phone, her voice "wistful and plaintive, like that of a lonely girl cast up on a desert shore. I did not know at that time that she really was lonely and troubled." Diana appeared to deflect the slings and arrows. "I didn't set out to point a moral," she explained. "[W]riting it has been a cleansing process . . . it's like psychiatry in a way." It helped her work through Bob's death and begin to heal. "I don't think there ever can be as many dark moments again . . . [a] lot of people are rooting for me."

One such person was Olga Dziedzic of Valley Falls, Rhode Island.

Home (NBC, 1954–57) was Diana's first stop on her promotional tour, April 15, 1957. She and host Arlene Francis discussed the book in between taped segments touring NYC locations pertinent to Diana and the Barrymores. The show brought their largest audience response to date, attracting piles of fan mail, some of which Diana kept, including this letter from Mrs. Dziedzic:

I know you'll succeed now, no matter what . . . there must be thousands who will be cheering for you, Dianna [sic]; so many will be famous in their own way, but take it from a housewife and mother: I'm with you all the way. Keep that certain something you possess! It came through on TV . . . one saying I'd like to end with when I've seen my own loved ones suffering . . . "those nearest to God suffer the most."

She did interviews on Tex McCrary and Jinx Falkenberg's *Closeup* and *The Ben Hecht Sho*w, and told journalist Charles McHarry discussing her past foibles was "not very pretty but at least I can face it and try to do something about it." The centerpiece of her book tour was an appearance on *The Mike Wallace Interview*. Even in its infancy, the show's reputation for hardball scared celebrities away in a manner "virtually a geometric theorem: We call star. We persuade star. Star says OK and sets date. Star contacts agent and/or press agent. Agent says over his dead body. Period, end of report." They made a good fit, Diana and Mike Wallace: his fresh style of interview, hard questions, no gloss; her "writing" the same kind of memoir. It wasn't quite full vulnerability, but it was close, and it was something people weren't used to seeing. Actor Kirk Douglas's commentary after being on with Wallace: "The public should have a chance to see an actor off balance every once in a while."

The introduction to Diana's July 14, 1957, show would put anyone off balance: "After a promising start on Broadway and in Hollywood, Miss Barrymore swapped her birthright for alcoholism, three tempestuous marriages, and professional failure." He quoted from *Time* magazine's review of her book: "'If a former glamour girl is down and out, shaken by the DTs and degraded by three nightmare marriages plus numerous vulgar affairs, how can she rehabilitate herself? She simply writes a book about it.' What about that?"

"Well, Mike," she said, smoke curling from her ever-present cigarette, "when we were talking a little bit before, you said the first one might be a tough one!" They chatted candidly about her revelations. Wallace thought they were "pretty nasty things about a good number of people" of whom the world thought highly. "Maybe they were nasty, but they were true," Diana replied. For thirty minutes, they discussed her father ("tortured"), her reluctance to blame herself for her problems ("if you make one false move, you've had it"), her desire to re-enter café society. Michael once told her "ladies and gentlemen wear well," and Diana thought after the "monsters" she'd mixed with, the old crowd was "refreshing."

She brought out her flirty former debutante. She loved to cook—"I make the best Yorkshire pudding this side of England"—and invited Wallace to dinner. "May I bring my wife?" he asked. "You certainly may," she replied coyly. The talk turned personal. She wanted to remarry, wanted to be "Mrs. Somebody" instead of Miss Barrymore. "I want to forget about being an actress and try being a wife." She also thought she'd make a good mother—"Don't ask me why or we'll need another program!" Manager Violla Rubber entered her life and gave her "someone [else] to cling to." The tight-laced Rubber, "a sort of old maid British spinster," previously worked with and befriended Marlene Dietrich and Bette Davis.

She tried to find solace in a return to Catholicism but still wrestled with the blasé attitude of her mother and Robin, who said Mass was a "marvel-ous show" with great costumes. Religion was a big part of the twelve steps, which Diana rejected as "too stringent." Would she prove an "exception" to the high recidivism rate? Her answer was noncommittal. "At the moment I don't drink, but I hope to be able to one day . . . to be able to drink like a normal human being." Being a regular ordinary "hausfrau" appealed greatly to Diana, who was dating Chilean actor Octavio Señoret Guevara. She and Guevara, previously known for spending a little too much time with Ava Gardner on the set of *The Barefoot Contessa* (1954), were serious enough to throw an engagement party with their friends a month earlier. "I fell for Octavio as soon as I met him," she told newspapers. "He's a combination of Jean-Pierre Aumont and Fernando Lamas and has charm to burn." She insisted to Wallace "a woman with a kitchen is happier than someone with a curtain going up and down." She wasn't planning to abandon the stage entirely, however. Was it a good idea, Wallace mused, placing herself back in the lap of "all the potential trouble" she experienced before? "Yes, because I think I've learned, Mike," she said. "I hope."

Jack Gould of the *New York Times* found her a "fascinating guest," "immensely likeable," and possessing "sardonic self-appraisal." A month later, Diana was back on stage for her eleventh summer stock as Tracy Lord, and no longer with Guevara. He allegedly began dating one of her relatives, and Diana moved on with bandleader Lester Lanin and actor John Ireland's brother, Mike. Equity continued needling her, sending a letter stating "Miss Barrymore has recently sold her biography for some $150,000.00 and has no further excuse not to clean up the matter." Violla Rubber finally stepped in and got Blaney talking with Charles Mintz, Diana's lawyer and, as luck would have it, Blaney's old friend. They settled and Mintz finally cut the $180 check on July 19, 1957.

While a guest on game show pilot *Make Up Your Mind* back in 1951, she remarked on the immense fortitude needed to "look in the mirror" and improve oneself. "I was on the wagon for three months, just by doing that," she later wrote. "I'd say, 'Look, do you remember what you were, what you could have become? . . . come on and pull yourself together.'" After *Too Much, Too Soon,* she committed herself to just that. She saw a (female!) therapist four times a week and was so cooperative that her summer stock[17] managers wanted to run a "good conduct" notice in *Variety.* Another *Glad Tidings* production, this time with original Broadway cast member Fay Sappington and John Heath as leading man. She did *Laura* in August, the show replacing *Gigi* with Margaret O'Brien, and thought she might return to Broadway next or revive *The Royal Family* for a 1958 road show. She dismissed rumors that *Good Night, Sweet Prince* was being adapted as a teleplay for *Playhouse 90,* starring her half-brother Johnnie as their father. "John hardly knew Daddy . . . [n]one of the Barrymores knew each other especially." She hosted a week of the TV soap *Modern Romances* (NBC, 1954–58) and did a few charity appearances, like the coin toss for a Jaycees/United Cerebral Palsy-sponsored football game in Pennsylvania that August. Columnist Bill McReynolds wondered if Diana's comeback was genuine, or if she would "combine her great inherited talents with stage prostitution" like her father. Trouble still found her, however. Earl Wilson witnessed Diana and an unidentified man in a 1 a.m. fight on Park Avenue just before Christmas 1957. The man struck her, then kicked her in the rear, knocking her to the pavement. "Aren't any of you gentleman enough to help a woman being slugged?" she shouted to the gathering crowd. "Diana isn't out of the woods yet, and she knows it as well as anyone," said Gerold Frank. "She can be just as great as she wants to be."

Jack Warner shelled out between $100,000 and $150,000 to snatch Diana's book from the galley proofs and planned it as Warner Bros. answer to M-G-M's Oscar-winning *I'll Cry Tomorrow.* A book this juicy, however, could mire the studio in lawsuits. Story analyst Helen Maloney set to work teasing out the VIPs from whom they needed clearance while Gerold Frank and screenwriter Irving Wallace started their step outline.

Bramwell Fletcher required several nonnegotiables of his character, among them:

- portrayal as "a person active as an actor," not someone "who sits idly at home"
- "not to be portrayed as a greying, aged or decrepit man."
- "not to be portrayed as living at his wife's expense"

and most inexplicably, since his real name was in the book and their marriage was common knowledge:

---

17. Nancy Reagan played a bit role as a maid in one production.

- "[o]nly use a fictitious name that does not phonetically suggest Bramwell Fletcher"

Frank and Wallace assured studio counsel Morris Ebenstein that he "emerges as a decent human being, thoughtful and considerate, a man who never sanctioned Diana's escapades—indeed, who did his best, while her husband, to help a confused, wilful [sic] girl make sense of her life. If he failed, the blame is not attached to him."

Tony Duke also didn't object to his real name in the book, but in a motion picture? His family probably would. This required delicacy. "[T]he first lover in Diana Barrymore's life will have to be a fictional character . . . you will, of course, have to fictionize the circumstances. For example, roughly speaking, he would have to be a poor man and it would have to take place in Florida, so as to avoid confusion with the rich man who wooed in chilly Tuxedo Park." They also tweaked their meeting to one arranged by their mothers at Diana's debut: "It's a sure thing Tony Duke's mother never did any maneuvering to bring Diana into Tony's life and into their family."

While the rest of the cast of characters was evaluated, Irving Wallace brought his notes to Dr. Marshall D. Schechter for an "anaylsis." Wallace and Frank valued the opinion of the highly regarded medical doctor and psychiatrist, later a professor emeritus of child and adolescent psychiatry, and felt it would clarify their script concept.

"People do not attempt suicide simply because they are depressed . . . . [Diana] didn't know who she was, what she was. She had no picture of herself as a human being.

"Diana has a masochistic structure. She hurts herself, repeating the same harmful episodes over and over again . . . [r]epetition of outrageous acts makes it clear the patient is not making sense in terms of reality."

He called her an "exhibitionist," a "textbook of pathology—and it's all bad. Not neurotic, but very near psychotic. . . . Diana has no feeling of value, of being worthwhile. She has no good feeling inside her." Her parents divorced at a time when children look to them for "authority, omnipotence, [and] strength." He claimed she regressed to "early childish ways of satisfying herself," believing "some kind of magic will accomplish things for her." She sought men who loved "tender and weak or cruel and sadistic. She could not put the two together." She adapted to them because "[s]he had no real single sustained good relationship in her life . . . such people become those around them."

He felt she'd try therapy because it would be "a lark . . . one more magical thing—like the job, the latest lay" but would drop it when it exposed her real feelings about her parents: "she would learn she hates their guts."

He summarized with the following underlined passage: "Diana never had the feeling of being loved. Hypersexuality is her way of getting love today. It is never satisfactory or satisfying. Because no man, ever, can give her what her mother and father should have given her and never did.

"[W]hen the book and movie are done . . . she will be wounded. And after that . . . ?"

The two men distilled this analysis for staff producer/production supervisor Henry Blanke: "[T]his is the story of a girl's search for love and affection that were denied by her parents too busy with their own extravagant careers . . . who tries to be first her mother's daughter—a social figure—and fails; then her father's daughter—an actress—and fails." One page outlines this emotional anguish:

> Diana's delirious dream:
> She is on a surrealistic stage in the shining armor of St. Joan of Arc, taking curtain call after curtain call. This is her triumph . . . now we see the audience—a thousand John Barrymores applauding wildly . . . a hundred Michael Stranges, strumming harps, heads bowed in acknowledgement of Diana's genius. And in the balconies—a dozen Bram Fletchers, a dozen John Howards, a dozen Bob Wilcoxes gesticulating their love, their love, their love. And now Diana as St. Joan again, pointing to her cast members, the hooded clergy, all bowing, all the faces of Farrell, of lust, of brutality, of love.

Blanke appreciated this, but was firm: Diana must "not emerge as a girl of low moral character." Despite its death throes, they must obey the Production Code.

The studio system was crumbling, thanks in part to the 1952 overturning of a 1915 Supreme Court ruling that films weren't protected under the First Amendment, and the 1954 retirement of Joseph Breen, previously of the National Legion of Decency and appointed by Will Hays to head the Production Code Administration. Yet "anti-scandal" sentiment still ran rampant, and after reading the script Breen "lieutenant" Jack Vizzard immediately arranged an emergency conference. "Are you trying to aim another blockbuster at the Legion of Decency?" he wrote. He and fellow censor Timothy Healy brought up a multitude of issues with Wallace, Frank, and screenwriter Finlay McDermid, the most immediate being Tom Farrell. "[H]er relationship with Farrell, as presently portrayed, is entirely too realistic and clinical in detail." They suggested he be edited "as forcibly as possible," and her other conquests be cut. Cut, too, were her suicide attempts, and a new character inserted "who would act as a voice for morality" during the "extreme degradation of her life." The call-girl sequence would also be "unacceptable under the Code," particularly "Diana's regrets after her father's death that she had not been more considerate and understanding of her father's needs for this." This could be corrected, they posited, by having the girl visit Jack "for some other purpose than sexual intimacies" and Diana, "thinking that the girl is trying to promote herself by exploiting the Barrymore name," throws her out.

Casting suggested box-office moneymakers like Elizabeth Taylor and Shirley MacLaine for Diana, Mary Astor for Michael, and Kirk Douglas or Vincent Price for Jack, but it wasn't easy finding actors willing to be involved with the project. Many of the Warner Bros. starlets, including Natalie Wood and Anne Baxter, chafed at playing Diana. "If they took out all of [the] things I objected to in the book, all they'd have left would be the covers," remarked actress Ann Blyth. Warner Bros. then assigned the role to Carroll Baker, who refused, having had her fill of controversy with the lurid *Baby Doll* (1956). The studio suspended her without salary, but public opinion sided with the actress, as evident in a letter sent to the studio by a fan named Mrs. Edith C. Vea: "Mr. Vea and I wish you to know that we are proud you stand for your own beliefs even to paying the terrific cost of suspension." She expressed disgust at the "filth" glorifying "characters such as Diana Barrymore and Lillian Roth (that alcholiac [sic] person)."

Finally, in August, Dorothy Malone was cast. She won the Academy Award for her role a year before as Marylee, a character eerily similar to Diana, in *Written on the Wind*. As film critic/historian Sheila O'Malley writes, "[Marylee] tries to be a vamp, but she's really just a damaged *kid* in the body of a bombshell." Robert Stack was Oscar-nominated for his performance of Marylee's brother Kyle, and Robert Keith played their father, Jasper.

The rest of the cast also took shape: radio and Broadway actress Neva Patterson as Michael Strange (a role which Bette Davis coveted); Efrem Zimbalist Jr. of *Maverick* (and later, *77 Sunset Strip*, and father of actress Stephanie Zimbalist) as pseudo-Bramwell Vincent Bryant; actor Ray Danton, winner of Most Promising Newcomer at the 1956 Golden Globes for his role in *I'll Cry Tomorrow*, as John Howard; Martin Milner, later of *Route 66* and *Adam-12*, as Lincoln "Linc" Forrester, the moral character loosely based on Tony Duke; and Murray Hamilton, best known by modern audiences as Amity mayor Larry Vaughn from *Jaws* (1975) and *Jaws 2* (1978) as Charlie Snow, a composite of Walter Wanger and the rest of Diana's directors. They hadn't yet chosen their John Barrymore, and after nixing Fredric March were now leaning heavily towards actor John Emery, called John Barrymore's illegitimate son due to their strong physical resemblance. Emery also knew Jack, and roomed for a time with him and his first wife, Katherine Corri Harris. Allegedly, somewhere in the crowd of extras, is Maila Nurmi, better known as Vampira.

Summer dwindled in a haze of rewrites. Yvonne, Aunt Ethel, Nita Naldi, Ann Andrews, and all the strong supportive women in Diana's life were merged into character Pauline Barnard, whose caring advice would save Diana from complete ruin. Robert Wilcox was now a "reformed drunkard" who helps Diana to quit, and the ending now revolved around the moral character, Lincoln Forrester (Martin Milner), a friend from Diana's past "whose family is in the social register." Diana walks home from the hospital after being in the "psycho and alcoholic section" when she runs into Linc, "the sweetheart of her deb days." She's broken and disheveled, clad in cheap lamé—a stark contrast to her white debutante dress—and offers to take her in, care for her, and pay her debts. She "resists the temptation to return once again to a life of ease . . . she intends to find herself first."

After numerous drafts and script problems, Gerold Frank and Irving Wallace handed over the reins to married writer/director team Art and Jo Napoleon. Columnist Erskine Johnson wondered how anyone could get "an acceptable screenplay" out of a book that was "merely a bound edition of *Confidential* magazine," but the Napoleons were determined to tell her story with grace and compassion. To them, Diana was "sensitive and intelligent," forced through a "bewildering maze of real life Alice in Wonderland characters—with Michael Strange as the Red Queen needling her on one side, and John Barrymore as the mercurial Mad Hatter constantly out of reach for comfort on the other." Art would even direct, after the departure of Irving Rapper and the refusal of Michael Curtiz to be associated with, in his opinion, a disreputable picture. "[W]e want to get the feeling that for the motion picture industry, for the columnists and for everything else she is a commodity—nothing more. But we do not want to play the producers as heavies, simply as solid businessmen . . . the punch-drunk fighter who everyone has taken advantage of."

Warner Bros. spent an inordinate amount of time and effort clearing the name of "Tassles Terhune," a fictional character billed alongside Diana at the burlesque club. "We have found four burlesque queens who wear or have worn in recent years, tassels variously attached in a manner designed to accomplish their agitation during a characteristic strip routine," wrote research department head Carl Milliken Jr. "[T]here is [also] a burlesque queen named Sally Keith who is known professionally as 'The Tassel Girl.'

Her specialty, which she claims to be unique, is that of attaching tassel adornments suitably fore and after and causing them to rotate in a marvelous manner. . . . Perhaps we can use 'Pom-Poms.'" They should've utilized it instead to reach Clara Bow, one of the most popular actresses of the 1920s and the original "It Girl." Milliken Jr. didn't bother to get permission from her, though mentioned by name, because he "stupidly thought she was dead. However, she is still alive and, according to the *Mirror News*, has been confined in a sanitarium in Culver City for five years." Whether he attempted to contact her is unclear; his memo ends with "I do not think she is compos mentis."

Some didn't wait to be contacted. "Please be advised," wrote Elaine Barrie in a September 1957 letter to Warner Bros., "that in the event that I, or any member of my family, is portrayed in said film, or is in any way libeled, slandered, defamed, or in any way injured in our reputation, we shall prosecute vigorously any and all causes of action available to us." Elaine, rumored to have been played by Linda Darnell, was quickly cut. John Howard, for whom permission was understood to be granted, threatened legal action and hired an attorney. "I have been trying to forget those old days. Warners told me not to worry and made me promises which they have not kept. If necessary, I certainly will sue them." Either his threats were empty, or the studio paid him off, because his decidedly unpleasant portrayal remained in the film. Diana didn't think John McNeill would sue over Tom Farrell since "he ha[d] been in the Tombs" and therefore didn't want to make waves. "It is hardly necessary to add that we should not rely on Diana Barrymore's judgment," wrote Ebenstein.

They felt there was nothing for Leonard to object to concerning his mother's portrayal. As for Johnnie and his father, "since he had become a notoriously seedy and decrepit character," wrote Morris Ebenstein, "it is hard for me to imagine that you could commit a criminal libel with respect to him even if you tried." Erskine Johnson called Art to ask if "anyone made any overtures toward John Barrymore Jr. for a part in the picture" (they had not). It's infuriating that Dede's opinion, or participation, wasn't even considered.

John Emery's screen test didn't impress the Napoleons, despite the resemblance. "He seems to think that to snort, to arch his eyebrows and to roll his r's is to play Barrymore. . . . [Barrymore] had infinitely more depth to his personality than the few exaggerated mannerisms he used to get laughs, and that fact must come through in our story. . . . [Emery] is unable to project the innate fire, intellect and tragedy of the man. The audience must believe that he was once the biggest actor of his time, and unfortunately, no one will believe that about Emery." Their choice? Errol Flynn.

They've come up with a dilly to play John Barrymore," blared Louella Parsons. They say to never meet your heroes; Flynn befriended and bonded with his over shared passions (and demons). "We both had boats and we both made a lot of headlines," he laughed. "I'm glad people think I'm a natural for the part. . . . I hope Jack, wherever he is, will also think I'm a natural for the part." If anyone could see past the caricature that was Jack in his last years, it was Flynn, who died at fifty a year after *Too Much Too Soon* was released. "I wanted to show a man with a heart," he wrote in *My Wicked, Wicked Ways*, "a man eaten up inside . . . full of regrets and ready to die, but with one last thing to live for, the love of his daughter."

That kind of complexity and pathos was the Napoleons' goal. Primarily known as the creators of (and occasional writers for) the Desilu-produced helicopter adventure series *Whirlybirds* (1957–60), they had few other credits to their name and labored to produce a script justifying their selection. "[W]e can really have a hell of a good picture, one that will be a wonderful credit for us and that, even in today's market, has every chance of making a bundle for you," they wrote studio vice president Steve Trilling. "[W]e have tried to use every device we could dream up . . . to give it 'snap,' excitement, vitality; to give it pace and shock, and to make the characters poignant and touching human beings." This was not easy to do with the censors still thwarting them at every turn. One, Geoffrey M. Shurlock, sent his objections directly to Jack Warner:

- cut a kissing scene that had "an objectionably sex suggestive flavor"
- any embracing between Diana and Vince Bryant must be vertical and fully-clothed
- "no silhouette of Diana in the shower"
- The scene with a wild, drunken Jack brandishing a broken bottle was "unduly gruesome and too easily imitated" and should be reshot with an empty, intact bottle.

The Napoleons conceded and cooperated, revised and rearranged, until Shurlock insisted on eliminating the burlesque scene. Neutering Tassels's performance wasn't enough, he said. The whole thing must go. Not a chance, said Jo Napoleon.

"[T]he burlesque involves the whole sense of the story . . . *[h]er great need for love* must lead her to a final wild act to obtain it. *The Barrymore name . . .* we must establish that she can no longer earn a living, even on the basis of the name . . . *[c]ontrast between what she was and what she has become . . .*"

The scene was staying, and Diana would be blotto in it:

"*Her drinking*—whether we like it or not we have now set it up as a manifestation of her problem—when she's lonely and unhappy she drinks . . . it would [be] unbelievable for her not to be loaded."

The censors, surprisingly, relented. But Diana's impressions during the scene raised other issues. Milliken Jr. recommended she impersonate only "happily defunct" celebrities, and provided a crowdsourced and somewhat befuddling list:

Fanny Brice
W. C. Fields
Joe McCarthy
Bela Lugosi
Oliver Hardy
Lon Chaney Sr. (added advantage "because of the present picture in release about him")
Bugs Bunny

Thanks, said the Napoleons. Very helpful.

By the time the film was submitted for final approval, things were complete save for some last-minute dubbing and editing. After talent, the $1.1 million budget went to costumes by Orry-Kelly, a mansion once owned by silent film stars Madge Kennedy and Pola Negri as Jack's palatial home on Tower Road, the recreation of several locations and the *Infanta* on a soundstage, and tennis champion Tony Trabert as technical advisor and coach to Ray Danton, who once showed up for training only to encounter Howard himself playing against tennis pro Frank Feltrop. "John wouldn't even shake [Danton's] hand," Feltrop said.

The Production Code Administration signed off in February 1958, and an invitation-only preview held at Warner Bros.' Manhattan headquarters on Fifth Avenue on March 20, 1958. *Too Much, Too Soon*'s official New York premiere was on May 9th at dual New York City theaters, the Odeon at 256 West 145th St and the Sutton at 205 East Fifty-seventh Street.

What could have been an uncompromising and very human portrait is toothless under the censor's hand. Gone are Tony Duke, "Pauline Barnard" (or any family/friends, save for Mom and "Linc"), the events at Garrison Forest, the "call girl" incident, and the shower scene. Diana's society debut gets only a few minutes and looks more like a Sunday buffet. This Diana is two-dimensional, a doomed figure of failure and loss.

We meet her as a starry-eyed teenager, reading a movie magazine with her father on the cover. She desperately wants a relationship with her father and writes him letters, about which an irritated Michael confronts her. Michael is a good deal softer here than in Diana's book, austere solely as protection from the lurking Barrymore miasma eager to consume her daughter. She eventually acquiesces to the trip aboard the *Infanta*.

Our first glimpse of Jack is fishing with Diana. He clearly loves his daughter but grows bored with her chatter, and when friends—shown only in shadow, specters from Jack's past—beckon from an adjoining yacht he jumps overboard, drink in hand and spouting Shakespeare, to join them. Flynn visibly enjoys playing his friend, and the first part of the film succeeds due to how beautifully he captures Jack's verve, volatility, and painful self-awareness.

Diana triumphs on Broadway (in *Alexander Hamilton*) as Michael and friend Linc watch from the wings. Linc beams for his friend and Michael scoffs. "Don't be a boy," she says flatly. "They're applauding her name." (Unfair, since she received good notices for her actual Broadway debut.) She comes to Hollywood, meets Vincent Bryant, and puts her feet in Clara Bow's (recreated) cement footprints. A promising future stretches before her with her father as self-appointed guide, and so when she refuses a cocktail at his home, his reply stabs them both in the heart: "Why not? They haven't proved it's hereditary!"

He walks her through Tower Road, a shell of what once was. They pause by an enormous cage housing "Uncle Sam," Jack's pet bald eagle. "Two old men who've flown pretty high and ended up caged," he muses. When Jack opens the cage during one of his episodes, a terrified Diana creeps through the darkened house to the clinking of the crystal chandelier on which the bird perches—sounding exactly like ice in a highball glass.

The more time they spend together, the more apparent his destruction becomes. One night, in a drunken rage, he threatens his nurse with a broken brandy bottle—yes, the Napoleons got their way—and Diana sent away so as not to see Jack wrestled into submission. His wails of anguish follow her all the way to the guest bedroom. There was little left of the man who, childlike and slightly maudlin, called his ex-wife and invited her to Tower Road so they could be a family one more time. (Flynn did redubs on this scene because he didn't sound drunk enough.)

Producer Charlie Snow mounts a massive ad campaign for Diana's first film, *Forever in my Heart*. Three huge billboards scream, "You've Loved Lionel Barrymore! You've Thrilled to John Barrymore! Now EXALT Diana Barrymore in 'Forever in my Heart'!" After the preview, however, it's agreed both the movie and Diana are a flop. Jack's nurse pulls up outside the theater and relays the news that her father is near death; she rushes to the hospital, pausing only to let two men wheeling a gurney exit the elevator. As they pass by, we see the toe tag on the sheet-covered body: John Barrymore.

Diana comes home to empty, cavernous Tower Road, dusts off a comically large copy of *Hamlet*, finds her father's brandy stash, and begins the film's second half by drinking herself unconscious.

She is now the Diana everyone thinks she was: a trollop in a wet bathing suit entertaining fair-weather friends while refusing Snow's pleas for retakes; walked out on by Vincent after being discovered with the oily John Howard (thus ensuring Bramwell Fletcher was not cuckolded), a cruel man who hits Diana in the face with a tennis ball after she calls him a "weak, sadistic tennis bum"; meeting an in-recovery Robert Wilcox, who unravels after marrying her; and scraping the bottom of the barrel with an impressionist's act in a tawdry burlesque house. Just who did she end up imitating? Garbo—"I vant to be ah-lone"—and, though never explicitly stated, Marilyn Monroe. Donning a blonde wig, she adopts the hands-on-knees pose and babbles in a breathy voice until, after goading from the men, she laughs and begins stripping. She is rushed off stage and out of the theater, leading us to one of the film's strongest scenes.

In this key scene, Diana is seen walking the midnight streets, sloshed. She passes a drugstore window, bright and cheerful with beautiful people advertising things like suntan lotion and deodorant. She mocks the poses of the models and giggles—until she catches her own bleary-eyed reflection in the glass. Her blonde wig is crooked, her garish makeup smeared. One imagines her thinking back to the days when she was the one endorsing soap and antiperspirant. Now, faced with the "ugly" truth, she smashes the window and obliterates the display. Police haul her off to the alcoholic ward, where Gerold Frank—an old colleague of her mother's, in this version—offers her redemption through telling her story. They kept the ending, with Linc's hope of, and her determination for, a better future.

Timelines skip, details blur, but in two instances the Napoleons' refrain of FAILURE drowns out facts: her father's later career, and Robert Wilcox.

"[Director Charlie Snow] is impressed with Barrymore's sobriety and says he will suggest that the studio star Barrymore in 'The Man Who Came to Dinner.' No studio had dared hire Barrymore."

This is an outright falsehood. While Bette Davis had indeed wanted Jack for the role of Sheridan Whiteside and lobbied the studio into giving him an ultimately disastrous screen test, he worked steadily until his death in films, several mocking his former greatness: *The Great Profile* (1940), *World Premiere* (1941), *Playmates* (1941).

"Diana gets no comforting words from [Wilcox] when she learns her mother has died. Wilcox hates Diana and dashes a whiskey glass in her face."

To the contrary, Wilcox adored Diana, and she had nothing but loving, kind things to say about Bob all throughout the book, even dedicating it "[t]o Robert, who understood." He resumed drinking the moment he left the clinic and never considered himself a recovering alcoholic; he never discouraged their relationship or blamed her for dragging him back into addiction. When Diana learns of her mother's death via telegram a day after her burial and complains of feeling nothing, he viciously throws a drink in her face and says now she feels "wet." Of all the studio's concerns about libel, if he were alive, Robert Wilcox would have had a hell of a case.

"Undaring and even unsurprising," wrote Howard Thompson for the *New York Times*, "a basically familiar case history of an insecure girl who mourns a sodden father by emulating him." Changing the dysfunctional love story that was Bob and Diana robbed the film of poignancy, as did excising "most of the soiled linen . . . perhaps the book's only real substance." Dorothy Malone made "a winsome, earnest protagonist," but Errol Flynn as "a moody, wild-drinking ruin of a great actor" stole the movie out from under her. "It is only in the scenes of his savage disintegration, as the horrified girl hangs on, that the picture approaches real tragedy." The *Daily News* thought the "pathetic, true-confession type story" bore "some resemblance" to *I'll Cry Tomorrow* but "failed to inject that particular ingredient into the story that arouses compassion in the beholder." They, too, felt Malone was "growing in stature as an actress" but Flynn's "penetrating portrait" of Jack was "one of the highlights of the picture."

The film went into wide release on May 31st, and critics nationwide largely agreed with their New York counterparts.

- "Mae Tinee" at the *Chicago Tribune*: "It's a sordid, unattractive tale, poorly written and badly acted. Miss Malone tries hard, but never manages to be very appealing, and the same goes for Mr. Flynn as the late actor . . . [a]s a whole, it's a deadly dull tale which seems endless."
- Philip K Scheuer for the *Los Angeles Tribune*: "'Too Much, Too Soon' is a libel on the memory of the Barrymores . . . Flynn is not the great profile and great actor of our time and I resented him in the part. I am mortified for Warner Bros. . . ."
- Harry MacArthur, the *Washington Evening Star*: "Mr. Flynn rolls around for more than an hour here impersonating a drunk. Miss Malone, being younger, displays more stamina and goes the full

distance, which tops two hours. It seems like at least six ... the pain is too much and never is too soon."

W. Ward Marsh of the *Cleveland Plain Dealer* was disgusted by the "stark, uninspirational tale" and its "unaccomplished" and "untalented" subject, Malone's inability to bring "the slightest ray of sympathy," and Flynn's "hollow caricature" of the great John Barrymore. "Sorry, my reader. I have so little use for Diana, her story and her film. The last two can be forgotten. If the family representative should come this way again, let's hope she does better."

Walter Winchell thought "[t]he flicker's highlight is Errol Flynn's portrayal of John Barrymore," but Hedda Hopper opined that it "never should have been made." *Time* magazine summarized: "It may make a lot of moviegoers feel that they have had one too many ... the booze flows a good deal more freely than the narrative."

Ticket sales started strong then sagged in week three, after the novelty factor wore off. The *Louisville Courier-Journal* called it "a dreary affair" attended by "a sparse audience that didn't seem too fascinated by it." Total box office take was a drab $1.5 million.

Modern reviews are kinder, particularly in regards to Flynn. A 2010 revisit by the *New York Post* deemed it "an essential and in some ways fascinating experience for students of Hollywood's studio era" with a "rather remarkable and disciplined performance" by the "magnificent ruin" Flynn. The *Post* deemed it an "oddly touching film."

For his role as pseudo-Bramwell Vincent Bryant, Efrem Zimbalist Jr. won the 1959 Golden Globe for Most Promising Newcomer. Dorothy Malone, "a much better actress than the one she is portraying," never met Diana, who threatened to sue Warner Bros. over the "lewd and misleading" portrayal. "WHAT SCANDAL ENDED DIANA BARRYMORE'S SCREEN CAREER SO SUDDENLY?" screamed the print ads. "THE HOTTEST HUNK OF FILM HOLLYWOOD EVER SHOT!" Some of the listings were stamped "Adult Entertainment," and a sultry-voiced woman did the radio spots. "They've just laid it on with too thick a brush," Diana said, annoyed. "I may have been a bad girl but I never hit the Bowery."

This new iteration of Diana lived in a modest apartment on East Sixty-first Street. It was small but neat, with a kitchenette/bar combo and red velvet loveseat. Yes, she had a bar, but purely for the "vicarious pleasure" of mixing cocktails for others. "I like to see them have fun, but I also like to watch them get sozzled and think, oh you poor dear creatures, you'll feel so bad in the morning." She was doing well on Antabuse, she told columnist Phyllis Battelle, and therapy had nothing to do with it. She stopped analysis after three months (as Dr. Schechter predicted) because "she had me hating my mother, really blaming her for everything. I knew I had only myself to blame." Her wake-up call was the daughter of the man she was seeing in December 1957. The seven-year-old was inconsolable after Diana, deep in her cups, screamed at her. "My Lord, I don't care what other slobs I frighten, but a child!" That little girl did more to help than most of her friends—"leeches" and "phonies" she called them, "a million sycophants."

Sometimes Diana faltered in mending her image, like the time she wandered backstage at the Ethel Merman musical *Happy Hunting*, proclaiming how "perfectly dreadful" it was until she was asked to leave. She regularly attended evangelist Billy Graham's revivals at Madison Square Garden, visibly shaking and tearful. "The broad is really trying," she told Earl Wilson, who reported she was drinking only coffee, ginger ale, and "no-cal orange juice." Secretly, she'd begun having a nip now and then. Vermouth.

CHAPTER 9

THE BOY

TENNESSEE WILLIAMS'S *GARDEN DISTRICT* TOURED THE COUNTRY IN THE spring of 1959 as a double bill of the one-act plays *Something Unspoken* and *Suddenly Last Summer.* The latter starred Diana as the emotionally disturbed Catherine Holly, whose Aunt Violet (Cathleen Nesbitt) wants to have her lobotomized to keep her quiet about a family scandal. Diana continued to astonish critics as she had over the last two years in *A Streetcar Named Desire* and *Cat on a Hot Tin Roof,* the "fine young star" finally achieving the "great acting recognition she deserves." "Her return as a woman of dignity and an actress of depth and sensitivity" had Sydney J. Harris of the *Chicago Daily News* "rejoic[ing] the restoration of a great name to the American theater." Boston critic Elliott Norton's review was poignant enough to run as a *Variety* ad:

> She was never really pretty. But she had lustrous eyes and lovely hair . . . [t]he girlish softness, which often gave way to hardness, has gone. She shows in her face everything she may have put into her book. It is all there and it is not pleasant. But somewhere along the line of the years, Diana has found something important that she didn't have as a youngster . . . a genuine love of acting and a deep desire for a career.

Esther Kupcinet met Diana when the tour played Chicago's Civic Theater. Essee was married to "Mr. Chicago," legendary *Chicago Daily Tribune* columnist Irv Kupcinet, whose long-running "Kup's Column" began in 1943 and spawned a weekly talk show with the local CBS affiliate. Essee booked most of the talent, not that it was hard; everyone loved Kup. Writer/broadcaster Studs Terkel respected his "unique trick" of balancing gossip with decency, and comedienne Phyllis Diller liked that he wasn't a "hatchet man." Essee could be "gracious" when working as a "tireless champion of the arts," but otherwise was a boisterous, sexy, chain-smoking broad who laughed and swore at top volume. "I either love a person or loathe him," Diana once wrote.

"When I love, I'll fight against odds for that love. When I loathe, I can be the most vindictive bitch in the world." Diana finally found someone who shared that outlook. "Violla is the only one who understands how much we adore each other really—quite a gal not a jealous bone—although in the beginning there was," Diana wrote in a letter to Essee. "Diana had always wanted a sister; Essee had always wanted a sister," said Irv. "In all the world to have found a sister who understands me is a miracle," read another of Diana's telegrams. "Thank brother [Kup] too. The nights will be easier."

Diana loved Chicago, especially the nightlife. She adopted Bram's love of jazz and often went to see the Horace Silver Quintet when they played the South Side; vocalist Jackie Paris, still early in his storied career, was allegedly her "singing protégé." She dated the aspiring actor son of Ric Riccardo, proprietor of Riccardo's, "the Montmarte of the Midwest." It was *the* place from the 1940s through the 1960s, attracting everyone from newspapermen to actors and artists. (Riccardo Sr. later cofounded Pizzeria Uno, and is sometimes credited with inventing Chicago-style deep dish pizza.) She was also connected with actor Hurd Hatfield. The rare nights she stayed in, she either watched *Gunsmoke, Maverick,* or *Perry Mason* on TV, or she painted. "I like to mess around with paints. Guess I'm what you'd call a Sunday painter. Not good, not bad. But anyway, when I'm making with the paint brush, I never know what I have until I stand back and take a good look. Often it's possible to make changes which bring about the desired effect. It's harder to stand back and take an honest look at oneself."

It was an upbeat, optimistic time in Diana's life. "[I'm] no longer a has-been, but reborn. . . . I think I've finally become a real Barrymore," she proclaimed. "Honey, you've no idea what it's like coming out of that fog." She was "radiant with health and energy," fresh-faced in her usual uniform of button-down shirt, slacks from the boys' department, and flats. Her beauty regimen? Soap and water—and she had plenty of Woodbury from her endorsement days. "I'm crazy to do a musical . . . [t]here might also be an opportunity to work in one of those divine foreign films—if I had enough sense to say the right things when I met Mr. Big."

She played a special show of *Streetcar* on July 8th at Pennsylvania's Bristol Theater. Tennessee Williams himself drove two hours from New York City to be in the audience that night. "He stood up and yelled 'Bravo' until hoarse," Diana wrote to Essee. "When he came backstage—shattered—he said and I quote—'you are a great artist—you had moments as Blanche that no one ever had, I have seen them all!'" An ecstatic Violla honored her "champion actress" with a ruby seahorse brooch: "Remember Tennessee Williams applauded you + SOON I PRAY so will the world!"

Williams's enthusiasm spilled into his letter to Maria St. Just the next day: "[S]he has the Barrymore madness and power . . . remarkable." In the same letter Williams mentioned Diana traded alcohol for "happy pills and sleepy pills" and her old vice, marijuana. She was down more than twenty pounds, which she attributed to sobriety and a bout of measles (she played Houston with a 101.2-degree fever), The truth about her rail-thin appearance? She was stoned. She landed in Lenox Hill Hospital a month earlier, second-degree burns to her right thigh, hip, and buttock severe enough to miss Aunt Ethel's June 22th funeral in Los Angeles. She was scrambling eggs in the nude when her sleeping pills kicked in and she nodded off, spilling hot butter on herself in the process. "What happens to actresses in my plays?" he remarked to St. Just. "I seem to push them over."

Williams liked Diana. She was *Streetcar*'s faded Southern belle Blanche DuBois; the deluded, genteel Amanda Wingfield of *The Glass Menagerie*; and his own beloved sister Rose, an emotionally unstable, sex-obsessed "failed" debutante. Meeting "Tom" was transcendent for Diana. He was Robin, Billy Flinn, and Daddy, all rolled into one. She worshipped him. "Williams began this ressurection [*sic*]," she wrote Elia Kazan. "He is the God of my idolatry," she wrote, citing *Romeo and Juliet* to mutual friend Marion Vaccaro, a writer for magazines like *Weird Tales* and the tutor and travel companion for Billie Burke and Florenz Ziegfeld's daughter Patricia. She and Tom bonded after he rented a cabin at her mother's mansion, Tradewinds, and considered themselves siblings, often traveling together. Diana also began thinking of him as a brother, another Robina with whom she could navigate the world. "You can make a career of playing Tennessee Williams, and I almost have," Diana told reporters, performing his oeuvre almost exclusively. She befriended his mother and exchanged copious letters and phone calls with his brother Dakin, the two referring to each other as "brother" and "sister," but the brass ring was always "the Boy," Diana's preferred pet name for Williams, her "savior on earth."

Shortly after *Streetcar* wrapped in Kennebunkport, Maine, she, Williams, his doctor friend, and Vaccaro spent four glorious days zooming around Cuba. "[D]riving in a Thunderbird with him is like the Coney Island Roller Coaster!" she wrote to Essee. Maybe it was all the pot she smoked, but Diana told everyone she would marry Tom and bear his child. Being gay was no obstacle, she wrote Essee. "We'll have a ménage a trois. His boyfriend will always be in bed with us. It will work." Williams didn't help, scattering crumbs of affection out of pity and amusement. He told her theirs was an "intense friendship," which Diana insisted she liked "better than any romantic item . . . what we now have, which is 'mutual admiration for each other's perspicacity'—(X-ray vision to us!)—is better." She and the Boy went everywhere together, "camping it up [and] being outrageous. "He looked at Kim [Hunter] and said, 'Honey, your face used to be just a blob . . . it's a face now!'" She became the male counterpart to "Mona," his drag persona, affecting a masculine tailored style that reminded people of her mother. "Appeal to his butch side!" Diana once scribbled in a note to herself.

Williams wrote *Sweet Bird of Youth* in 1959. Alexandra del Lago/Princess Kosmopolis, the alcoholic, drug-addicted actress struggling to make a comeback, was allegedly inspired by Tallulah Bankhead but is clearly Diana, down to the injections for neuritis. In one scene, she tells failed actor-turned-gigolo Chance Wayne of the "crown" that exists "in the cells of my blood and body from the time of my birth." The Princess, like Diana, proudly looks her failure in the eye: "out of the passion and torment of my existence I have created a thing that I can unveil, a sculpture, almost heroic." She knows "monsters don't die early; they hang on long . . . their vanity's infinite, almost as infinite as their disgust with themselves." "The Monster" was Jack's affectionate nickname among friends. John Decker, in a piece about Jack's last days for *Esquire*, wrote "there are no clocks. Not even calendars—for time means nothing and goes on tiptoe in the presence of the 'Monster.'"

Tom gave her a charm bracelet with a little gold "10" that Diana showed to everyone, saying the role of the Princess came with it. Williams disagreed, felt her "too much like the princess to play the princess well," but Diana pushed—hard. She wrote to director Elia Kazan, begging "Gadge" for sympathy: "I'm a f——ing desperate woman pleading for her life . . . [l]et me do her for you—give me some small measure of that 'compassion' I've heard about, but haven't seen yet—I'm not a star, but really you know that—wouldn't you like to help me at long last live up to that fabulous name—? . . . [s]ee me—Please—I can't wait anymore with sanity." Kazan refused, and the play opened on March 10, 1959, at the Martin Beck Theatre with Geraldine Page as del Lago. Writer Gilbert Maxwell remembered Diana watching rehearsals, constantly smoking or biting her nails, "a sort of urchin girl-woman, too thin, high strung, supersensitive, and somehow touching." Page earned a Tony nomination (and later an Oscar nomination for the 1962 film version). "My hatred for Kazan burns black," Diana wrote Dakin. In his memoirs, actor Christopher Plummer recounts Kazan's version of events: she showed up for the audition "so goddamn drunk they had to help her out of the theatre." Plummer knew Diana, and the two often spent hours discussing her father in her hotel room, Diana in the nude, "a dark animal look about her, not beautiful, but sensual . . . sultry [and] brooding."

Her focus shifted to an astrologer's prediction she'd be in London by November 1960, which obviously meant starring in a UK tour of *Sweet Bird of Youth*. At a party that December, Gilbert Maxwell witnessed Diana badgering Williams, shaking a finger in his face, until the latter finally snapped: "All right. I've told you I don't think it's for you, but if you want it this bad, I will do all I can." Diana thanked God and prayed the astrologer was correct. She had grown spiritual, collecting inspirational clippings and talking religion with Dakin when he visited Chicago that past April. He wrote a book about Catholic versus Protestant beliefs and sent her a copy, which she credited with making her want to attend Mass again. Dakin connected her with his close friend Father Wilkerson, and the three met for dinner in St Louis that May.

Faith had changed a lot for Diana since the days of her lithograph daydreams. "I don't know—things happened to me in life and things that I saw happen to other people made me not believe in God," she said. "I think the first thing that put me very much down in the belief of God was when Robin died . . . when Mother could talk about it, one minute she'd say, 'I'll see my catkins again,' and she'd make these pilgrimages to the grave—she'd drag me along in the spring especially—and we'd kneel down and pray . . . [t]hen she'd leave and get into these fits of depression and say maybe there isn't a God." She remembered her mother's words about losing the only thing she loved. "If she loved [Robin] that much, why didn't He take me or Leonard?"

She corresponded with Fr. Wilkerson through the summer, and he spent hours with her on the phone untangling the ecclesiastical red tape of her three marriages. It went a long way toward sweetening her view of the clergy, especially after Jack's death. "I thought, this is a bunch of baloney . . . [a priest] trying to tell me what a good Catholic my father was, and he died a Catholic; I said he died a Catholic, but you just threw the sacrament in his face—he didn't know anything. Don't tell me that my father was a good Catholic." Marrying Bob, she said, "completely fixed" her because "he was an agnostic," their conversations about faith organic, not organized. She began talking with God again regularly. "[He] has given me at least 9 chances," she wrote, praying the role of the Princess would be her "10th and final one."

Four days before Christmas and seventeen years after his death, her father's estate closed $31,000 "in the red." Any assets left after settling his debts went to his attorneys, leaving nothing for Diana, Johnnie, or Dede. Diana was unbothered and cheerful, joking about Tom's Christmas gift of a magnum of champagne—"the absolutely perfect and intelligent gift for a woman who doesn't drink . . . [he] forgot about me until the last minute."

She regifted the bubbly to Violla, or so she said; alcohol had already crept back into her life. She started dating Glenn Stensel, a flaky Illinoisan who ditched his family's multimillion-dollar funeral home business for acting and met Diana while playing the bartender in *Sweet Bird of Youth*. Black theater royalty Edna and Nick Stewart warned their friend in a letter: "Don't let anything distract you—not even Another Dog, UNLESS you are SURE of his BREEDING—never mind HIS BREED." Diana ignored the advice as always, and she and her new beau—variously described as "nutty," "too slick," and a "crumb"—spent their evenings drinking and making trouble.

On January 4, 1960, two days after Diana's appearance on NBC's radio magazine *Monitor*, Glenn roughed up Sinatra impersonator Frankie Domino during their night out at a West Forty-fifth Street night spot. Diana stayed out of it: "I had on my good mink and I wasn't going to soil it." Glenn, who wasn't hurt, said he merely "tweaked" Domino's hat. "He almost broke my neck," replied Domino, who demanded Glenn cover the medical bills for his cracked ribs and black eye.

Upbeat, fresh-faced Diana vanished. Four policemen were forced to eject her from the audience of Broadway's *The Andersonville Trial* after she "made a scene." Her conversations with Essee were "full of concern about dying," convinced she was "running out of time." "She told me, 'I want you to get a nice black hat and a veil for my funeral—it's going to be soon.'" It was harder now to chase away Diana's "dark thoughts," and Essee missed her infectious laugh. "Life is too much," Diana told her friend. "Sometimes I wish I had never glimpsed the side of the moon where genius presides—it knocks you for a f——ing loop." Now and then she spoke of a baby as a way to heal her own broken heart, someone to lavish with the unconditional love of which she was starved as a child and denied as an adult. There were tests and several attempts, but motherhood ultimately eluded her. Dr. Colton Rule, who later became a "chemical addiction specialist," was a doctor and psychiatrist known for taking on difficult patients. He treated her as her physical health declined; along with advanced cirrhosis, she was now having chest pains. Tom said he regularly felt her heart "pounding like a hammer on an anvil."

Diana invited a few friends over for a Sunday night get-together on January 24th. Essee, of course, and Glenn, and Glenn's two friends, Edward "Guy" Thomajan and John Cook. Thomajan was Elia Kazan's assistant and stage manager on *Bird*, a "brooding Armenian" known for his short fuse and quick fists, and twenty-four-year-old John, or "Jack," worked as a charter/commercial pilot. One of the men brought booze—likely Thomajan, who boasted his efficiency supplying Williams with bourbon—but Essee confiscated Diana's drink as soon as it was poured. They chatted a while, then Essee left around

11 p.m., with Thomajan departing shortly after. Stensel stayed until 2 a.m., leaving Diana looking at old photos with Cook, who finally went home sometime after 2:15 that morning. Diana then called The Colony, begged them to send over a bottle, and when they refused, she called Stensel to come back over. He declined, saying he had work in the morning. She tried to invite herself over to his place, but he hung up. She went to bed.

Diana's maid Eva Smith arrived at 9 a.m. on January 25th and found her in bed, as always, nude and sound asleep. Smith busied herself straightening up the apartment until 3 p.m., when Violla Rubber called with news: they wanted Diana for a new Canadian production of *Streetcar*. When Smith said Diana was still sleeping, Rubber insisted she wake her. Eva couldn't. "She's cold and white," she told Rubber. "You better come over." Rubber rushed from her apartment across the street. They called Dr. Rule,[18] but it was too late for him to do anything but call the police. Diana, for all appearances, had died quietly in the night. Deputy inspector John Sexton's report noted "no signs of violence," only empty liquor bottles in the kitchen—scotch, gin, and vermouth—and bottles of Seconal and other sedatives by the bed. Essee, who officially identified Diana's body, hid her marijuana so it wouldn't be included.

Dr. Rule and chief medical examiner Dr. Milton Halpern both felt Diana's cause of death was a heart attack brought on by years of "large amounts" of alcohol and "small amounts" of barbiturates, and while the autopsy was inconclusive, there was no indication of suicide. Any possible overdose was accidental. Despite Williams insisting Rubber mentioned "blood streaming from [Diana's] mouth and other evidence of struggle," it was likely as her attorney Aaron Frosh put it: "Diana just went to sleep and didn't wake up."

---

18. Colter Rule III, email to author, January 20, 2022.

CHAPTER 10

NOBODY CARED

JANUARY 29, 1960, WAS WINDY AND UNUSUALLY WARM OUTSIDE THE FRANK E. Campbell Funeral Home on Eighty-first and Madison. Diana's body lay inside, in a simple black dress, earrings, and sheer scarf at her throat. Over 350 people attended the standing room only service conducted by Williams's cousin, Episcopal priest Sidney Lanier, with Leonard, Ethel Colt Miglietta, and Uncle Charles Oelrichs the only family present. More than thirty-five floral tributes thronged the casket blanketed in two thousand violets—a tribute from Williams, who had done the same for his grandfather. Nestled among the sprays was a large red apple from Anne Francine, a nod to the Barrymore opening-night tradition. She and Diana's paths had crossed multiple times over the years, most recently in *Garden District*. "We used to talk about her quitting drinking, and she would, for awhile," Anne told reporters. "Diana shouldn't be dead. She should be here right now!"

"She was a sweet, nice, honest, good kid, and yet people will giggle at you for saying so," said Gerold Frank. In his eulogy, he praised her "fever and fury" and "terrifying honesty about herself," ending the only way he knew how: "Goodnight, my sweet, my bewildered, my lost Diana." Essee was in town to see her daughter Karyn with Pat O'Brien in a New Jersey production of *Father of the Bride*. "You're here to spend six weeks with your daughter," Diana had remarked. "Do you know that in all my entire life put together, I never spent that much time with my mother?" Essee finished her visit with "Cookie" after Diana's death, "very strong [but] visibly shaken and tearful."

Journalists scrambled to show compassion they denied her in life, and the *New York Daily News*—worst of the exploiters—poignantly declared "Death Stills the Storm for Diana Barrymore." Of course, they also mentioned her nudity and lowly $230 per month apartment. "A soul in anguish," they wrote. "[C]heap, melodramatic bilge," countered Gilbert Maxwell. Articles and headlines repeated an old chestnut: "the Barrymore curse."

148

The dark cloud that enveloped the family was common knowledge. Fredric March couldn't stop "copycatting" Jack for months after playing Tony Cavendish—the Jack character in the Barrymore satire *The Royal Family*—on Broadway and the 1930 film version. "The Barrymore curse has got me," he joked. Several Drews and Barrymores suffered from (or succumbed to) addiction and mental instability. Ethel managed to quit drinking in 1939, but Lionel's morphine and intermittent cocaine use continued until his death in 1954. "Barrymore Curse Trips Diana Too," read the *Toronto Daily Star*. Her brother Johnnie's substance abuse and mental health problems derailed his Hollywood career, ruined his marriages, and led to arrest or jail several times by 1960. Diana herself called it "a curse—an inheritance from my father, his father probably, way down the line."

Diana inscribed Dolores's copy of *Too Much, Too Soon* "to my second mother," and now that mother wept. "She was badly treated all her life," she said, and distilled Diana's life into two words: "nobody cared." Dede concurred: "[S]he came to us, but it was too late. She didn't come to us as a child, but as a beaten woman."

A grieving Marion Vaccaro wrote a poem in Diana's voice:[19]

> *Yellow, yellow roses, for the loves I have known . . .*
> *Valley lillies [sic] for loves I never knew . . .*
> *Violets to say farewell to all that might have been . . .*

Before long, salaciousness took over. "Nobody can accuse the 42nd St. grind houses of not keeping up with the headlines," wrote Dorothy Kilgallen in February. "Currently they're offering flickers featuring Diana Barrymore." She also mentioned that "[o]ne of the 5th Ave. book shops" couldn't keep *Too Much, Too Soon* in stock after dumping it in the bargain bin "just before her death." Gossip rags like *On the Q.T.* dramatized Diana's last days as unhinged, Norma Desmond performing *Bird* to her bedroom mirror, and invented a "taunting blonde" at the holiday party she'd attended with Williams, whose name-calling drove her to that "tragic drink." Even her memoir was spoofed, along with *I'll Cry Tomorrow*, in *I Made My Bed*, "the outrageous confessions of the naughtiest girl of them all" written by "'Kathy O'Farrell' as told to Rube Goldberg." Humorist H. Allen Smith called its fictional subject's fall from "screen siren" to "lying drunk in the rain" in the gutter outside the Ed Sullivan Theater "sharp satire . . . a lot of fun to read." A talentless drunk with a famous name and ignoble end: thus became the legacy of Diana Barrymore.

---

19. Tennessee Williams, *The World of Tennessee Williams*, ed. Richard F. Leavitt (New York: Putman, 1977).

"I feel very deeply, as anyone would, the passing of a good friend," wrote Tennessee Williams, subdued, pitying, almost impersonal. She was "an engine running away . . . great talent but no control." The man whom Diana crowned "the Shakespeare of the 20th Century" dismissed her "only true love" as being "her struggle to become a good artist."

Her estate was estimated at $50,000. She left $10,000 to Violla, $5,000 each to Ann Andrews, Nita Naldi, and Uncle Charles Oelrichs, and another $10,000 to her friend Emil Sorrento. "He was a lovely, lovely person," Diana wrote. "[A] rather short, bulky man with a very lovely smile . . . when he smiles you see beauty because you see a lot of pathos." The blind gentleman was a fixture in Astoria, Queens, NY: travel agent in the 1930s and 1940s (he claimed to have met her when she was ten, planning a European trip to Europe for Michael and Harry), women's shop proprietor in the 1950s, investment fund salesman and chairman of the 114th Precinct Youth Council in the 1960s. The two lived in the same building and formed a friendship around their shared love of the theater. He knew she was broke and bought her groceries on his tab, requesting Diana read or sing to him as payment. In 1952, "the period when I was borrowing money from Aunt Ethel and everybody," he overheard her telling someone how dire things really were. "[T]hree days later I received a check for five hundred dollars in the mail with a note saying, 'Don't even bother to thank me—I know that your genius will pay it back.'" Later, when things improved, she gifted him a Saint Christopher medal which he never took off. "I was very indebted to him. . . . I cried of course upon opening the envelope because I thought, this man who I don't really know that well—how can he do such a thing when these society bastards that I called said, 'Oh, I'm so terribly sorry but my taxes are too much . . . I can't lend you money.'" He came to see her in Bristol, Pennsylvania, when she did *Streetcar*. Diana claimed the whole restaurant "stood up and applauded" when she met him afterwards for dinner.

The remainder of her estate went to the Actors Fund, and her furniture and personal effects auctioned by the Savoy Art and Auction Gallery on April 16th. Her mink coat netted $1,900; her furnishings, a paltry $176. It was reminiscent of her father's auction, where a man named Edward Molen posed triumphantly for pictures holding Jack's girdle, a steal at $4.50. At the final valuing of Diana's estate in November 1964—delayed in part by Frankie Domino's ongoing $50,000 suit—lawyers tallied her outstanding bills, income tax, and other debts at $36,579. "Since the estate has insufficient assets . . . the legacies set forth will lapse, and the interest of each legatee is nil." All bequests were cancelled, and "like most of the chapters in her autobiography," the *Daily News* wrote, "the posthumous court development was a dismal one."

Diana touched more lives than she knew. In late 1960, the New York Public Library featured her scrapbooks and other memorabilia alongside that of her father, mother and Aunt Ethel in their main lobby exhibit. Essee kept her own scrapbook about her beloved friend, titled " . . . Much Too Soon," for the rest of her life. She was "one of the late Diana Barrymore's dearest friends," Kup wrote in 1962. "We have never forgotten her." Author, actress, and culinary anthropologist Vertamae Smart-Grosvenor, who had a small part in a production of *Streetcar*, said: "Everyone had warned me what a bitch Diana Barrymore was, but she was the only person I talked to during the whole week I was there." They shared an interest in the occult, "voodoo and vibrations and stuff like that." Journalist and one-time actress Elaine Shepard fondly recalled their "furious" gin rummy competitions in between acts of *The Land is Bright*: "[She was] the most fun to be with of any girl I've ever known . . . I have not read her book [and] probably never will, preferring to remember her sweetness, generosity, and loveliness." Studs Terkel remembered her kindness during an interview the year before, when *Garden District* opened in Chicago. "It's no concern of mine," he told her, refusing to ask questions about her personal life. "I find out about you as a person through your art." The day after, Terkel—who liked cigars—received a gift box of them, with a note: "No one ever said that to me before." It wasn't signed, but Terkel knew exactly who it was from. "[A] Tennessee Williams vulnerable heroine on the stage being a Tennessee Williams heroine in the flesh," he said.

Aspiring actor Orin Kennedy met Diana through Williams at a cocktail party in 1959. "So you want to be an actor?" she asked. "Well . . . act!" He nervously performed Heathcliff's bedside farewell to Cathy from *Wuthering Heights*. "YES!" she exclaimed, and the two promised to stay in touch. At one visit to her Manhattan apartment Kennedy found her "distraught" over her relationship with Williams. After they talked, Diana gave Kennedy her private phone number and told him to call collect. Her December 4, 1959, telegram to Kennedy only weeks before her death was jovial: "I will see you at Christmas / what a nice present you will make / Love, Diana."

In *Elegy in Manhattan*, poetic reflections on stars of the past, entertainment legend George Jessel writes in Diana's voice, defining herself as merely "[a] barfly." As her father, however, Jessel is tender:

My girl-child, Diana / Is no longer mixed-up. / She's at peace now.[20]

---

20. George Jessel, *Elegy in Manhattan* (New York: Holt, Rinehart & Winston, 1961).

Two years after her own suicide attempt on March 16, 1961, Brenda Frazier wrote "My Debut—A Horror" for *Life*. "At least a half dozen of my friends of debutante days have committed suicide," she wrote, blaming the "superficial kind of life" they shared. Like Diana, she used sleeping pills; like Diana, she was, "at the age of 39, at the end of my line." She died of cancer in 1982.

Cobina Jr., whose parents divorced, in part, over Cobina Sr.'s grooming her for stardom—what her father called "prostitution"—acted on radio and in movies until her husband insisted she retire in 1943. She was also a recovering alcoholic and devoted her later life to charities working in the anti-alcohol crusade. She treasured her copy of *Too Much, Too Soon*, which Diana inscribed "from the ugly one!" Cobina Jr. died in 2011.

Francis Kellogg was a philanthropist, ambassador, and diplomat who served as special assistant for secretaries of state William P. Rogers and Henry Kissinger. He and Fernanda Wanamaker Munn had two children; they divorced in 1971 after twenty-nine years of marriage. He died in 2006.

Johnny Galliher lived a chic, cosmopolitan lifestyle until the end, dying peacefully in his sleep in 2003. He left $2 million in bequests, including $25,000 to each of thirty-five needy friends; the remainder was split between City Harvest, GMHC, and God's Love We Deliver. Every lady received a posthumous orchid, every man a case of wine.

Patricia Howard (1924–2014) filed for divorce a year after Diana's death, citing "extreme cruelty." (Later, as Patricia Wilder, her historic landmark restoration work[21] made the National Registry.) In 1962, John Howard was arrested in Florida attempting to cash US savings bonds stolen in a heist at New York's Idlewild (now Kennedy) Airport. Howard denied knowledge of the scheme, saying he was only helping a drinking buddy who paid him $200 and promised more after the bonds were cashed. The buddy, whose name was on forty-five of the bonds, was . . . "John Barry." (Really.) Howard spent five years in prison for possession/passage of forged savings bonds. At the time of his arrest, press described him as a "suave playboy," flashily dressed, "unshaven [but] deeply tanned and slightly paunchy." He died in 2001.

Some say Essee was an overbearing stage mother, controlling her daughter's weight with diet pills and arranging for plastic surgery, but Karyn ended up in only a handful of roles. A turbulent relationship with actor Andrew Prine (1936–2022) resulted in an abortion and her stalking him when he ended things. She was found dead in her apartment about a week after the JFK assassination, leading conspiracy theorists to suggest she knew something, which her parents vehemently denied. The cause of death was

---

21. The First National Bank (Carson City, NV); Blake Hammond Manor (Ben Lomond, CA); and especially the Golden Gate Villa (Santa Cruz, CA).

strangulation, and a cryptic note at the scene read: "There's nothing only phony motives, selfish egoists, selfless people, fat heads and drunks." Essee and Irv both felt Prine had murdered her, and Essee devoted the rest of her life to a "personal vendetta" against him, visiting psychics for clues. When Essee died in 2001, she was buried with a pack of her preferred Pall Malls in her casket. Irv followed in 2003, and their son Jerry, a five-time Emmy winner best known for *Judge Judy*, died in 2019. The playhouse at Shimer College in Illinois and the Kupcinet-Getz Program at Canada's Weizmann Institute of Science were both founded by Essee and Irv in Karyn's memory.

John McNeill was "a captain at Regent's Row" in 1959, then moved to upstate New York and became an auto salesman. He was married with two sons at the time of his death, following a long illness, in 1973.

Emil Sorrento went on to create and coach the children's tennis clinic in Astoria, Queens. He died in 1998 and is still remembered fondly in the neighborhood.

Karl Schanzer acted in several 1960s cult classics like *Dementia 13* (1963) and *Spider Baby* (1967), and his work as a private investigator inspired Francis Ford Coppola's *The Conversation* (1974). He worked as a reader for Paramount—he discovered the hit *48 HRS.* (1982)—and an executive for 20th Century Fox. He died in 2014.

Audrey Gray was front-page news after badly injuring fourteen-year-old Wilfred Jr. and ten-year-old Gerard Martineau in a 1939 hit-and-run. She was fined $200 for reckless driving and her license suspended six months, after which the boys' irate family sued for $50,000 damages. They settled out of court, $17,500 for Wilfred (whose crushed left arm required amputation) and $11,000 for Gerard (who suffered a fractured skull). She married twice, the first to an RAF pilot, and died in 1984.

Bramwell Fletcher remarried in 1950 and had three children. He wrote and acted in the critically acclaimed play *The Bernard Shaw Story* (1965) and was married to his fourth wife at the time of his death in 1988.

Leonard Jr., described as a "mountaineer, financier, restauranteur, lodge owner, and sportsman," went missing ten miles east of Aspen in October 1954. He was hunting with some friends on Bald Knob and walked away from camp carrying his Geiger counter to search for uranium. He had no food or weapons, and heavy snow and subfreezing temps were no match for his light denim jacket, but he turned up completely fine two days later, wanting a sandwich and saying he spent the time "swimming in a beaver pond to clear [his] head." On June 14, 1968, he was found dead of smoke inhalation next to the phone in the burned-out ruins of the Red Mountain House, his home in Aspen, Colorado.

Yvonne Navello Thomas became a renowned New York-based abstract expressionist and one of the first women invited to join The Club, the avant-garde group borne from the historic Ninth Street Show. She was friends with many in the field, including Marcel Duchamp, Jackson Pollock, and the de Koonings, and continued making and showing her art up until her death at age ninety-five in 2009. She and Leonard had two daughters and three grandchildren.

Billy Flinn never married. He was a Good Humor ice cream man at the time of his death from cancer on August 30, 1960, only seven months after Diana. He was forty.

Octavio Señoret produced *GOAL!* (1966) for Columbia, a documentary about World Cup Soccer still considered one of the best sports documentaries ever made. He died of a self-inflicted gunshot wound in 1990.

Winnie Hoveler's "small segment of the Rockettes"—the Winnie Hoveler Dancing Darlings, later the Winnie Hoveler American Ballet—toured the world performing their innovative shows, like the all-aerial routine Winnie choreographed on swings. She co-owned the troupe with her sister Audrey, who also designed their costumes. As for acting, she joined the Grand Detour Stock Company the summer of 1940, billed as "John Barrymore's Chicago Girl" or his "Chicago protégé." Like Elaine, she called their brief time together among "the happiest memories of my life." She died in 2003.

Glenn Stensel did some TV and uncredited movie roles after he was rejected for the film version of *Sweet Bird of Youth*. He tried producing, but after unsuccessful proposals for the Billy Carter-starring *Peanuts* (1978) and a low-budget 1980 movie about Chappaquiddick, he returned home to Illinois, where he died of cancer in 1983 at age fifty-three.

Anne Francine replaced Bea Arthur as Vera Charles in *Mame* on Broadway in 1966 and again briefly in 1983. She was in *Juliet of the Spirits* (1965) and *Crocodile Dundee* (1986), and played Flora Simpson Reilly on *Harper Valley PTA* (ABC, 1981–82). She taught a cabaret symposium at the Eugene O'Neill Theater, continuing even after a stroke robbed her of her speech in 1992. She died in 1999.

In addition to producing and directing summer stock, Violla Rubber managed and cast-directed various regional theaters and was executive of creative affairs for ABC Pictures Corp., a subsidiary of ABC-TV. She died in 1981.

Ann Andrews performed in multiple Broadway plays and roadshows through the 1940s, and became reclusive in later years, sharing her apartment with several cats. She died in 1986.

Nita Naldi endured heart disease, vision problems, and poverty in her last years, though she remained vampy as ever; she appeared at her last public event, her April 1959 induction into the Ziegfeld Club, with her hair "defiantly black," nails "impeccably manicured," and "quick wit still in evidence." The Actors' Fund paid half her rent on a single room at the Wentworth Hotel in Times Square, by then a "seedy dive," and friends gave what they could. Diana's bequest would have helped Nita immensely, but she died on February 17, 1961, before probate was completed.

Johnnie—professionally known as John Drew Barrymore—had a life as tumultuous as his half-sister. He debuted in *The Sundowners* (1950) and worked erratically in film and TV through the 1970s. He married four times and had four children, including actors John Blyth Barrymore III and Drew Barrymore, from whom he was estranged for many years. He lived a largely reclusive existence until his death from cancer in 2004. Dede is in her 90s and still enjoys being active with family and friends.

Gerold Frank penned the critically acclaimed *The Boston Strangler* (1966), adapted into the 1968 movie with Tony Curtis and Henry Fonda, and *An American Death* (1972), about the assassination of Dr. Martin Luther King Jr. *Judy* (1975), his biography of Judy Garland, is considered one of the best on the singer-actress. He died in 1998.

Diana's name recognition lasted as late as the 1970s. *National Lampoon* magazine's July 1970 "Bad Taste" issue titled one (unrelated) article "Diana Barrymore Drinking Songs." The punk/glam rock band the New York Dolls named their 1974 album *Too Much, Too Soon*, dedicating it to Diana. Today, she pops up on the occasional "Old Hollywood" list, in articles about the Barrymore family, or mislabeled on social media as Drew Barrymore's mother. Green Day had a song titled "Too Much, Too Soon" on their 2004 album *American Idiot*, and experimental musician Eddie Palmer included a "sound collage" named after Diana on Studio Noir's 2014 album *Sunset Boulevard.*

The "Barrymore curse" continued through the public struggles of three of Johnnie's children. "Make no mistake, substance abuse is a Barrymore curse," wrote John Blyth Barrymore III in 1990. "Portrayals of me as the troubled, drug-addicted brother [of Drew] and of my father as a mean-spirited, hopeless, waste of a man and a parent from hell are accurate . . . a truthful picture of what it is like to be a child with the name Barrymore." Jessica Blyth Barrymore died in 2014 from an overdose just days before her forty-eighth birthday. And Drew. . . .

Drew's story, that of the most famous Barrymore of modern times, eerily parallels the aunt she never met: the "explosive, wild father" and "dark, beautiful mother," the expectations she called a "7,000-pound bag on my shoulders," even the booze-as-dessert first drink (ice cream sundaes topped with Bailey's Irish Cream, when the *E.T.* actress was seven). "I liked the feeling . . . dizzy and happy and glorious and on top of the world," she said, echoing Diana almost exactly thirty years earlier: "There's nothing sweeter-feeling to my bones." Drew also shared Diana's magical view of Jack, thanks to stories from Johnnie. "I would listen as if I was being let into this fairy-tale world, where dangers lurk but fantastical magical things can occur." A memoir penned at fourteen, *Little Girl Lost*, received the same criticism as *Too Much, Too Soon,* accusing Drew of seeking notoriety for a flagging career while offering dubious hope of her recovery. But, unlike her aunt and father (who, like Diana, called treatment programs "bullshit"), Drew sought help through Alcoholics Anonymous, therapy, and rehab. "I know where Drew is coming from," continued her half-brother. "If she stays sober that will be a greater achievement than that made by any Barrymore to date." Drew stayed sober and today is a highly successful writer, actress, and brand, with her company, Flower, offering everything from cosmetics to home furnishings to Flower Films, her own production company. She even hosts her own popular talk show, an achievement of which her aunt would no doubt be very proud.

It's unfortunate that Diana didn't live to see the radical cultural shift of the 1960s. She leaned progressive politically, supported sexual freedom and autonomy for all genders, fiercely loved her LGBTQIA+ friends and family, and understood the pitfalls of addiction. "I've never been wicked, really wicked or really nasty or malicious to anyone in my life," she said. "[T]he only sins I have committed are sins against myself." Bob once said, "[She was] a girl who was always trying to put her best foot forward and always wound up by putting it in her mouth."

She wholly embraced the mystical and at the time of her death was writing the story of an intersex person who meets God—and finds She is a woman. Would she fade in public memory with the dawning decade, or suffer the "*Mommie Dearest* effect" and become a caricature of the grossly accentuated low points of her life? I like to imagine, once and for all, her talent vanquishing the Sisyphean burden of her surname. "That name is magic—it spells magic everywhere," Diana once said. "All the chances that I've had . . . my career would have run along different lines, perhaps, if I had been named Brown."

SOURCE NOTES

CHAPTER 1: NEWPORT, PHILADELPHIA, MANHATTAN

4   "It seemed to me": Strange, *Who Tells Me True*, 19.
4   "Society as a business": Strange, 48.
4   "sumptuous," "a waltz-time aura": Strange, 49.
4   "gnome," "wretched-looking": Strange, 51–52.
5   "hoping he would now say something": Strange, 36.
5   "tossing about": *New York Press*, May 16, 1904.
6   "the hardest punishment of all": *Morning Journal-Courier* (New Haven), March 23, 1908.
6   "My daughter and I are supremely happy," "[Leonard] is not looking": *Philadelphia Inquirer*, September 12, 1909.
6   "I was fantastically spoiled by everyone": Strange, 114.
6   "frumps, fools, and knaves": Strange, 123.
6   "monster": "Not So Easy to Head a Big Parade, Says Suffrage Worker," *Post-Star* (Glens Falls), October 22, 1915.
6   "the white and gold banner": "10, Men in the Ranks Join Biggest Demonstration Ever Held in New York," *Evening World* (New York), October 23, 1915.
6   "it is not enough to believe" *Post-Star* (Glens Falls), October 22, 1915.
6   "paragon of conventionality," "he was terribly against" Bound Notes G, box 1, Gerold Frank papers, Manuscripts and Archives Division, New York Public Library.
7   "one of the most brilliant": "Louisa Lane Drew," *Encyclopedia Britannica*, March 12, 2023. https://www.britannica.com/biography/Louisa-Lane-Drew.
7   "Of those days in Philadelphia I have few memories": Barrymore, *Confessions of an Actor*, unpaginated.
8   "This incident": Barrymore, *Confessions*.
8   "seemed to be thrown in": Bound Notes E, box 1, Gerold Frank papers, Manuscripts and Archives Division, New York Public Library.
8   "I didn't want to be an actor": Barrymore, *Confessions*.
8   "the greatest journalist": "Brisbane is Widely Mourned; Editor's Rites Set for Monday." *Brooklyn Times-Union*, December 26, 1936.
8   "I only went back to the theater": Barrymore, *Confessions*.

9   "vivid and exquisitely sensitive," "the monstrous nightmare quality": *New York Times*, April 9, 1916.

10   "a being transformed": *New York Times*, April 4, 1916.

10   "finely imaginative," "at its great moments": *New York Times*, April 19, 1916.

CHAPTER 2: A UNION OF GENIUS

11   "leading designer of the New Stagecraft in America": Morrison, *John Barrymore Shakespearean Actor*, 58.

11   "vivacious creature with sparkling, snapping eyes": Davidson, *Between Sittings*, 5.

12   "dazed," "drooping mustache": Strange, 144.

12   "he looked elfin and forsaken": Strange, 152.

12   "as if he were at sea": Bound Notes D, box 1, Gerold Frank papers, Manuscripts and Archives Division, New York Public Library.

12   "My God, that's a fascinating woman": Nesbitt, *A Little Love and Good Company*, 104

12   "society bitches": Nesbitt, 104.

12   "like a mast on a ship," "somebody put lemon," "[s]he wore outrageous clothes": Bound Notes E, box 1, Gerold Frank papers, Manuscripts and Archives Division, New York Public Library.

12   "smart clans of the beach": Ada Patterson, "John Barrymore's Romance," *Photoplay*, November 1920.

12   "[t]he work of this young man": George Keppel Thomas, "Books and Authors: Why is Futurism." *Pittsburgh Post*, January 20, 1917.

12   "his [sic] soul": Gordon Ray Young, "New Books—Book News," *Los Angeles Times*, June 24, 1917.

12   "unconventional in her thinking": "Reviews of Recent Books: Strange Book of Ultra Modern Free Verse Poems," *Daily News and The Independent* (Santa Barbara), January 6, 1917.

13   "and we are all sure we will like Michael": "Mrs. Leonard Thomas, Poetess of Fashionable Society," *San Francisco Examiner*, May 4, 1919.

13   "Mr. Barrymore is distinctly arriving": *Theatre Magazine*, November 1918.

13   "During the first entr'acte": Strange, 158.

13   "Once again the Barrymore brothers have shown": *Vanity Fair*, June 1919.

13   "so unusual and so outstanding": *New York Times*, May 25, 1919.

13   "I am waiting so patiently for the time when I can put my arms around you": John Barrymore, letter to Michael Strange, undated, circa summer 1917, Michael Strange papers, New York Public Library.

13   "horribly sorry": John Barrymore, John, letter to Michael Strange, undated, circa summer 1917, Michael Strange papers, New York Public Library.

13-14   "restless poet": Strange, 148.

14   "[i]t is terrible to think how much our happiness depends on Len": John Barrymore, letter to Michael Strange, July 11, 1919. Michael Strange papers, New York Public Library.

14   "heavy armor in which he was required": Morrison, 116.

14   "[H]e gave so much, revealed so much": Morrison, 117.

14   "I could play [*Richard III*]": Barrymore, *Confessions*.

14-15   "[I]t is no secret": "Whom Will Beautiful, Poetic, Mrs. Thomas Marry Next?" *Buffalo Times*, August 8, 1920.

15 "Michael was always on a play," "[s]he had been snubbed": Bound Notes G, box 1, Gerold Frank papers, Manuscripts and Archives Division, New York Public Library.

15 "Indeed, there is something almost ludicrous": "Inside Stuff on Legit," *Variety*, April 23, 1920.

15 "Muldoon conceives his job": "John Barrymore Is Cast in New 'Role' at Muldoon's Farm," *Brooklyn Daily Eagle*, April 18, 1920.

15 "My boy—ye seem that to me": Ada Patterson, "John Barrymore's Romance," *Photoplay*, November 1920.

15 "A very nervous sort of man": Morrison, 126–27.

16 "huge ego, supreme self-confidence": Peters, 204.

16 "in spite of the Four Horsemen," "entrenched in the Reading Room": Strange, 163.

16 "union of genius": *Philadelphia Inquirer*, September 19, 1920.

16 "But has he married the Baby": Strange, 163.

16 "Fifth Avenue Ella Wheeler Wilcox," "America's Most Beautiful Woman": *Philadelphia Inquirer*, September 19, 1920.

16 "I am the happiest man in the world," "I'll be hanged if I can tell you": "John Barrymore Weds Mrs. Leonard Thomas, Noted Society Writer," *Times-Herald* (Washington, DC), August 6, 1920.

16 "temperament[s] with a big T": *Philadelphia Inquirer*, September 19, 1920.

CHAPTER 3: JOAN STRANGE BLYTH

17 "Mr. B was a worshipping father," "Now and then Michael": Bound Notes A, box 1, Gerold Frank papers, Manuscripts and Archives Division, New York Public Library.

17 "wandered the dark, lonely streets": Barrymore and Frank, 28.

17 "She did not visit the nursery often," "Barrymore was there more often": Bound Notes A, box 1, Gerold Frank papers, Manuscripts and Archives Division, New York Public Library.

18 "the play-room of an institution": *Life*, May 5, 1921.

18 "clumsy [and] at times grotesque": *Arts & Decoration*, June 1921.

18 "decaying rose leaves": *The Billboard*, May 7, 1921.

18 "For the love of Mike": *Chicago Tribune*, Apr 24, 1921.

18 "[H]e wrote a long letter": Diana Barrymore and Frank James Singer. "Meet My Fabulous Family . . . the Barrymores" (unpublished manuscript, undated, circa pre-1947), typescript, page 51, Gerold Frank papers, Manuscripts and Archives Division, New York Public Library.

18 "maimed by loving kindness": Barrymore, *Confessions*.

18 "it reads better than it acts": *Brooklyn Daily Eagle*, May 1, 1921.

18-19 "[*Clair de Lune*] wore itself out": *Photoplay*, September 1921.

19 "Diana was quite a celebrity" through "she was a spoiled beauty": Bound Notes A, box 1, Gerold Frank papers, Manuscripts and Archives Division, New York Public Library.

19 "If John Barrymore fails": *New York Times*, November 26, 1922.

19 "[H]e hasn't had time": John Barrymore, letter to Michael Strange, October 21, 1922. Michael Strange papers, New York Public Library.

19 "frightening[ly] high ceilings": Barrymore and Frank, 31.

19 "more fun than anything I have ever done": Barrymore, *Confessions*.

19   "I don't suppose two people": John Barrymore, letter to Michael Strange, October 18, 1922, Michael Strange papers, New York Public Library.

19   "violent clashes" "something out of a Russian novel": Barrymore and Frank, 21.

20   "a tennis game in hell": Strange, 175.

20   "a strangely exhilarated state of mind," "proceeded to express his affection," "on the arm": "'No Truth In It,' Says Barrymore of 'Marital Rift.'" *New York Daily News*, December 3, 1920.

20   "I know that just over the edge": John Barrymore, letter to Michael Strange, October 18, 1922. Michael Strange papers, New York Public Library.

20   "If ever two egotists crashed down": Strange, 174.

20   "aired": Barrymore and Frank, 32.

20   "you cannot devote your *life*": John Barrymore, letter to Michael Strange, April 1922. Michael Strange papers, New York Public Library.

20   "Love and marriage and motherhood": *Theatre*, November 1922.

20   "North Shore summer colony": "Mrs. John Barrymore Makes Stage Debut." *New York Times*, June 30, 1925.

21   "Miss Treadwell wrote it" through "attributed to his wife": "Says Actor's Wife Copied Her Work," *Buffalo Times*, October 17, 1924.

21   "charging libel and slander": "Author of 'Poe' is Sued by Wife of Barrymore," *Buffalo Times*, October 28, 1924.

21   "subjecting her to withering attacks": Terry Ponick, "Treadwell: Light and Dark," *DC Theatre Scene*, June 1, 2010, https://dctheatrescene.com/2010/06/01/treadwell-bright-and-dark/.

22   "gloom, trouble and strife": Ray W. Harper, "The Premiere: A Nice Evening of Gloom," *Brooklyn Citizen*, March 20, 1926.

22   "fortunate choice for leading man": "The New Plays: At the Princess Theatre," *Brooklyn Daily Times*, March 19, 1926.

22   "very capable showing": *Brooklyn Citizen*, March 20, 1926.

22   "performed last night with a skill": *Brooklyn Daily Times*, March 19, 1926.

22   "[Michael Strange] made her New York debut": Alexander Woollcott, "Second Thoughts on First Nights," *Buffalo News*, March 27, 1926.

23   "The wonderful colors," "the native cruelty": Bound Notes C, box 1, Gerold Frank papers, Manuscripts and Archives Division, New York Public Library.

23   "If Robin had been there": Bound Notes D, box 1, Gerold Frank papers, Manuscripts and Archives Division, New York Public Library.

23   "the face of a Romney portrait and the spirit of a US Marine": Fowler, *Good Night Sweet Prince*, 187.

24   "You're going to meet a genius": Barrymore and Frank, 45.

24   "How frenzied the neighborhood": Strange, 245.

24   "It's the deadest": *Life*, July 6, 1922.

24   "When did I realize": Bound Notes F, box 1, Gerold Frank papers, Manuscripts and Archives Division, New York Public Library.

24   "a nice Robin": *Chicago Tribune*, December 5, 1934.

25   "I should have been the girl": Barrymore and Frank, 47.

25   "I was the ugliest child I knew," "jaundice": Barrymore and Frank, 33.

25   "dank-haired," "sallow-faced": Strange, 51.

25   "stringy bangs": Barrymore and Frank, 33.

25   "devil's hair": Barrymore and Frank, 38.

25 "I think she played boy's parts": Bound Notes D, box 1, Gerold Frank papers, Manuscripts and Archives Division, New York Public Library.

25-26 "She lay there without moving," "something that was to become": Barrymore and Frank, 40.

26 "understanding of meanings": "The New Play," *Brooklyn Daily Times*, December 27, 1927.

26 "very—and obvious": "'L'Aiglon' Suffers in English Version." *New York Times*, December 27, 1927.

26 "the perfection of love": "Ex-Barrymore Wife Sings Best Wishes in Wistful Vein." *New York Times*, January 3, 1929.

26 "[W]hen we were at Montauk Point": Bound Notes F, box 1, Gerold Frank papers, Manuscripts and Archives Division, New York Public Library.

26 "unheard-of practice": Cavett, 233.

26 "pathos," "clear and consoling": Strange, 278–79.

27 "She wasn't like a mother": Bound Notes D, box 1, Gerold Frank papers, Manuscripts and Archives Division, New York Public Library.

27 "as she is quite grown up enough as she is": Barnes, *The Man Who Lived Twice*, 231.

27 "I thought, *well, I'm like this man*": Bound Notes F, box 1, Gerold Frank papers, Manuscripts and Archives Division, New York Public Library.

27 "When you were about two or three": Bound Notes G, box 1, Gerold Frank papers, Manuscripts and Archives Division, New York Public Library.

28 "[f]or the first time an adult was interested": Barrymore and Frank, 63.

28 "Barrymore streak": Barrymore and Frank, 87.

28 "I guess I was just acting all the time": Bound Notes F, box 1, Gerold Frank papers, Manuscripts and Archives Division, New York Public Library.

28 "small, proper, exclusive": Barrymore and Frank, 65.

28 "peppermint": Barrymore and Frank, 53.

28 "She had a very engaging smile": Bound Notes E, box 1, Gerold Frank papers, Manuscripts and Archives Division, New York Public Library.

28 "mulberry-colored lips": Lambert, *The Ivan Moffat File*, 130.

29 "If I am pushy, Mother": Lambert, 132.

29 "I'm John Barrymore's son": Lambert, 135.

29 "They've saddled you," "Pillows and false faces": Barrymore and Frank, 71.

29 "seventeen and always ready for fun": Barrymore and Frank, 69.

30 "It's exactly like a milk shake": Barrymore and Frank, 73.

30 "John visited [Diana] at a boarding school": Power-Waters, 105–6.

31 "Barrymore, Doc, and I," "more mettlesome": Bound Notes A, box 1, Gerold Frank papers, Manuscripts and Archives Division, New York Public Library.

31 "[w]hen I came back": Bound Notes D, box 1, Gerold Frank papers, Manuscripts and Archives Division, New York Public Library.

31-32 "Dearest Diana": excerpt from telegram by John Barrymore, "no reply to this appeal," Fowler, *Good Night, Sweet Prince*, 393.

32 "displaying much of the ability": *Boston Globe*, December 20, 1935.

32 "Barrymore headache": Barrymore and Frank, 68.

32-33 "His place was lovely" through "he looks like an anteater": Bound Notes A, box 1, Gerold Frank papers, Manuscripts and Archives Division, New York Public Library.

33 "I'm having a good time here": 1938-39 Notes, book A, box 2, Gerold Frank papers, Manuscripts and Archives Division, New York Public Library.

33 "rose and white": Barrymore and Frank, 90.

34   "like any girl waiting": 1938–39 Notes, book A, box 2, Gerold Frank papers, Manuscripts and Archives Division, New York Public Library.

35   "electrical nymph," "windblown hair": *Buffalo Evening News*, February 7, 1942.
35   "exaggerated as the early silent movie heroines": Thompson, 155.
35   "Wasn't here also an audience?" "magnificent discovery": Bound Notes C, box 1, Gerold Frank papers, Manuscripts and Archives Division, New York Public Library.
35   "Society's all right": *Philadelphia Inquirer*, October 13, 1939.
35   "disgusting": *Life*, December 6, 1963.
35   "vain little girls": *Pittsburgh Press*, January 27, 1937.
36   "revolving in his grave": *New York Daily News*, October 29, 1938.
36   "[She] is a very nice, sweet": 1938–39 Notes, book A, box 2, Gerold Frank papers, Manuscripts and Archives Division, New York Public Library.
36   "a hooped skirt and Marie Antoinette fichu": *Chattanooga Daily Times*, October 5, 1941.
36   "the most beautiful, the most talented": Barrymore and Frank, 12.
36   "[L]ike a young lawyer": Bound Notes G, box 1, Gerold Frank papers, Manuscripts and Archives Division, New York Public Library.
37   "[y]ou're a society girl": Barrymore and Frank, 114.
37   "Tony is marvelous": Barrymore, Diana, letter to Michael Strange, undated, circa summer 1939. Diana Barrymore papers, New York Public Library.
37   "Tony was to be my husband": Barrymore and Frank, 110.
38   "Dark, pert Diana Blythe": *Indianapolis Star*, January 1, 1939.
38   "progressive": Washington Duke, phone discussion with author, April 11, 2022.
38   "Country club life": Anthony Drexel Duke and Richard Firstman, *Uncharted Course*, 99.
38   "devote all of his fortune": *New York Daily News*, May 24, 1937.
38   "I don't know if I loved her": Duke and Firstman, *Uncharted*, 104.
38   "[L]ast night, when all those people were at dinner": Diana Barrymore, letter to Michael Strange, undated, circa 1940, Diana Barrymore papers, New York Public Library.
38   "Michael was always against Diana's decisions": Bound Notes A, box 1, Gerold Frank papers, Manuscripts and Archives Division, New York Public Library.
39   "excitem": *Reading Times*, June 13, 1939.
39   "That he has picked a bride": *New York Daily News*, June 10, 1939.
39   "Mother said be very very careful": Bound Notes F, box 1, Gerold Frank papers, Manuscripts and Archives Division, New York Public Library.
39   "subdued, winsome": *Boston Globe*, July 22, 1941.
39   "eyes inflamed from artificial eyelashes": *Buffalo Evening News*, December 9, 1939.
39   "not a middle-aged actress": *Philadelphia Inquirer*, October 13, 1939.
39   "She IS theater": *Buffalo Evening News*, February 7, 1942.
39   "I am simply marvelous": *Scrantonian Tribune*, August 13, 1939.
40   "pudgy, plain and pug-nosed": Jean Lightfoot, "Gloria Vanderbilt: Eighteen Years on Society's Merry-Go-Round," *Spokesman-Review*, November 16, 1941.
40   "round, saucy-lipped": "New York's No. 1 Society Girl Fails to Keep On Easy Footing." *Arizona Republic*, November 25, 1938.
40   "When I'd see a pretty girl," "take well," "[they] photograph looking like Donald Duck":

40   "Noses, Eyes, Chins," *Pathfinder*, February 27, 1937.

40   "The ideal figure": "This Is Ideal Figure That Modern Women Want," *Life*, August 15, 1938.

40   "[N]either too slim or too ample": "Top Notch Allure Bars Straight Line Silhouette," *Philadelphia Inquirer*, August 8, 1939.

40   "scrawny": *Collier's*, October 7, 1942.

40   "a diet would help": *New York Daily News*, December 21, 1940.

40   "good start," "Young lady, people very big in the theatre": Bound Notes G, box 1, Gerold Frank papers, Manuscripts and Archives Division, New York Public Library.

41   "I wanted to make good": 1938–39 Notes, book A, box 2, Gerold Frank papers, Manuscripts and Archives Division, New York Public Library.

41   "Diana holds up the high tradition": *Hanover Evening Sun*, October 14, 1939.

41   "genuinely affecting": *Philadelphia Inquirer*, October 15, 1939.

41   "When I heard that applause," "Where are the actors staying": 1938–39 Notes, book A, box 2, Gerold Frank papers, Manuscripts and Archives Division, New York Public Library.

41   "[held] her own": *Boston Globe*, October 24, 1939.

41   "the only one of them": Catherine Turney and Jerry Horwin, *My Dear Children* (New York: Random House, 1940).

41   "make a fool of himself": Preminger, *Preminger*, 59.

41   "beneath human dignity": Kobler, 332.

41   "He has such a wonderful sense of humor": *Buffalo News*, December 9, 1939.

41   "*My Dear Children* is a good time": John Barrymore, "There Must Be a Play," Turney and Horwin, preface.

41   "She's the best thing I ever produced": *Harrisburg Telegraph*, November 30, 1939.

41-42 "We went to my apartment first" through "work like an S.O.B.": 1938–39 Notes, book A, box 2, Gerold Frank papers, Manuscripts and Archives Division, New York Public Library.

42   "constant friend and companion": "Happy About the Whole Thing." *Salem News* (OH), February 7, 1940.

42   "You-will-leave," "almost like a little boy": Barrymore and Frank, 137.

43   "wastrel youth," "infantile worldview," "he thought her more realistic": Fowler, *Good Night, Sweet Prince*, 432–33.

43   "nice young man" through "bottomless spoons": 1938–39 Notes, book A, box 2, Gerold Frank papers, Manuscripts and Archives Division, New York Public Library.

43   "a little quieter": *Portland Press-Herald*, July 21, 1940.

43   "readable," "pretentious": Katherine Woods, "The Story of Michael Strange," *New York Times*, May 12, 1940.

43   "consented to make a one-week appearance": Emmie B. Whitney, "Social Economy Engrosses Michael Strange, Author, Poet, Playwright, Now in Maine," *Lewiston Sun-Journal*, August 24, 1940.

43-44 "tough," "after those sweet ingénues," "anything crawl out": Diana Barrymore, letter to Francis Kellogg, undated, circa summer 1940. Diana Barrymore papers, New York Public Library.

44   "I shall always love you," "I respect you": Diana Barrymore, letter to Francis Kellogg, undated, circa before September 1942. Diana Barrymore papers, New York Public Library.

44   "but I couldn't do it": Bound Notes F, box 1, Gerold Frank papers, Manuscripts and
       Archives Division, New York Public Library.
44   "I haven't experienced such a chill": Power-Waters, 245.
44   "Hope springs eternal": *Hartford Courant*, February 2, 1940.
44   "[t]wo Barrymores": *Buffalo News*, May 4, 1939.
44   "I'm in the peculiar position": *New York Daily News*, February 2, 1940.
44   "I can't bear to see Jack": Barrymore and Frank, 137.
44-45 "The theatre is a strange cruel depressing place": John Barrymore, letter to Michael
       Strange, October 11, 1922. Michael Strange papers, New York Public Library.
45   "Hamlet comes home a clown": *New York Daily News*, February 1, 1940.
45   "Mr. Barrymore ceased to be an artist": Arthur Pollock, "Playthings: George Abbott
       Takes a Vacation from His Talents and John Barrymore Suffers Comparison With
       Wits, Improvisators," *Brooklyn Eagle*, February 18, 1940.
45   "thumbing his Grecian profile": Burns Mantle, "Putting a Great Actor to Bed," *New
       York Daily News*, February 11, 1940.
45   "at 58, the star looks 45 and acts 30": *Pittsburgh Post-Gazette*, January 9, 1940.
45   "that of a fine virtuoso" "The Strange Case of—John Barrymore: Back on Broadway,"
       Life, February 12, 1940.
45   "stenographer's spread": *Buffalo News*, January 21, 1939.
45   "like Death itself": Elaine Barrie Barrymore and Sanford Dody, *All My Sins Remembered*,
       252.
45   "She's dressed for battle": Barrymore and Frank, 138.
45   "If it comes to blows": *Fort Worth Star-Telegram*, February 1, 1940.
45   "Please allow your father": Barrymore and Dody, 253.
45   "Treepee . . . perhaps": Barrymore and Frank, 138.
45   "I can't stand it anymore": Thompson, 162.
45   "Stop trying to be a Barrymore": *New York Daily News*, December 17, 1939.
45   "the satisfied smile": Thompson, 162.
45   "One would've never thought": Barrymore and Dody, 254.
45   "Goddam[n] it, I'm asking you": Barrymore and Dody, 254.
46   "twenty-four hours": *Tampa Tribune*, February 2, 1940.
46   "Miss Jacobs": Barrymore and Frank, 139.
46   "This is like the gentle rain," "We are Barrymores," "confused and torn," "Maybe so":
       Brooklyn Daily Eagle, February 1, 1940.
46   "Daddy, either this woman leaves": Barrymore and Frank, 139.
46   "Well, you leave . . . goodnight, Treepee": Barrymore and Dody, 254.
46   "Very well": *Cincinnati Post*, February 1, 1940.
46   "self-appointed protector," "Everybody knows what happened": *New York Daily News*,
       February 2, 1940.
46   "vitamin deficiency": *Birmingham Post*, February 7, 1940.
46   "I am very definitely," "crude," "hated and loved," "he's not a person": *Brooklyn Daily
       Eagle*, February 2, 1940.
47   "DIANA LOSES TO PAPA": *Indianapolis News*, February 1, 1940.
47   "ELAINE AND DIANA TANGLE": *Wisconsin State Journal*, February 1, 1940.
47   "ELAINE WINS—DAUGHTER FURIOUS": *Boston Globe*, February 1, 1940.
47   "public squabble": Barrymore and Dody, 204.
47   "A genius—therefor a little abnormal": *Wisconsin State Journal*, March 10, 1940.

47   "Barrymore Brat": *Collier's*, October 7, 1942.

47   "Everything is just fine," "the best thing under the circumstances," "We are still very good friends": folder "1950–1955," box 1, Gerold Frank papers, Manuscripts and Archives Division, New York Public Library.

47   Woodbury ad ("take a tip"): *Chicago Tribune*, January 14, 1940.

47   Nobility Plate ad ("Nobility of the American stage"): *House & Garden*, February 1942.

47   "garbed as a Turk": *New York Daily News*, May 11, 1940.

47   "attack of vertigo": *San Francisco Examiner*, June 7, 1941.

48   "no half-brother and sister": *Detroit Evening Times*, July 25, 1941.

48   "on the threshold of theatrical success": *New York Daily News*, September 4, 1940.

48   "too decadent to be sent on tour," "hot-potato," "a promising rookie": *Chicago Tribune*, March 13, 1935.

48   "Mother had a bust of Apollo": Barrymore and Frank, 82.

48   "take the first battleship home": *Fresno Bee*, January 18, 1941.

48   "showed their affection openly": Arce, *The Secret Life of Tyrone Power*, 67.

48   "with endless rolls": Guiles, *Tyrone Power: The Last Idol*, 98.

49   "All right my dear": Barrymore and Frank, 144.

49   "I can never forget the eggs": Barrymore and Frank, 146.

49   "reached the state of premeditated marriage," "He's a very fine man": Diana Barrymore, letter to Francis Kellogg, undated, circa 1940–41, Diana Barrymore papers, New York Public Library.

49   "[t]hey're bitches. A woman always has an excuse": GFP 1950–55, Box 1.

49   "fourth and final love": "Fourth Generation of Barrymore's on Stage in New York," *Columbus (Nebraska) Telegram*, December 3, 1940.

49   "middle-aged philanderings": Brooks Atkinson, "THE PLAY: 'Romantic Mr. Dickens' Gives Diana Barrymore Her First Broadway Part," *New York Times*, December 3, 1940.

49-50 "Would [Robert] mind coming up" through "the only thing your father would have": 1938–39 Notes, book A, box 2, Gerold Frank papers, Manuscripts and Archives Division, New York Public Library.

50-51 "I took a swift look," "darling all the luck in the world," "I had my entrance—I walked": Bound Notes C, box 1, Gerold Frank papers, Manuscripts and Archives Division, New York Public Library.

51   "a bit of a boob": *St. Louis Post-Dispatch*, December 8, 1940.

51   "a vibrant young lady": *New York Times*, December 3, 1940.

51   "what you make of acting": Barrymore and Frank, 150.

51   "real surprise of the cast": "Klepfer," *Variety*, May 14, 1941.

51   "There was a deathly hush": 1938–39 Notes, book A, box 2, Gerold Frank papers, Manuscripts and Archives Division, New York Public Library.

51   "Miss Barrymore is going places": *Brooklyn Citizen*, May 14, 1941.

51   "unwritten Royal Family law": *Bangor Daily News*, September 15, 1941.

51   "spirited girl of 20": *Fort Worth Star-Telegram*, August 16, 1941.

51   "thrill-seeking flapper": *Variety*, November 5, 1941.

52   "I felt I knew what this woman was," "Well honey you're hired," "My eyes must have shown it": 1938–39 Notes, book A, box 2, Gerold Frank papers, Manuscripts and Archives Division, New York Public Library.

52   "overplayed," "just enough to turn": *The Billboard*, November 8, 1941,

52   "if anything lifted the last two": Goldstein, 155.

52 "the last of the Barrymores": "A Quip Off the Old Block: Diana is Last Barrymore," *Des Moines Register*, March 29, 1942.

52 "Movie acting is nothing": *Collier's*, October 7, 1942.

52 "they weren't thinking of me for the part": Bound Notes C, box 1, Gerold Frank papers, Manuscripts and Archives Division, New York Public Library.

52 "I don't need it at present": *Buffalo Evening News*, December 9, 1939.

52 "I'm simply mad about jewelry;" "I stopped even trying to learn arithmetic" Dee Lowrance, "A New Barrymore Beauty Takes a Bow," *Salt Lake Tribune Sunday Magazine*, March 22, 1942.

52 "my father, John, beat me": *Oakland Tribune*, April 5, 1942.

52 "department store window": *New York Daily News*, December 7, 1941.

52 "Don't be dull," "oh, how idiotic": *Tennessean*, October 5, 1941.

52 "dull," "most devastating," "if you wanted to ruin or crush anybody": Bound Notes G, box 1, Gerold Frank papers, Manuscripts and Archives Division, New York Public Library.

52-53 "they are aptly named": Bound Notes C, box 1, Gerold Frank papers, Manuscripts and Archives Division, New York Public Library.

53 "[I]f I ever get blue": *Des Moines Register*, March 29, 1942.

53 "a raven nesting in the hollow" *Esquire*, January 1943.

53 "married and dabbles": *New York Daily News*, December 7, 1941.

53 "a primitive wilderness": *Cincinnati Enquirer*, April 20, 1943.

53 "irregular teeth," "strange assortment of gifts": *Collier's*, October 7, 1942.

53 "Two parents like mine": *New York Daily News*, October 18, 1937.

53 "What I want most of all": *Buffalo Evening News*, December 9, 1939.

53 "great physical beauty": *The Age* (Melbourne, Victoria, Australia), October 19, 1951.

53 "I'm just going along on my own": *Tampa Tribune*, May 31, 1942.

53 "hint of violence," "animal vitality," "I'm living": Barrymore and Frank, 155–56.

53 "The Sardi's set is all a-twitter": *Tampa Bay Times*, December 10, 1941.

CHAPTER 5: THE BARRYMORE BRAT

54 "dignified manner consonant with [her] position as an artist": Barrymore and Frank, 154

54 "I remember I was terribly disappointed": 1938–39 Notes, book A, box 2, Gerold Frank papers, Manuscripts and Archives Division, New York Public Library.

54 "it's wonderful to have a daughter": *San Bernardino County Sun*, January 15, 1942

54 "divine house," "huge swimming pool": Diana Barrymore, letter to Francis Kellogg, undated, circa late 1941, Diana Barrymore papers, New York Public Library.

54 "castle out of fairyland": Barrymore and Frank, 164.

55 "He went right across the room," through "when they were tiny enough, they played in that pool": Bound Notes G, box 1, Gerold Frank papers, Manuscripts and Archives Division, New York Public Library.

55 "Jack's been talking": Barrymore and Frank, 166.

55 "He'd always been a stranger": Barrymore and Frank, 168.

56 "I'm in love with a man I can't have," "Sweetie, don't let Hollywood," "I have to pull": Barrymore and Frank, 173.

56 "Mr. Lawrence," a "major producer": Barrymore and Frank, 174.

56-57   "common sense," "Getting into movies was a big deal for girls those days," "putting out for a role": Lake and Bain, 16.

57   "Most natural thing in the world," "Let's have fun and then we'll talk": Lake and Bain, 18.

57   "Look . . . I'm not under contract" through "You're quite a girl": Barrymore and Frank, 174–75.

57   "[He] was very fond of me": Bound Notes D, box 1, Gerold Frank papers, Manuscripts and Archives Division, New York Public Library.

57   "I'd sort of look around at people": Bound Notes F, box 1, Gerold Frank papers, Manuscripts and Archives Division, New York Public Library.

58   "The First Great Picture of the Second World War!": *Film Daily*, June 8, 1942.

58   "[w]e concentrate on Europe because": *Lewiston Sun-Journal*, August 24, 1940.

58   "[h]ere is Britain bleeding and dying": 1938–39 Notes, book A, box 2, Gerold Frank papers, Manuscripts and Archives Division, New York Public Library.

58   "intangible factors of war," "what are we fighting for?": *Harrison's Reports*, July 4, 1942.

58   "Profile Jr.": *South Bend Tribune*, May 16, 1942.

58-59   "They didn't allow me to see any of [the makeup tests]": Bound Notes F, box 1, Gerold Frank papers, Manuscripts and Archives Division, New York Public Library.

59   "extremely painful": *Buffalo Evening News*, February 7, 1942.

59   "An extraordinary face": Barrymore and Frank, 169.

59   "This doll isn't even good looking": *Collier's*, October 3, 1942.

59   "I didn't buy a pretty face": Barrymore and Frank, 170.

59   "huge inhuman eye": Barrymore and Frank, 170.

59   "a brat," "spitting in a director's eye": *Collier's*, October 3, 1942.

59   "lousy," "as an actor," "I didn't really dislike Diana," "many of the outer trappings": Robert Stack and Mark Evans, *Straight Shooting*, 90–91.

59   "The public has a new awareness of good work," "no more 'personality,'" "scenes": *Photoplay*, March 1942.

59   "on the make for every man": James Kotsilibas-Davis, *The Barrymores*, 305.

59   "If Diana and I had ever gone near a bowling ball": Stack and Evans, 63.

60   "Divinely beautiful," "archangel": Barrymore and Frank, 198.

60   "He never seemed old": Fowler, *Good Night, Sweet Prince*, 460.

60   "a witty and willful playboy" through "he was still a superb actor": *New York Times*, April 20, 1941.

60   "He had a most meticulous regard," No matter how careless he may have been": Fowler, *Minutes*, 273.

60   "I don't think John would like that," "by all means": "Old Friends Pay Last Tribute to Barrymore." *San Francisco Examiner*, June 2, 1942.

60   "He and Daddy adored each other," "When Robin went to the coast": Bound Notes F, box 1, Gerold Frank papers, Manuscripts and Archives Division, New York Public Library.

61   "cyclonic vitality": John Barrymore, letter to Michael Strange, undated, circa summer 1917. Michael Strange papers, New York Public Library.

61   "often reiterated that there": Bound Notes E, box 1, Gerold Frank papers, Manuscripts and Archives Division, New York Public Library.

61   "so divine": Bound Notes F, box 1, Gerold Frank papers, Manuscripts and Archives Division, New York Public Library.

61   "puffed, white, bloodless": Flynn and Conrad, 305.

61   "Jack was a great patron of prostitutes": Peters, 464.

61   "like Valentino's funeral": Bound Notes F, box 1, Gerold Frank papers, Manuscripts and Archives Division, New York Public Library.

61   Arthur Hopkins telegram: cited in Fowler, *Minutes*, 220.

61-62   "finest girl I ever met," "no hypocrisy," "shocked him": *New York Daily News*, June 1, 1942.

62   "honest tears as large": *Santa Cruz Sentinel*, June 2, 1942.

62   "How could she be here?" "You can't stop her": Bound Notes F, box 1, Gerold Frank papers, Manuscripts and Archives Division, New York Public Library.

62   "worth more than 50 years": *New York Times*, July 8, 1982.

62   "what a vulgar display": *Daily News*, June 3, 1942.

63   "the prostitution of his dignity": *Boston Globe*, June 1, 1942.

63   "John Barrymore is dead at sixty": *New York Daily News*, June 1, 1942.

63   "the last of the bravura performers": Frank Gill, "Barrymore—An Actor Off Stage and On," *Detroit Free Press*, May 31, 1942.

63   "quick-witted, literate, articulate . . . a grand subject to interview": *New York Daily News*, June 1, 1942.

63   "the greatest Hamlet the world has ever known": *Fort Worth Star-Telegram*, May 31, 1942.

63   "Thousands who saw him in that circus": *New York Daily News*, June 1, 1942.

63   "a pain and eloquence which no one could have imagined," *Do you remember* (love letter excerpt): Bound Notes C, box 1, Gerold Frank papers, Manuscripts and Archives Division, New York Public Library.

63-64   "I think back night after night," "I think she figured [I] was pretty safe": Bound Notes D, box 1, Gerold Frank papers, Manuscripts and Archives Division, New York Public Library.

64   "believed 100% in a man's God-given right to destroy himself": Mank, 145.

64   "For five minutes, 35 seconds": *Time*, February 9, 1942.

64   John Barrymore cable to Michael Strange: cited in Fowler, *Good Night, Sweet Prince*, 458.

64   "take [him] out of the kind of roles he has been doing lately": *Buffalo Evening News*, February 7, 1942.

64   "You are going on to great things": Barrymore and Frank, 184.

64   "I am doing the work of a whore": Fowler, *Minutes*, 190.

65   "Aren't you going to check up," "disgusting": Barrymore and Frank, 187.

65   "That god damned boarding school *bitch*": Bound Notes D, box 1, Gerold Frank papers, Manuscripts and Archives Division, New York Public Library.

65   "what happened on his yacht": Bound Notes C, box 1, Gerold Frank papers, Manuscripts and Archives Division, New York Public Library.

65   "Ever f——d her?": Louise Guinness, *The Vintage Book of Fathers*, 56.

65   "My mother loved the fact": Terry Chester Shulman, *Film's First Family*, 187.

65   "little monster": Bound Notes C, box 1, Gerold Frank papers, Manuscripts and Archives Division, New York Public Library.

65   "We wrestled a lot": *New York Daily News*, July 29, 1951.

65   "exposing her breasts": Shulman, 187.

65   "prime brat," "broke rules": *Salt Lake Tribune Sunday Magazine*, March 22, 1942.

65   "He could be really frightening": Shulman, 185.

65   "slipping some of the family silver": Bound Notes C, box 1, Gerold Frank papers, Manuscripts and Archives Division, New York Public Library.

65   "glimmer of hope": Jeffrey Weissman, phone conversation with author, March 2021.

66   "one of the strangest families": *TV Radio Mirror*, August 1962.

66   "man-child": Drew Barrymore, caption excerpt: "He was a mad poet hedonist man child!," *Instagram*, June 21, 2020, https://www.instagram.com/p/CBsxHGtjD_4/

66   "neither were available": Shulman, 185–86.

66   "he had never had real love": *TV Radio Mirror*, August 1962.

66   "brilliant entertainment": *Film Daily*, June 6, 1942.

66   "the camera rides the sky with its pilots": *Modern Screen*, May 1942.

66   "Diana Barrymore does not photograph" *Variety*, June 17, 1942.

66   "inadequate and extremely affected": *New York Times* July 3, 1942.

67   "The film I'm now doing is the top": Diana Barrymore, letter to Francis Kellogg, undated, circa spring 1942, Diana Barrymore papers, New York Public Library.

67-68 "clever comedy," "an amazingly good account" "Reviews of the New Films: 'Between Us Girls,'" *Film Daily*, September 3, 1942.

68   "It is the excellent performance": *Harrison's Reports*, September 6 1942.

68   "her right for a crown": *Minneapolis Daily Times*, September 5, 1942.

68   "first-rate funny": *Pittsburgh Sun-Telegraph*, September 20, 1942.

68   "not too kind," "eat their words": *Pittsburgh Sun-Telegraph*, September 15, 1942.

68   "directors and producers," "the mistake was theirs": *Cincinnati Enquirer*, September 18, 1942.

68   "Diana Barrymore is tops": *Motion Picture Herald*, December 26, 1942.

68   "whimsical," "noisy and exhausting": *Variety*, September 2, 1942.

68   "The picture is as futile," "even her late and illustrious sire": *Pittsburgh Sun-Telegraph*, November 19, 1942.

68   "No doubt even the offspring": "T. S.," *New York Times*, September 25, 1942.

68   "the picture should help establish" "Hobe," *Variety*, September 2, 1942.

68   "a young she-wolf": *San Francisco Examiner*, October 20, 1942.

69   "trashed," "last real Hollywood movie": Michael O'Hanlon, "FILMS: Between Us Girls (1942)," *Kay Francis' Life & Career*, August 3, 2013, https://kayfrancisfilms.com/between-us-girls-1942/.

69   "knockabout comedian": Barrymore, *Confessions*.

69   "brand-new brilliant Barrymore": ad in *Pottsville Republican and Herald*, September 14, 1942.

69   "I think she had some of the mental difficulties": Ronald L. Davis, *Just Making Movies*, 9–10.

69   "lead pipe," "I'll never walk on a set": *Tyler Morning Telegraph*, April 9, 1947.

69   "Diana has as yet no grasp," "headstrong," "change her tone": *Pittsburgh Press*, July 29, 1942.

70   "took her lickings," "supposed to ride to stardom": *Time*, October 5, 1942.

70   "[Critics] hard put to say nice things": *New York Daily News*, October 18, 1942.

70   "I would marry him right now": *Salt Lake Tribune Sunday Magazine*, March 22, 1942.

70   "I only wish Jack were here to see you now": Barrymore and Frank, 206.

70   "Brian and I had many love scenes": Barrymore and Frank, 208–9.

70-71 Donlevy telegram excerpt, "I hardly knew him but he had been kind": Harry Evans, "Hollywood Diary," *The Family Circle* 12 no. 16 (October 16, 1942).

71   "full of vitality": Barrymore and Frank, 209.

71   "Of course I was married to Bram": Bound Notes D, box 1, Gerold Frank papers, Manuscripts and Archives Division, New York Public Library.

71   "taut and suspenseful melodrama": *Motion Picture Daily*, November 9, 1942.

71   "fairly entertaining": *Hollywood*, February 1943

71   "draggy": *Variety*, November 11, 1942.

71   "believable" *Showmen's Trade Review*, November 14, 1942.

71   "wooden": *Screenland*, February 1943.

71   "In spite of her efforts": *New York Daily News*, November 20, 1942.

71   "as great as Bette Davis": John Todd, "What's Doing in the Film Capital," *Richmond Independent*, September 25, 1942.

71   "cleaning up": *Philadelphia Inquirer*, January 20, 1943.

71   "whiz-ding": *Chico Record*, August 30, 1942.

71   "wooed and won," "darling of the [Universal] lot": *Hollywood*, January 1943.

71   "changed girl," "no other Barrymore": *Detroit Free Press*, June 28, 1943.

71   "always had a soft spot in his heart for me": Bound Notes D, box 1, Gerold Frank papers, Manuscripts and Archives Division, New York Public Library.

72   "comparable to the talent,": "cheapened," "the fact that you offer Diana Barrymore": Case No. 3242. Cummings v. Universal, Date: 1/7/43, Clerk, US District Court, Sou. Dist. of Calif. Louis J. Somers, Deputy Clerk.

72   "all the airy freshness": *Pittsburgh Post-Gazette*, December 6, 1943.

72   "Not very funny": *Philadelphia Inquirer*, November 27, 1943.

73   "Action compensates": *Miami News*, August 18, 1943.

73   "reversed the usual order of Hollywood": *New York Daily News*, August 14, 1943.

73   "ooz[ed] out of her bodice": *Louisville Courier-Journal*, August 27, 1943.

73-74   "entire exhibition branch," "Top Ten Stars," "most promising for development," "unusually versatile," "carrie[d] on the 'Royal Family' tradition": *Motion Picture Herald*, September 4, 1943.

74   "overact[ed] like mad," "it's hard to tone down": *Salt Lake Tribune Sunday Magazine*, March 22, 1942.

74   "flock of mascaraed glamor girls": *Philadelphia Inquirer*, May 31, 1944.

74   "Ladies Outrageous": Leslie Haynsworth and David Toomey, *Amelia Earhart's Daughters*, 117–18.

74   "Hysterics, bickering, and unladylike": *New York Times*, March 16, 1944.

74-75   "Judging by their actions": *Time*, April 3, 1944.

75   "hackneyed": Leonard Maltin, "Leonard Maltin Movie Review: Ladies Courageous (1944)," *Turner Classic Movies*, http://www.tcm.com/tcmdb/title/80577/Ladies -Courageous.

75   "patronizing" through "mopping up": "Ladies Courageous," Box 3520, Motion Picture Reviews and Analysis: Entry NC 148 567, Record Group 208, Records of the Office of War Information, National Archives at College Park, MD.

75   "making the public believe that 'Ladies Courageous' is a good picture": *Harrison's Reports*, April 22, 1944.

76   "I was an ass": *Philadelphia Inquirer*, June 29, 1947.

76   "eccentric country squire": Barrymore and Frank, 215.

76   "not a mink": Bound Notes B, box 1, Gerold Frank papers, Manuscripts and Archives Division, New York Public Library.

76   "you'll know soon enough": Barrymore and Frank, 216.

76   "I'm sorry to do this to Robin": Barrymore and Frank, 217.

76   "looking like what mother used to say": Bound Notes D, box 1, Gerold Frank papers, Manuscripts and Archives Division, New York Public Library.

76   "Robin loved mother deeply," "You understand about Billy": Bound Notes E, box 1, Gerold Frank papers, Manuscripts and Archives Division, New York Public Library.

77   "Bram came back": Bound Notes D, box 1, Gerold Frank papers, Manuscripts and Archives Division, New York Public Library.

77   "if you don't understand": Bound Notes E, box 1, Gerold Frank papers, Manuscripts and Archives Division, New York Public Library.

77   "I got on my knees" through "Bramwell drove him out": Bound Notes D, box 1, Gerold Frank papers, Manuscripts and Archives Division, New York Public Library.

77   "nervous breakdown": *Indianapolis Star*, April 4, 1944.

77   "he died of a broken heart": Bound Notes F, box 1, Gerold Frank papers, Manuscripts and Archives Division, New York Public Library.

78   "They've taken the one thing I love": Barrymore and Frank, 270.

78   "long, dusky, atmospheric tunnel," "dry and uphill path": *Time*, January 29, 1945.

78   "tedious," "mainly talk," "lifeless": *New York Times*, January 19, 1945.

78   "curiously disappointing" and "woefully contrived," "a much improved young actress": *The Billboard*, January 27, 1945.

78   "rarely received less cooperation," "gold mine," "It does not remain": Clarence Derwent, *The Derwent Story*, 207–8.

78   "less than five hours' work": Barrymore and Frank, 224–25.

78   "[Carson] was an affable, charming, big, tall, very attractive guy": Bound Notes F, box 1, Gerold Frank papers, Manuscripts and Archives Division, New York Public Library.

78-79   "old reliable Barrymore touch": *New York Daily News*, April 2, 1944.

79   "I was sweet-talked by all the MCA people": Bound Notes F, box 1, Gerold Frank papers, Manuscripts and Archives Division, New York Public Library.

79   "receiv[ing] the traditional blessing of the fabulous Barrymore clan," "Ethel Barrymore passed the apple": "Star of Rebecca Receives Blessing of Barrymores," *Sacramento Bee*, September 1, 1945.

79   "Diana liked to say": David Patrick Columbia, "John Galliher. A Life of Style," *New York Social Diary*, July 27, 2021, https://www.newyorksocialdiary.com/biography -of-a-classic-man-of-style-john-galliher-a-life-of-style/.

79   "my time was my own": Bound Notes G, box 1, Gerold Frank papers, Manuscripts and Archives Division, New York Public Library.

79   "Why don't you hit a woman?" Barrymore and Frank, 227.

79   "knuckle-duster": *Philadelphia Inquirer*, June 29, 1947.

79   "It's exactly what I thought would happen": Barrymore and Frank, 227–28.

80   "I started thinking the more I went out": Bound Notes G, box 1, Gerold Frank papers, Manuscripts and Archives Division, New York Public Library.

80   "I lost something I could hold on to": Bound Notes D, box 1, Gerold Frank papers, Manuscripts and Archives Division, New York Public Library.

80   "chill," "coal shortage": *New York Daily News*, February 27, 1946.

80   "I wouldn't remain here": Barrymore and Frank, 231.

80   "as though a live eel": Barrymore and Frank, 232.

81   "We understood each other completely": Barrymore and Frank, 234.

81   "I think he did definitely love me": Bound Notes F, box 1, Gerold Frank papers, Manuscripts and Archives Division, New York Public Library.

81   "second billing to a motion picture," "humiliating": Barrymore and Frank, 225.

81   "I'd go to see him as often as I could": Bound Notes E, box 1, Gerold Frank papers, Manuscripts and Archives Division, New York Public Library.

81   "underneath the mask": Barnes, 228.

81-82   "I was made to go to church," "horrible horrible blow," "I felt as if I had lost contact with God": Bound Notes E, box 1, Gerold Frank papers, Manuscripts and Archives Division, New York Public Library.

CHAPTER 6: *THE DIANA BARRYMORE SHOW*

83   "with a smile that could win": *Louisville Courier-Journal*, April 16, 1947.

83   "then let's make love": Barrymore and Frank, 237.

83   "the antithesis of Bramwell," "unabashed animal vigor": Barrymore and Frank, 238.

83   "divorce party," "I guess I slapped him back," "we are if John says so": *Philadelphia Inquirer*, May 16, 1946.

83   "John isn't divorced yet," "How can anyone discuss marriage": *Sacramento Bee*, June 29, 1946.

83   "gentleman tennis player," "health": Barrymore and Frank, 240.

84   "I'd use the wrong muscles," "Keep him as a lover": Barrymore and Frank, 241.

84   "[i]t was not love": Barrymore and Frank, 243.

84   "[T]hey live on the wrong street for you": Barrymore and Frank, 244.

85   "same damned cop-and-robber": *Rochester Democrat and Chronicle*, January 18, 1946.

85   "Miss Barrymore set out," "fire and brimstone": *New York Daily News*, May 2, 1948.

85   "finish and sincerity," "natural and easy performance": *Wilmington Morning News*, January 3, 1948.

85-86   "She looked beautiful—always looked good": Bound Notes E, box 1, Gerold Frank papers, Manuscripts and Archives Division, New York Public Library.

86   "the most sacredly enimagtic": Strange, 319.

86   "Miss Barrymore lives up to everything": *Atlanta Constitution*, January 20, 1948.

86   "'She strode up to me. Her lips brushed my cheek'": Barrymore and Frank, 252.

86   "no doubt [done by Zuloaga]": Strange, 207.

87   "we both had lumps on our cans": Bound Notes B, box 1, Gerold Frank papers, Manuscripts and Archives Division, New York Public Library.

87   "The problem is you have no faith": Diana Barrymore, letter to Michael Strange, undated, circa late 1939, Diana Barrymore papers, New York Public Library.

87   "began to turn in bitterness," "scatterbrained," "Michael was beside herself," "the last relic remaining," "utterly brutal": Bound Notes E, box 1, Gerold Frank papers, Manuscripts and Archives Division, New York Public Library.

87   "Mother has been seeing a lot of Bram": Diana Barrymore, letter to Francis Kellogg, November 1947, Diana Barrymore papers, New York Public Library.

87   "[Michael] invited us up one week-end": Bound Notes B, box 1, Gerold Frank papers, Manuscripts and Archives Division, New York Public Library.

88   "magnificent shock of black hair," "dark and flashing eyes": Barrymore and Frank, 271.

88   "hunks of ice": *St. Louis Star and Times*, January 6, 1949.

88   "no reaction . . . like a clam": Bound Notes D, box 1, Gerold Frank papers, Manuscripts and Archives Division, New York Public Library.

89   "For months everywhere I looked": Barrymore and Frank, 266.

89   "wham down the stairs": *New York Daily News*, December 16, 1949.

89   "very embarrassing": Bound Notes D, box 1, Gerold Frank papers, Manuscripts and Archives Division, New York Public Library.

89   "marihuana[*sic*]-happy gunmen," "ex-GIs," "[w]e are on the marihuana [*sic*]," "mumbling," "poor child . . . I guess this makes her": *New York Daily News*, December 21, 1949.

89   "started taking up with John Barrymore," "No one had ever talked back": Barrymore and Frank, 254.

89   "home run [after] two errors" Barrymore and Frank, 249–50.

90   "In God's green earth," "a couple of equestrians," "cocked at a similar devastating angle": Bound Notes G, box 1, Gerold Frank papers, Manuscripts and Archives Division, New York Public Library.

90   "trigger-happy young Texan": *Bangor Daily News*, June 8, 1950.

90   "dipsomania": *Olean Times Herald*, June 2, 1950.

90   "the ordinary girl in business and social life," "head start," "plenty of work": Fraser et al., *The Charming Woman*, 36.

90   "delightful[ly] throaty": *Buffalo Evening News*, February 7, 1942.

91   "Be natural. Be yourself": Fraser et al., 83.

91   "Diana Barrymore has a trick of switching her eyes": Frank Vreeland, *Opportunities in Acting: Stage, Screen, Radio, Television* (New York: Vocational Guidance Manuals, 1946).

91   "hadn't been playing much tennis lately," "blonde model," "call girl," "I don't demand money": *New York Daily News*, March 12, 1950.

91   "prostitute," "lavishly furnished": *New York Daily News*, October 29, 1950.

91   "women simply like[d] to support him": *New York Daily News*, December 19, 1950.

91-93 "Jules, you talked to us . . ." through "and your money is safe": Bound Notes E, box 1, Gerold Frank papers, Manuscripts and Archives Division, New York Public Library.

93   "to discourage hoarding and combat communism": *Lewiston Sun-Journal*, August 3, 1950.

93-94 "I think I'm going have a lot of trouble" through "you're absolutely wonderful": Bound Notes E, box 1, Gerold Frank papers, Manuscripts and Archives Division, New York Public Library.

94   "I failed Robin": Barrymore and Frank, 268.

95   "there were 97 photographers there": Bound Notes B, box 1, Gerold Frank papers, Manuscripts and Archives Division, New York Public Library.

95   "white slavery": *New York Daily News*, October 29, 1950.

95   "before someone else does": Leonard Marcus, Leonard, *Awakened by the Moon*, 252.

95   "BARRYMORE EX DEAD AT 60": paraphrase of several headlines, such as in *New York Daily News*, November 6, 1950.

96   "the tall actress with the Byronic hairbob": *New York Times*, November 6, 1950.

96   "socialistic socialite": *Louisville Courier-Journal*, November 6, 1950.

96   "an extraordinary girl": Bound Notes E, box 1, Gerold Frank papers, Manuscripts and Archives Division, New York Public Library.

96   "Michael was a flamboyant, bombastic, most unusual person": Bound Notes A, box 1, Gerold Frank papers, Manuscripts and Archives Division, New York Public Library.

96   "I've had a few myself," "this is not going to be": Barrymore and Frank, 272.

96   "everyone I've ever loved": Barrymore and Frank, 364.

96   "swallow's-wing eyebrows": Barrymore and Frank, 272.

96 "I've never seen such a beautiful thing," "A Catholic priest came to her home," "reeked of Newport and good breeding," "could let down her hair": Bound Notes B, box 1, Gerold Frank papers, Manuscripts and Archives Division, New York Public Library.

96 "something of my own life": Barrymore and Frank, 273.

96-97 "collapsed, actually . . . watching that hole swallow her mother": Bound Notes B, box 1, Gerold Frank papers, Manuscripts and Archives Division, New York Public Library.

97 "[Mother] thought she was successful": Bound Notes E, box 1, Gerold Frank papers, Manuscripts and Archives Division, New York Public Library.

97 "more valuable to her than life itself": Bound Notes B, box 1, Gerold Frank papers, Manuscripts and Archives Division, New York Public Library.

CHAPTER 7: BOB AND MUZZY

98 "Hello children. . . . I'm absolutely green and untried": *Boston Globe*, March 28, 1951.

98 "back-breaking assignment": *Variety*, March 17, 1951.

98 "hitching up": *Variety*, May 16, 1951.

98 "dubious vocalizing": *Variety*, March 14, 1951.

98 "I'm not very good": *San Francisco Examiner*, September 20, 1951.

98 "This is the first time": *New York Buffalo News*, April 18, 1951.

98 "satirist and singer": *Pittsburgh Press*, February 27, 1951.

98-99 "every bit as volatile," "let's get going," "[h]e sounds like he needs a lot of rehearsing": *Pittsburgh Post-Gazette*, May 30, 1951.

99 "if they so much as rattled a single dish": Plummer, *In Spite of Myself*, 48.

99 "lengthy long-distance calls": Barrymore and Frank, 281.

99 "'they say I'm a buffoon'": Barrymore and Frank, 282.

99 "nauseating ad-libs," "she tried to sing a hillbillly number": *Dayton Journal-Herald*, June 20, 1951.

99 "off-script remarks": *New York Daily News*, July 17, 1951.

99 "beginning to pull a B.S. Pulley [*sic*]": *Brownsville Herald*, July 19, 1951.

99 "John let the family down": *Bangor Daily News*, July 30, 1951.

99 "suddenly freed prisoner[s]": Barrymore and Frank, 284.

99 "cheap spectacle": Barrymore and Frank, 285.

99 "I said, 'Diana, you're letting this thing prey'": Bound Notes B, box 1, Gerold Frank papers, Manuscripts and Archives Division, New York Public Library.

100 "brilliant characterization," "exasperated," "brash personality": *The Age* (Melbourne, Victoria, Australia), November 10, 1951.

100 Dec. 25, 1951 diary excerpt, "offered to put up a $1500 bond," "personal triumph": Robert Wilcox diary, 1951-52, box 2, Gerold Frank papers, Manuscripts and Archives Division, New York Public Library.

100 "star[ing] blankly at each other," "superb drunken clowning": *The Age* (Melbourne, Victoria, Australia), December 31, 1951.

100 "[S]he becomes bored very quickly": Bound Notes B, box 1, Gerold Frank papers, Manuscripts and Archives Division, New York Public Library.

100 "[T]he 'director,' and I use that word with a great deal of care": Robert Wilcox diary, 1951-52, box 2, Gerold Frank papers, Manuscripts and Archives Division, New York Public Library.

100   "temperamental outbursts": *New York Daily News*, January 12, 1952.
100   "salty," "offended the audience," "many walked out,": *St. Joseph News-Press*, February 13, 1952.
100-101 Friday, January 4, 1952, Saturday, January 5, 1952, January 7, 1952, diary excerpts: Robert Wilcox diary, 1951–52, box 2, Gerold Frank papers, Manuscripts and Archives Division, New York Public Library.
101   "All I want to do is sleep": *St. Joseph News-Press*, February 13, 1952.
102   "We spent wildly": Barrymore and Frank, 289.
102   "never going back," "fifty years behind the times," "it's all right for a night club [*sic*] master of ceremonies": *Honolulu Star-Bulletin*, March 10, 1952.
102   "Why are people so mean to me": *Boston Globe*, April 24, 1955.
102-103 "Let me say honestly" article excerpt, "discipline, guidance, [and] encouragement," "As I explained, the editors found much of the material," "kindest personal regards": Bound Notes C, box 1, Gerold Frank papers, Manuscripts and Archives Division, New York Public Library.
103   "hospital operating room": Barrymore and Frank, 295.
103   "pinned-up shrine," "Hollywood mores and backlot intrigue": Howard Hampton, "BULLSEYE: Howard Hampton on Vincente Minnelli's *The Bad and the Beautiful* (1952)," *Artforum*, November 21, 2019, https://www.artforum.com/film/ howard-hampton-on-vincente-minnelli-s-the-bad-and-the-beautiful-1952–81335.
103   "an unhappy hangover of family fame," "irritated and sometimes disgusted": *Philadelphia Inquirer*, June 29, 1947.
103   "radiant," "vital [and] electrifying": Barrymore and Frank, 296.
104   "You know, I did Juliet" through "clippings or myself": Bound Notes D, box 1, Gerold Frank papers, Manuscripts and Archives Division, New York Public Library.
104   "Good evening, ladies and gentlemen." "Now, tell me, Miss Paterno": Barrymore and Frank, 304.
104   "seesaw in hell": Barrymore and Frank, 305.
104   "skin and bones, [she] weighed less than 100 pounds . . . I used to get up and feed her": Bound Notes F, box 1, Gerold Frank papers, Manuscripts and Archives Division, New York Public Library.
105   "a wife, two children and a Buick": *New York Daily News*, June 10, 1953.
105   "One night I hadn't come home" Bound Notes D, box 1, Gerold Frank papers, Manuscripts and Archives Division, New York Public Library.
105   "professional vagabond" Barrymore and Frank, 312.
105   "John Howard with a Bramwell Fletcher technique": Barrymore and Frank, 312.
105   "Noël Coward said women should be struck": *New York Daily News*, June 10, 1953.
105   "sexual pervert": S. A. August C. Kempff, "Albert Frabotta, aka," Chicago, IL: Federal Bureau of Investigation, Nov 10, 1963.
105   "peddled heroin": folder "1950–1955," box 1, Gerold Frank papers, Manuscripts and Archives Division, New York Public Library.
105   "the whole plot of my life is now twisting and turning": Bound Notes G, box 1, Gerold Frank papers, Manuscripts and Archives Division, New York Public Library.
106   "There are big names involved," "special vice exhibitions," "red-headed starlet from the coast": *New York Daily News*, March 23, 1953.
106   "one of the screen's hottest young musical comedy stars" *Cincinnati Enquirer*, March 30, 1953.

106 "human weakness," "transcontinental vice procurer," "psychopath": *San Francisco Examiner*, March 27, 1953.

106 "schizophrenic tendencies": *New York Daily News*, March 27, 1953.

106 "Your lover boy just came through it": Barrymore and Frank, 321.

106 "The big fight started over three simple lines," "it would be awfully messy," "rare confusion": *New York Daily News*, June 10, 1953.

106-107 "I suppose Bob was in the right," "Isn't that dreadful," "she keeps me": *New York Daily News*, June 10, 1953.

107 "That man broke up my home," "amicable and decent," "after all, darling," "very cagey guy": *New York Daily News*, June 11, 1953.

107 "the Grand Guignol," "horsewhipped," "That man will do you in," "[b]efore she could remove her coat": Barrymore and Frank, 327.

107 "live volcano": *Des Moines Tribune*, May 4, 1939.

107 "He's the kind of man who will get up," "great kindness": *Boston Globe*, April 24, 1955.

107 "Hold[ing] the aerial": Bound Notes B, box 1, Gerold Frank papers, Manuscripts and Archives Division, New York Public Library.

107 "Poor darling, every time anything happened": Bound Notes D, box 1, Gerold Frank papers, Manuscripts and Archives Division, New York Public Library.

108 "his fist crashed into my face": Barrymore and Frank, 331.

108 "lacerations, a shiner," "love tokens," "Don't be silly, darling": *Los Angeles Daily News*, August 12, 1953.

108 "illiterate foreign peasant," "vile and indecent things": *New York Daily News*, December 11, 1953.

108 "Dear Muzzy, you seem to think": Robert Wilcox, letter to Diana Barrymore, September 17, 1953, Diana Barrymore papers, New York Public Library.

108 "Was I trying to hurt myself?" "gentleman callers," "[they] would order food": folder "1950–1955," box 1, Gerold Frank papers, Manuscripts and Archives Division, New York Public Library.

109 "I used to love Diana. Now I dismiss her": Bound Notes A, box 1, Gerold Frank papers, Manuscripts and Archives Division, New York Public Library.

109 "minus lingerie and not caring who knew it": *Pittsburgh Post-Gazette*, September 15, 1953.

109 "Years earlier, my doctor had warned me": Bound Notes C, box 1, Gerold Frank papers, Manuscripts and Archives Division, New York Public Library.

109 "She had absolutely no self-respect": Bound Notes A, box 1, Gerold Frank papers, Manuscripts and Archives Division, New York Public Library.

109-110 "It happens to be urgent," "I do need a Broadway show,": Diana Barrymore, letter to Leonard Thomas Jr., undated, circa 1954, Diana Barrymore papers, New York Public Library.

110 "Simply dressed in slacks" through "sweetness and other qualities": Bound Notes H, box 1, Gerold Frank papers, Manuscripts and Archives Division, New York Public Library.

110 "the damndest, longest, dullest," "lost a bet": *Tampa Tribune*, October 6, 1946.

110 "audition[ed] for General Artists," "some strange Club de Nuit": Diana Barrymore, letter to Leonard Thomas Jr., undated, circa 1954, Diana Barrymore papers, The New York Public Library.

110 "spitfire prostitute": *Variety*, August 4, 1954.

111   "and kept it up through the end of the play": Bound Notes H, box 1, Gerold Frank papers, Manuscripts and Archives Division, New York Public Library.

111   "explod[ing] upon the stage": *Wilmington Morning News*, July 28, 1954.

111   "more like a police blotter than a playbill": *New York Daily News*, June 3, 1956.

111   "a deeply cut flaming red evening gown": *Miami Herald*, August 8, 1954.

111   "up to him to get the wheels rolling," "probably an idiot," "no gentleman sticks around": *San Francisco Examiner*, August 8, 1954.

111   "I said, 'You know I would'": Bound Notes H, box 1, Gerold Frank papers, Manuscripts and Archives Division, New York Public Library.

111   "as delicate and subdued as a circus calliope": *Philadelphia Inquirer*, January 18, 1955.

111   "definitely not Broadway": *Hartford Courant*, February 11, 1955.

111   "Diana has one thing her father bequeathed her": *Hartford Courant*, February 11, 1955.

111   "more than a twinge," "leering trash": *Chicago Tribune*, November 29, 1954.

111   "I thought, my uncle is dead": Barrymore and Frank, 347.

111   "Nobody's trying to fool anybody": *Chicago Tribune*, November 26, 1954.

112   "rough," "a snob," "little hardships": Bob's diary entry, December 1, 1954.

112   "a small Christmas tree," "[r]egardless of the bitch she may tend to be": Bound Notes H, box 1, Gerold Frank papers, Manuscripts and Archives Division, New York Public Library.

112   "embarrassingly bawdy": *Detroit Free Press*, February. 21, 1955.

112   "I was mad about that fascinating woman," "she started telling me how to make up": *Boston Globe*, April 24, 1955.

112   "because you have spent so many years": Barrymore and Frank, 349.

112   "we decided to be friends no matter what": *Boston Globe*, April 24, 1955.

112   "entirely different," "kind, gentle yet hard": Bound Notes B, box 1, Gerold Frank papers, Manuscripts and Archives Division, New York Public Library.

112   "the poor man's Tallulah": Davis, *Just Making Movies* 9–10.

112   "but Diana doesn't want to be Diana": Bound Notes B, box 1, Gerold Frank papers, Manuscripts and Archives Division, New York Public Library.

112   "general restraint of a Jerry Lewis": *Philadelphia Inquirer*, January 18, 1955.

112   "I wasn't tight but I wasn't sober": Bound Notes G, box 1, Gerold Frank papers, Manuscripts and Archives Division, New York Public Library.

112   "sell[ing] the Barrymore name": Barrymore and Frank, 351.

112-113 "blue jackets and yellow jackets," "a succotash to oblivion," "double shot of Four Roses": Barrymore and Frank, 353.

113   "I only tried to calm my nerves,": *Boston Globe*, April 28, 1955.

113   "breathing heavily": *New York Times*, April 29, 1955.

113   "[a]nyone else probably would have died": *Boston Globe*, April 28, 1955.

CHAPTER 8: TOO MUCH, TOO LOUDLY

114   "stock farce," "like commuters hurrying," "limited in scope": *Pittsburgh Post-Gazette*, May 18, 1954.

114   "where even the obscenities on the walls": *Life*, June 29, 1959.

114   "rather personable": *Waterloo Courier*, April 21, 1972.

114   "His directness and enthusiasm excited me": Barrymore and Frank, 359.

114   "many of the mannerisms," "[A]l eyes were on her": *Akron Beacon Journal*, June 9,
         1955.

114   "in an alcoholic ward": Barrymore and Frank, 360.

115   "Does she really enjoy the men?": Bound Notes A, box 1, Gerold Frank papers,
         Manuscripts and Archives Division, New York Public Library.

115   "When I slept with men": 1938–39 Notes, book A, box 2, Gerold Frank papers,
         Manuscripts and Archives Division, The New York Public Library.

115   "liver disease": *Buffalo News*, June 11, 1955.

115   "breakdown": *Variety*, November 9, 1955.

115   "suspected heart attack": *The Age* (Melbourne, Victoria, Australia), October 28, 1955.

115   "ready to go": *Variety*, November 9, 1955.

115   "How does one explain such things": Barrymore and Frank, 373.

115   "a fiasco," "The Last Straw," "there will probably be no more two for one legits":
         Variety, November 9, 1955.

116   "Miss Barrymore's cancellation of her contract": *Little Hut*, aka *Bamboo Bed*: claim
         against Diana Barrymore and other company correspondence, 1955–57; Actors'
         Equity Association Records, WAG 011, Box 295, Folder 1, Tamiment Library/Robert F.
         Wagner Labor Archives, New York University.

116   "My immediate thought" "shambles": Bound Notes H, box 1, Gerold Frank papers,
         Manuscripts and Archives Division, New York Public Library.

116   "monstrously untidy": Bound Notes D, box 1, Gerold Frank papers, Manuscripts and
         Archives Division, New York Public Library.

116   "pathetic, absolutely beat": Bound Notes H, box 1, Gerold Frank papers, Manuscripts
         and Archives Division, New York Public Library.

116   "I saw myself already on the skids": Bound Notes G, box 1, Gerold Frank papers,
         Manuscripts and Archives Division, New York Public Library.

116-117 "She went on Monday, July 4," "an outstanding performance," "[She] starts from A
         and works through Z," "She has a schedule": Bound Notes H, box 1, Gerold Frank
         papers, Manuscripts and Archives Division, New York Public Library.

117   "Either I am talking or telephoning or drinking or moving, or if nothing's happening
         I've got to pick up a telephone and say hi," "I can't relax": folder "1950–1955," box 1,
         Gerold Frank papers, Manuscripts and Archives Division, New York Public Library.

117   "click[ed]," "and she almost goes berserk": Bound Notes H, box 1, Gerold Frank
         papers, Manuscripts and Archives Division, New York Public Library.

117   "What do records do to me? . . . the actress [comes] out": Bound Notes F, box 1,
         Gerold Frank papers, Manuscripts and Archives Division, New York Public Library.

117-118 "I said don't do it, the boy is very Catholic," "Well, some morning when he gets up,"
         "perfectly guilty," "There was a difference": Bound Notes H, box 1, Gerold Frank
         papers, Manuscripts and Archives Division, New York Public Library.

118   "earnestly, seriously and well" through "only in the love-making scene": Harold L.
         Cail, "Diana Barrymore Is Standout In K'Port's 'Glad Tidings,'" *Portland Press Herald*,
         August 4, 1955.

118   "I couldn't sit up, I had to lie on my back": folder "1950–1955," box 1, Gerold Frank
         papers, Manuscripts and Archives Division, New York Public Library.

118-119 "cured" "while she had [a] drink her [her] other hand" through "amazed": Bound
         Notes H, box 1, Gerold Frank papers, Manuscripts and Archives Division, New York
         Public Library.

119   "There are two Diana Barrymores": folder "1950–1955," box 1, Gerold Frank papers, Manuscripts and Archives Division, New York Public Library.

119   "Oh please . . . I can take one or two" "flipped": Bound Notes H, box 1, Gerold Frank papers, Manuscripts and Archives Division, New York Public Library.

119-120 "[H]e said, 'I met you when you were sixteen" through "champagne, then stingers": folder "1950–1955," box 1, Gerold Frank papers, Manuscripts and Archives Division, New York Public Library.

120   "[Diana] said she was going to be married": Bound Notes H, box 1, Gerold Frank papers, Manuscripts and Archives Division, New York Public Library.

120-121 "to hell with love" through "I just said, 'My God, what have I done to deserve this": folder "1950–1955," box 1, Gerold Frank papers, Manuscripts and Archives Division, New York Public Library.

121   "[what] took your father sixty years to do": Barrymore and Frank, 372.

122   "rock to cling to": Barrymore and Frank, 375.

122   "[H]e can afford to put his little sister away": *New York Newsday*, January 12, 1956.

122   "never want[ed] to see a sleeping pill again": *New York Daily News*, June 3, 1956.

122   "licked alcoholism": *Springfield Reader and Press*, February 16, 1956.

122   "I spent January and February": *Miami Herald*, June 17, 1956.

122   "limp-haired, unsteady, disheveled woman": *Life*, Jun 29, 1959.

122-123 "shabby Hell's Kitchen hotel" through "But I didn't want not to die": letter dated June 6, 1955, from Gerold Frank to editor Howard Cady at Henry Holt & Co., Warner Bros. Archives, School of Cinematic Arts, University of Southern California.

123   "I lied to him," "oh, you son of a bitch," "people seem to think," "why must he do Zsa Zsa," "the world's most eminent": *Life*, June 29, 1959.

123   "rich with incident and utterly lacking in respect for chronology": Ted Bonnet, "You Can't Keep Good Actor Down, John Barrymore Proves Once More." *Knoxville News-Sentinel*, December 12, 1937.

123   "It is apparent that if you didn't drink" through "I'm glad she had the guts": GFP 1950–55.

123   "atrocity," "stumble[d] badly": Jefferson, *Phylon*, no. 3 (1956).

123   "deplorable": *Variety*, May 30, 1956.

123-124 "Miss Diana Barrymore certainly succeeded," "Darling . . . Daddy's ghost": *New York Daily News*, June 3, 1956.

124   "strikingly modern": Fiona Gregory, *Histrionic Heroines*, 117.

124   "You will observe that a cute was made . . . I trust you're having a ball": letter dated February 1, 1957, to Gerold Frank from Margery Darrell, book editor for *Look* magazine, Folder "Correspondence A," box 1, Gerold Frank papers, Manuscripts and Archives Division, New York Public Library.

124   "I am sorry, too . . . [u]mgrammatical, but exciting": letter dated February 4, 1957, to Margery Darrell from Gerold Frank, Folder "Correspondence A," box 1, Gerold Frank papers, Manuscripts and Archives Division, New York Public Library.

124   "the possibility of Diana's appearance . . . published April 8 by Henry Holt & Company!": letter dated February 8, 1957, to Gerold Frank from Betty Ringler, publicity for Henry Holt & Co. Folder "Correspondence A," box 1, Gerold Frank papers, Manuscripts and Archives Division, The New York Public Library.

124   "There must be a lot of cringing" "For Diana, bless her heart": Luther Nichols, "BOOKS: Diana Barrymore: Her Story Is a Tale of Total Wreckage," *San Francisco Examiner*, April 7, 1957.

124   "Hollywood doesn't like *Too Much, Too Soon*": *Photoplay*, July 1957.
124   "'Too Much, Too Late—Too Bad,'" "'Long Day's Journey into Oblivion'": *Chicago Tribune*, April 12, 1957.
124   "much to tell": *Chicago Tribune*, January 31, 1957.
124   "too much, too loudly": *Arizona Republic*, March 31, 1957.
124   "cost[ing] her the few friends she had left": *Miami Herald*, April 8, 1957.
125   "Diana's a total stranger to me": *Pittsburgh Press*, February 23, 1957.
125   "why should all this dirty linen," "the book is full of sex": *Detroit Free Press*, April 7, 1957.
125   "dramatic rehab," "Diana Barrymore had neither the moral fiber": *Tucson Citizen*, April 6. 1957.
125   "the sort of lurid book": *Washington Post and Times-Herald*, April 7, 1957.
125   "because it isn't until we take the full responsibility": Day Tuttle, letter to Diana Barrymore, April 12, 1957, Diana Barrymore papers, New York Public Library.
125   "the 'fatal flaw' in this": *Oakland Tribune*, April 7, 1957.
125   "a cheap, cruel piece of exhibitionism," "tune of jingling cash registers": *Chicago Tribune*, April 7, 1957.
125   "admire[d] her guts" *New York Daily News*, April 16, 1957.
125   "an admirable collaborator," "compelling": *Roanoke Times*, April 7, 1957.
125   "shocker," "thoughtless genius of a father": Mel Heimer, "My New York," *Beaver Dam Daily Citizen*, April 6, 1957.
125   "a detestable book": *St. Joseph News-Press*, April 29, 1957.
125   "setting yourself up as a clay pigeon": Battelle, Phyllis. "Assignment: America—Gypsy Rose Lee Is Distressed by Lack of Big Sins for Her Autobiography," *Springfield Daily News*, April 9, 1957.
125   "spiritually naked," "wistful and plaintive": William F. McDermott, "McDermott on Barrymores: Relationships Often Confused; Diana's Book Bares Her Soul to Point of Embarrassment," *Cleveland Plain Dealer*, May 10, 1957.
125   "I didn't set out to point a moral," "writing it has been a cleansing process": *Cincinnati Enquirer*, April 30, 1957.
125   "I don't think there ever can be as many dark moments": *Los Angeles Times*, April 23, 1957.
126   "I know you'll succeed now": Olga Dziedzic, undated note to Diana Barrymore, circa 1956, Diana Barrymore papers, New York Public Library.
126   "not very pretty but at least I can face it": *Orlando Sentinel*, July 29, 1956.
126   "virtualy a geometric theorem," "the public should have a chance": Michael Wallace, "Who's Between Me and You?," *Variety*, January 8, 1958.
126-127 "After a promising start on Broadway" etc. unless noted: *The Mike Wallace Interview*, season 1, episode 12, "Diana Barrymore," July 14, 1957. Accessed February 2, 2021 via The Mike Wallace Interview Collection, Digital Collections, Harry Ransom Center, University of Texas at Austin, https://hrc.contentdm.oclc.org/digital/collection/p15878coll90/id/19/.
126   "if a former glamour girl is down and out": *Time*, April 15, 1957.
127   "a sort of old-maid British spinster": Sikov, *Dark Victory*, 369.
127   "too stringent": *Orlando Sentinel*, July 29, 1956.
127   "I fell for Octavio as soon as I met him": *San Francisco Examiner*, May 16, 1957.
127   "immensely likeable," "sardonic self-appraisal": *New York Times*, July 15, 1957.

127   "Miss Barrymore has recently sold her biography": *Little Hut*, aka *Bamboo Bed*: claim against Diana Barrymore and other company correspondence, 1955–57, Actors' Equity Association Records, WAG 011, Box 295, Folder 1; Tamiment Library/Robert F. Wagner Labor Archives, New York University.

127   "look in the mirror": *Make Up Your Mind* (Audition), August 20, 1951, box 47, folder 12, Arthur Henley Papers, Collection Number 08663, American Heritage Center, University of Wyoming.

127-128 "I was on the wagon for three months": folder "1950–1955," box 1, Gerold Frank papers, Manuscripts and Archives Division, New York Public Library.

128   "John hardly knew Daddy": Akron *Beacon-Journal*, May 6, 1957.

128   "combine her great inherited talents": *Amarillo Globe-Times*, April 16, 1957.

128   "Aren't any of you gentleman enough to help a woman being slugged?": *Detroit Free Press*, December 24, 1956.

128   "Diana isn't out of the woods": *New York Daily News*, Jun 3, 1956.

128-129 "a person active as an actor" through "does not phonetically suggest Bramwell Fletcher": interoffice memo dated March 25, 1957, *Too Much, Too Soon* (1958) collection, Warner Bros. Archives, School of Cinematic Arts, University of Southern California.

129   "emerges as a decent human" through "the blame is not attached to him": letter from Gerold Frank to Morris Ebenstein, February 22, 1957, *Too Much, Too Soon* (1958) collection, Warner Bros. Archives, School of Cinematic Arts, University of Southern California.

129   "The first lover" through "Tuxedo Park," "It's a sure thing Tony Duke's mother": letter to Steve Trilling from ? dated December 11, 1956, *Too Much, Too Soon* (1958) collection, Warner Bros. Archives, School of Cinematic Arts, University of Southern California.

129-130 "analysis" through "And after that . . . ?": Analysis of Diana Barrymore by Dr. Marshall D. Schechter, MD and psychiatrist, transcript of interview by Irving Wallace, March 18, 1957, *Too Much, Too Soon* (1958) collection, Warner Bros. Archives, School of Cinematic Arts, University of Southern California.

130   "[T]his is the story of a girl's search for love and affection": interoffice memo dated March 27, 1957, to Henry Blanke from Gerold Frank and Irving Wallace, *Too Much, Too Soon* (1958) collection, Warner Bros. Archives, School of Cinematic Arts, University of Southern California.

130   "Diana's delirious dream": undated *Too Much, Too Soon* step outline page, *Too Much, Too Soon* (1958) collection, Warner Bros. Archives, School of Cinematic Arts, University of Southern California.

130   "not emerge as a girl of low moral character": interoffice memo dated March 27, 1957, from Blanke to Wallace and Frank, *Too Much, Too Soon* (1958) collection, Warner Bros. Archives, School of Cinematic Arts, University of Southern California.

130   "Are you trying to aim another blockbuster at the Legion of Decency?": interoffice memo dated March 28, 1957, from Trilling to Finlay McDermid, *Too Much, Too Soon* (1958) collection, Warner Bros. Archives, School of Cinematic Arts, University of Southern California.

130-131 "[H]er relationship with Farrell, as presently portrayed" through "thinking that the girl is trying": "Memo for the files" dated April 2, 1957, synopsis of meeting between Vizzard, Healy, McDermid, Blanke, Wallace, and Frank. *Too Much, Too Soon* (1958) collection, Warner Bros. Archives, School of Cinematic Arts, University of Southern California.

131   "if they took out all of [the] things I objected to": *Santa Barbara News-Press*, September 28, 1957.

131   "Mr. Vea and I wish you to know": undated letter from Mrs. Edith C. Vea to Warner Bros. Studios, *Too Much, Too Soon* (1958) collection, Warner Bros. Archives, School of Cinematic Arts, University of Southern California.

131   "she tries to be a vamp": Sheila O'Malley, "TCM Diary: Dorothy Malone Knows," *Film Comment*, July 31, 2018, https://www.filmcomment.com/blog/tcm-diary-dorothy -malone-knows/.

132   "reformed drunkard" through "resists the temptation": "Memo for the files" dated April 2, 1957, synopsis of meeting between Vizzard, Healy, McDermid, Blanke, Wallace, and Frank, *Too Much, Too Soon* (1958) collection, Warner Bros. Archives, School of Cinematic Arts, University of Southern California.

132   "an acceptable screenplay": interoffice memo dated August 29, 1957, from Art Napoleon to Walter MacEwen, *Too Much, Too Soon* (1958) collection, Warner Bros. Archives, School of Cinematic Arts, University of Southern California.

132   "sensitive and intelligent," "bewildering maze": interoffice memo dated August 6, 1957, from Art and Jo Napoleon to Walter MacEwen, *Too Much, Too Soon* (1958) collection, Warner Bros. Archives, School of Cinematic Arts, University of Southern California.

132   "[W]e want to get the feeling": miscellaneous notes dated August 8, 1957, *Too Much, Too Soon* (1958) collection, Warner Bros. Archives, School of Cinematic Arts, University of Southern California.

132   "We have found four burlesque queens": miscellaneous notes by Carl Milliken Jr., dated November 7, 1957, *Too Much, Too Soon* (1958) collection, Warner Bros. Archives, School of Cinematic Arts, University of Southern California.

132   "[T]here is [also] a burlesque queen": miscellaneous notes by Carl Milliken Jr., dated November 8, 1957, *Too Much, Too Soon* (1958) collection, Warner Bros. Archives, School of Cinematic Arts, University of Southern California.

133   "stupidly thought she was dead": miscellaneous notes by Carl Milliken Jr., dated October 31, 1957, *Too Much, Too Soon* (1958) collection, Warner Bros. Archives, School of Cinematic Arts, University of Southern California.

133   "Please be advised": letter from Elaine Barrie Barrymore dated September 19, 1957 to Warner Bros. Studios, *Too Much, Too Soon* (1958) collection, Warner Bros. Archives, School of Cinematic Arts, University of Southern California.

133   "I have been trying to forget those old days": Harrison Carroll, "Diana's Ex-Mate Hires Lawyer, May Sue Over Movie," *Los Angeles Herald-Express*, November 11, 1957.

133   "he ha[d] been in the Tombs," "[i]t is hardly necessary to add": interoffice memo from dated April 12, 1957, from Morris Ebenstein to Henry Blanke, *Too Much, Too Soon* (1958) collection, Warner Bros. Archives, School of Cinematic Arts, University of Southern California.

133   "since he had become a notoriously seedy": interoffice memo from dated May 2, 1957, from Morris Ebenstein to Henry Blanke, *Too Much, Too Soon* (1958) collection, Warner Bros. Archives, School of Cinematic Arts, University of Southern California.

133   "anyone made any overtures": interoffice memo dated August 29, 1957, from Art Napoleon to Walter MacEwen, *Too Much, Too Soon* (1958) collection, Warner Bros. Archives, School of Cinematic Arts, University of Southern California.

133   "He seems to think that to snort": interoffice memo dated August 21, 1957, from Art and Jo Napoleon to Steve Trilling, *Too Much, Too Soon* (1958) collection, Warner Bros. Archives, School of Cinematic Arts, University of Southern California.

134   "They've come up with a dilly": *Arizona Republic*, September 28, 1957.

134   "I wanted to show a man with a heart": Flynn, *Wicked*, 427.

134   "[W]e cam really have a hell of a good picture": interoffice memo dated January 3, 1958, from Art and Jo Napoleon to Steve Trilling, *Too Much, Too Soon* (1958) collection, Warner Bros. Archives, School of Cinematic Arts, University of Southern California.

134   "an objectionable sex suggestive flavor," "no silhouette," "unduly gruesome": interoffice memo dated November 6, 1957, from Geoffrey Shurlock to Jack Warner, *Too Much, Too Soon* (1958) collection, Warner Bros. Archives, School of Cinematic Arts, University of Southern California.

134-135   "[T]he burlesque involves the whole sense of the story," "*Her drinking*—whether we like it or not": interoffice memo dated January 3, 1958, from Art and Jo Napoleon to Steve Trilling, *Too Much, Too Soon* (1958) collection, Warner Bros. Archives, School of Cinematic Arts, University of Southern California.

135   "happily defunct," "because of the present picture": interoffice memo dated November 14, 1957, from Carl Milliken Jr. to Jo Napoleon, *Too Much, Too Soon* (1958) collection, Warner Bros. Archives, School of Cinematic Arts, University of Southern California.

136   "Don't be a boy," "Why not? They haven't proved," "[t]wo old men who've flown pretty high," "You're Loved Lionel Barrymore!": *Too Much, Too Soon*, directed by Art Napoleon (1958, Warner Bros.).

137-138   "[Director] Charlie Snow is impressed," "Diana gets no comforting words": synopsis of *Too Much, Too Soon*, *Too Much, Too Soon* (1958) collection, Warner Bros. Archives, School of Cinematic Arts, University of Southern California.

135   "John wouldn't even shake [Danton's] hand": *Palm Spring Desert Sun*, February 14, 1992.

138   " Undaring and even unsurprising," "scenes of savage disintegration": *New York Times*, May 10, 1958.

138   "winsome, earnest": *New York Times*, May 10, 1958.

138   "pathetic, true-confession type story" through "one of the highlights of the picture": *New York Daily News*, May 10, 1958.

138   "A sordid, unattractive tale": *Chicago Tribune*, June 10, 1958.

138   "A libel on the memory of the Barrymores," "resented," "mortified," "excellent": *Los Angeles Times*, May 16, 1958.

138-139   "Mr. Flynn rolls around for more than an hour": *Evening Star* (Washington, DC), May 16, 1958.

139   "stark, uninspirational tale": Ward W. Marsh, "BARRYMORES AND BOOZE—Diana Tells Her All but Gladly." *Cleveland Plain-Dealer*, June 5, 1958.

139   "the flicker's highlight": *Buffalo Courier Express*, May 11, 1958.

139   "never should have been made": *Buffalo Courier Express*, May 31, 1958.

139   "[I]t may make a lot of moviegoers feel": *Time*, May 19, 1958.

139   "a dreary affair" "a sparse audience": "Audience Not Too Fascinated by 'Too Much, Too Soon,'" *Louisville Courier-Journal*, May 31, 1958.

139   "oddly touching": *New York Post*, Mar 18, 2010.

139   "a much better actress": *Louisville Courier-Journal*, May 31, 1958.

139   "lewd and misleading": *Miami News*, May 28, 1958.

139   "WHAT SCANDAL ENDED," "THE HOTTEST HUNK OF FILM": ads in several
           newspapers, such as *New York Daily News*, May 9, 1958.

139   "They've just laid it on": *Miami News*, May 28, 1958.

139   "I may have been a bad girl": *New York Daily News*, May 23, 1956.

139-140   "vicarious pleasure" through "a million sycophants": Phyllis Battelle, "Assignment:
           America—Diana Barrymore Saw What Was Wrong and Now Everything Is Fine,"
           Springfield Daily News, July 29, 1958.

140   "perfectly dreadful": *Miami Herald*, May 30, 1957.

140   "The broad is really trying," "no-cal orange juice": *New York Newsday*, February 14,
           1958.

CHAPTER 9: THE BOY

141   "fine young star," "acting recognition": *Windsor Star* (Windsor, Ontario, Canada),
           March 5, 1959.

141   "Her return as a woman of dignity": *Chicago Daily News*, referenced in *Rochester
           Democrat and Chronicle*, April 19, 1959.

141   "She was never really pretty": *Variety*, September 17, 1958.

141   "unique trick": *New York Times*, August 14, 2002.

141   "hatchet man": "Karyn 'Cookie' Kupcinet," FindADeath.com, https://findadeath.
           com/karyn-cookie-kupcinet/.

141   "gracious," "tireless champion of the arts": *Chicago Tribune*, June 17, 2001.

141-142   "I ether love a person": Bound Notes C, box 1, Gerold Frank papers, Manuscripts
           and Archives Division, The New York Public Library.

142   "Violla is the only one who understands": Diana Barrymore, undated letter to Essee
           Kupcinet, private collection, courtesy Sue Kupcinet, used with permission.

142   "Diana had always wanted a sister": Irv Kupcinet and Paul Neimark, *Kup*, 133.

142   "in all the world to have found a sister": Diana Barrymore, telegram to Essee Kupcinet.
           November 16, 1959, private collection, courtesy Sue Kupcinet, used with permission.

142   "singing protégé": *Detroit Free Press*, October 17, 1958.

142   "I like to mess around with paints": Bound Notes C, box 1, Gerold Frank papers,
           Manuscripts and Archives Division, New York Public Library.

142   "[I'm] no longer a has-been," "radiant with health and energy": *Miami Herald*, June
           1, 1959.

142   "Honey, you've no idea": *Philadelphia Inquirer*, April 19, 1959.

142   "I'm crazy to do a musical": Bound Notes C, box 1, Gerold Frank papers, Manuscripts
           and Archives Division, New York Public Library.

142   "He stood up and yelled 'Bravo' until hoarse": Diana Barrymore, letter to Essee
           Kupcinet, undated, circa 1959, private collection, courtesy Sue Kupcinet, used with
           permission.

142   "Champion actress," "[r]emember Tennessee Williams": Violla Rubber, letter to Diana
           Barrymore, February 12, 1959, Diana Barrymore Papers, New York Public Library.

143   "[S]he has the Barrymore madness and power": Lahr, *Mad Pilgrimage*, 395

143   "happy pills and sleepy pills," "what happens to actresses in my plays?" Lahr, 396.

143   "Williams began this resurrection [*sic*]": Diana Barrymore, letter to Elia Kazan,
           undated, circa 1959, Diana Barrymore papers, New York Public Library.

143 "He is the God of my idolatry": Diana Barrymore, letter to Marion Vaccaro Black, undated, circa 1959, The Fred W. Todd Tennessee Williams Collection, MSS 562, Box 39, Folder 657, Williams Research Center, The Historic New Orleans Collection.

143 "You can make a career out of playing Tennessee Williams": *Miami Herald*, June 1, 1959.

143 "savior on earth": Diana Barrymore, letter to Dakin Williams, April 1959, referenced in Lahr, 398.

143 "[D]riving in a Thunderbird with him": Diana Barrymore, card to Essee Kupcinet, undated, circa 1959, Diana Barrymore papers, New York Public Library.

143 "We'll have a menage-a-trois": Kupcinet and Neimark, 133.

143-144 "intense friendship," "better than any romantic item": Diana Barrymore, letter to Essee Kupcinet, undated, circa 1959, Diana Barrymore papers, New York Public Library.

144 "camping it up, "he looked at Kim [Hunter]": Diana Barrymore, Diana, letter to Essee Kupcinet, undated, circa 1959, Diana Barrymore papers, New York Public Library.

144 "appeal to his butch side!" Diana Barrymore, Diana, undated note to herself, circa 1959, Diana Barrymore papers, New York Public Library.

144 "crown," "in the cells of my blood," monsters don't die early": Williams, *Sweet Bird of Youth*, 116.

144 "out of the passion and torment": Williams, *Sweet Bird of Youth*, 120.

144 "there are no clocks": *Esquire*, January 1943.

144 "too much like the princess": Lahr, 399.

144 "I'm a f—-ing desperate woman": Diana Barrymore, letter to Elia Kazan, undated, circa 1959, Diana Barrymore papers, New York Public Library.

144 "a sort of urchin girl-woman": Maxwell, *Tennessee Williams and Friends*, 234.

144 "My hatred for Kazan burns black": Diana Barrymore, letter to Dakin Williams, referenced in Lahr, 399.

144 "so goddamn drunk they had to help her out of the theatre": Plummer, 281–83.

144 "a dark animal look about her": Plummer, 48–49.

145 "All right. I've told you I don't think it's for you": Lahr, 401.

145 "I don't know—things happened," "If she loved [Robin] that much," "I thought, this is a bunch of baloney," "completely fixed," "he was an agnostic": Bound Notes G, box 1, Gerold Frank papers, Manuscripts and Archives Division, New York Public Library.

145 "[God] has given me at least 9 chances": Diana Barrymore, draft of letter to unknown recipient, possibly Elia Kazan, undated, circa 1959, Diana Barrymore papers, New York Public Library.

145 "the absolutely perfect and intelligent gift": *Philadelphia Inquirer*, January 5, 1960.

146 "[d]on't let anything distract you" Edna and Nick Stewart, letter to Diana Barrymore, undated, circa spring 1958, Diana Barrymore papers, The New York Public Library.

146 "nutty," "too slick," "a crumb": *LA Weekly*, February 14, 1980.

146 "I had on my good mink": *New York Newsday*, January 4, 1960.

146 "tweaked," "he almost broke my neck": *Miami News*, January 9, 1960.

146 "made a scene": *Windsor Star* (Ontario, Canada), January 27, 1960.

146 "full of concern about dying," "running out of time," "she told me 'I want you to get a nice black hat'": *Tampa Tribune*, January 26, 1960.

146 "dark thoughts": *Pensacola News-Journal*, January 27, 1960.

146   "Life is too much": Diana Barrymore, letter to Essee Kupcinet, undated, circa 1959,
        Diana Barrymore papers, New York Public Library.
146   "pounding like a hammer on an anvil": *Pensacola News-Journal*, January 27, 1960.
146   "brooding Armenian": *New Castle News*, May 23, 1950.
147   "She's cold and white": *New York Daily News*, Jan 26, 1960.
147   "large amounts," "small amounts": *Cincinnati Post*, February 2, 1960.
147   "blood streaming from her mouth": Williams, *Memoirs*, 224.
147   "Diana just went to sleep and didn't wake up": *New York Daily News*, January 26, 1960.

                          CHAPTER 10: NOBODY CARED

148   "We used to talk about her quitting drinking": *Philadelphia Daily News*, August 28,
        1967.
148   "She was a sweet, nice, honest, good kid": *San Francisco Examiner*, February 7, 1960.
148   "fever and fury," "terrifying honesty," "goodnight, my sweet": *Durham Herald Sun*,
        January 30, 1960.
148   "You're here to spend six weeks with your daughter": Kupcinet and Neimark, 136.
148   "Death Stills the Storm for Diana Barrymore": *New York Daily News*, January 26, 1960.
148   "a soul in anguish": *Banning Daily Record*, January 27, 1960.
148   "[C]heap, melodramatic bilge": Maxwell, 275.
149   "Copycatting," "the Barrymore curse": Hedda Hopper, "Myths Stars Believe About
        Themselves," *Modern Screen*, July 1949.
149   "Barrymore Curse Trips Diana Too": *Toronto Star*, January 28, 1960.
149   "a curse—an inheritance from my father, his father probably, way down the line":
        Modern Screen, May 1960.
149   "she was badly treated all her life": *New York Daily News*, January 26, 1960.
149   "nobody cared," "[S]he came to us, but it was too late": *St. Louis Post-Dispatch*, Febru-
        ary 7, 1960.
149   "Nobody can accuse the 42nd St. grind houses" through "just before her death":
        Dorothy Kilgallen, "Gotham Gossip," *Cincinnati Enquirer*, February 25, 1960.
149   "taunting blonde," "tragic drink": *On the Q.T.*, September 1960.
149   "the outrageous confessions," "screen siren," "lying drunk in the rain," "sharp satire
        . . . a lot of fun to read": *New York Times*, May 8, 1960.
150   "I feel very deeply, as anyone would": *Tampa Tribune*, January 27, 1960.
150   "an engine running away": *Miami News*, January 26, 1960.
150   "the Shakespeare of the 20th Century": Kupcinet and Neimark, 133.
150   "only true love . . . her struggle to become a good artist": Lahr, 401.
150   "He was a lovely, lovely person" through "stood up and applauded": folder "1950-
        1955," box 1, Gerold Frank papers, Manuscripts and Archives Division, New York
        Public Library.
150   "Since the estate has insufficient assets," "like most of the chapters in her autobi-
        ography": *New York Daily News*, November 29, 1964.
151   "one of the late Diana Barrymore's dearest friends": Kupcinet, *Kup's Chicago*, 26.
151   "everybody had warned me what a bitch Diana Barrymore was": Smart-Grosvenor,
        Vibration Cooking, 107.

151   "the most fun to be with of any girl I've ever known": *San Francisco Examiner*, February 7, 1960.

151   "It's no concern of mine": Brian, *Murderers and Other Friendly People*, 291.

151   "[A] Tennessee Williams vulnerable heroine": Terkel, *The Spectator*, 141.

151   "So you want to be an actor?" Orin Kennedy, email message to author, March 7, 2021.

151   "I will see you at Christmas": Diana Barrymore, telegram to Orin Kennedy, December 4, 1959, private collection, via Orin Kennedy, used with permission.

152   "At least a half dozen of my friends," "superficial kind of life," "at the age of 39": *Life*, December 6, 1963.

152   "suave playboy," "unshaven [but] deeply tanned": *Miami Herald*, February 22, 1962.

153   "there's nothing only phony motives" "personal vendetta": "Karyn 'Cookie' Kupcinet," FindADeath.com, https://findadeath.com/karyn-cookie-kupcinet/.

153   "a captain at Regents Row": Lee Mortimer, "New York Confidential." *Glens Falls Post-Star*, August 14, 1959.

153   "financier, restauranteur, lodge owner": *Grand Junction Daily Sentinel*, December 21, 1958.

153   "mountaineer," "sportsman": *Grand Junction Daily Sentinel*, October 13, 1954.

153   "swimming in a beaver pond to clear his head": *Elmira Star-Gazette*, October 14, 1954.

154   "small segment of the Rockettes": *Montreal Star*, June 25, 1962.

154   "John Barrymore's Chicago Girl": *Brooklyn Eagle*, August 19, 1940.

154   "Chicago protégé": *Brooklyn Citizen*, August 22, 1940.

154   "the happiest memories of my life": *Miami Herald*, February 6, 1940.

155   "defiantly black," "impeccably manicured," "quick wit still in evidence," "seedy dive": Donna Hill, Joan Myers, and Christopher S. Connelly. "Act 3: Marriage, Later Years—Final Years," https://nitanaldi.com/biography-2/act-3-marriage-later-years/.

155   "make no mistake": *Lansing State Journal*, April 2, 1990.

155-156 "explosive, wild father," "7,-pound bag," "I liked the feeling": *Rochester Democrat and Chronicle*, February 1, 1990.

156   "[t]here's nothing sweeter-feeling": *Modern Screen*, May 1960.

156   "I would listen": Barrymore, *Wildflower*, 26.

156   "I know where Drew is coming from": *Lansing State Journal*, April 2, 1990.

156   "I've never been wicked": folder "1950–1955," box 1, Gerold Frank papers, Manuscripts and Archives Division, New York Public Library.

156   "[she was] a girl": Bound Notes B, box 1, Gerold Frank papers, Manuscripts and Archives Division, New York Public Library.

156   "That name is magic," "all the chances I've had": Bound Notes F, box 1, Gerold Frank papers, Manuscripts and Archives Division, New York Public Library.

156   "My career would have run": *Boston Globe*, April 24, 1955.

SELECT BIBLIOGRAPHY

Abelman, Lester. "Diana's Will Generous, But Estate Is Nil." *Daily News*, November 29, 1964.

Acosta, Mercedes. *Here Lies the Heart: A Tale of My Life.* New York: Reynal and Co., 1960.

Anderson, Mark. "Real Life His Best Role." *Bloomington Pantagraph*, January 3, 1981.

Arce, Hector. *The Secret Life of Tyrone Power.* New York: Morrow, 1979.

Associated Press. "Actress in Hospital: Diana Barrymore Felled by 'Accidental Dose' of Pills." *New York Times*, April 28, 1955.

Associated Press. "Australia Pains Diana Barrymore." *Baltimore Sun*, March 11, 1952.

Associated Press. "Diana Barrymore Sees US In White Slave Case of Ex." *New York Daily News,* March 24, 1953.

Associated Press. "Diana's Insult Trial Is Put Off." *New York Daily News*, December 11, 1953.

Associated Press. "Howard Trial On Vice Count Begins Today." *New York Daily*, March 25, 1953.

Associated Press. "She's Off Australia for Life." *New York Daily News*, March 14, 1952.

Associated Press. "Ambitions Unfulfilled, Diana Barrymore Buried." *Los Angeles Times*, January 30, 1960.

"'Bamboo Bed' (Ex-'Little Hut') a Foldo, Fiasco Souring Roch. on Twofers." *Variety*, November 9, 1955.

Barnes, Eric Wollencott. *The Man Who Lived Twice: The Biography of Edward Sheldon*. New York: Charles Scribner's Sons, 1956.

Barrymore, Diana, correspondence to Edwina Dakin Williams, Fred W. Todd Tennessee Williams Collection, MSS 562, Boxes 7.7 and 7.8, Williams Research Center, Historic New Orleans Collection.

Barrymore, Diana, correspondence to Marion Black Vaccaro, Fred W. Todd Tennessee Williams Collection, MSS 562, Box 7.9, Williams Research Center, Historic New Orleans Collection.

Barrymore, Diana, and Gerold Frank. *Too Much, Too Soon.* New York: Henry Holt & Company, 1957.

Barrymore, Elaine (Barrie), and Sanford Dody. *All My Sins Remembered: The Story of my Life with John Barrymore.* New York: Appleton-Century, 1964.

Barrymore, John. *Confessions of an Actor.* Indianapolis: Bobbs-Merrill, 1926.

Barrymore, John. *We Three* (Little Big Books). Akron: Saalfield Publishing, 1936.

"Between Us Girls (1942)." *AFI Catalog of Feature Films: The First 100 Years, 1893–1993.* https://catalog.afi.com/Catalog/moviedetails/27137.

Blaetz, Robin. *Visions of the Maid: Joan of Arc in American Film and Culture.* Charlottesville: University of Virginia Press, 2001.

"Books: Ei-lu-lu . . . Baby." *Time*, April 15, 1957.

Brennan, Edwin F. "Diana Barrymore Like Dad." *Pittsburgh Post-Gazette*, May 30, 1951.

Brian, Denis. *Murderers and Other Friendly People: The Public and Private Worlds of Interviewers.* New York: McGraw-Hill, 1973.

Brown, Peter H. "Chappaquiddick: The Motion Picture Cash-In." *LA Weekly*, February 14, 1980.

Cahall, Gary. "Too Much, Too Soon (1958): Too Much Diana Barrymore, Too Little John." *MovieFanFare! The Movie Collector's Blog*, August 14, 2015. http://www.moviefanfare.com/?p=47245.

Cavett, Dick. *Talk Show: Confrontations, Pointed Commentary, and Off-Screen Secrets.* New York: Times Books, 2010.

The Charming Woman. Edited by Helen Fraser. New York: Charming Woman, 1950.

Cohen, Harold V. "Diana Barrymore Is the Star of Nixon's 'Separate Rooms.'" *Pittsburgh Post-Gazette*, May 18, 1954.

Crowther, Bosley. "'Eagle Squadron,' Action Film of Americans in R.A.F., With Diana Barrymore, Jon Hall and Robert Stack, at Globe." *New York Times*, July 3, 1942.

Cummings v. Universal, Case No. 3242, US District Court (Southern District of CA), January 7, 1943.

Davis, Ronald L. *Just Making Movies: Company Directors on the Studio System.* Jackson: University Press of Mississippi, 2005.

Decker, John. "The Unpredictable Profile." *Esquire*, January 1943.

Derwent, Clarence. *The Derwent Story: My First Fifty Years in the Theatre in England and America.* New York: H. Schuman, 1953.

"Diana Barrymore Acts in Royal Family Style." *Life*, July 31, 1939.

"Diana Barrymore in Clever Play." *The Age* (Melbourne, Victoria, Australia), November 10, 1951.

Diana Barrymore papers. *T-Mss 1960-002. Billy Rose Theatre Division, New York Public Library.

"Diana Barrymore Shows Liking for Western Role." *Louisville Courier-Journal*, August 27, 1943.

"'Don't Whitewash Me,' Said Barrymore." *New York Times*, April 20, 1941.

Duke, Anthony Drexel, and Richard Firstman. *Uncharted Course: The Voyage of My Life.* Thomaston: Bayview Press, 2007.

"Eagle Squadron (1942)." *AFI Catalog of Feature Films: The First 100 Years, 1893–1993.* https://catalog.afi.com/Catalog/moviedetails/27210.

"Fallen Angels Fails Badly." *The Age* (Melbourne, Victoria, Australia), December 31, 1951.

Fidler, Jimmie. "Diana Decides Not to Follow Pater's Pranks." *Detroit Free Press*, June 28, 1943.

"'Fired Wife' with Robert Paige, Louise Allbritton and Diana Barrymore." *Harrison's Reports*, October 9, 1943.

"Fired Wife (1943)." *AFI Catalog of Feature Films: The First 100 Years, 1893–1993.* https://catalog.afi.com/Catalog/moviedetails/428.

Flynn, Errol, and Earl Conrad. *My Wicked, Wicked Ways.* New York: G. P. Putnam's Sons, 1959.

"Forget It, Says Star of Movie." *Uniontown Morning Herald*, April 7, 1947.

Fowler, Gene. *Good Night Sweet Prince: The Life and Times of John Barrymore.* New York: Viking Press, 1944.

Fowler, Gene. *Minutes of the Last Meeting.* New York: Viking Press, 1954.

Frazier, Brenda. "My Debut—A Horror." *Life*, December 6, 1963.

"Frontier Badmen (1943)." *AFI Catalog of Feature Films: The First 100 Years, 1893–1993.* https://catalog.afi.com/Catalog/moviedetails/439.

Gary, Amy. *In the Great Green Room: The Brilliant and Bold Life of Margaret Wise Brown.* New York: Flatiron Books, 2017.

Gerold Frank papers (MssCol 1067). Manuscripts and Archives Division, New York Public Library.

Gill, Ted. "She'll Go Along On Her Own—'Profile Junior' Is Witty, Too." *Fort Worth Star-Telegram,* May 31, 1942.

Goldstein, Malcolm. *George S. Kaufman : His life, His theater.* New York: Oxford University Press, 1979.

Gould, Jack. "TV-Radio: 2 New Comics." *New York Times,* July 15, 1957.

Gregory, Fiona. *Actresses and Mental Illness: Histrionic Heroines.* Oxfordshire: Routledge, 2018.

Guiles, Fred Lawrence. *Tyrone Power: The Last Idol.* Garden City: Doubleday & Co., 1979.

Guinness, Louise, *The Vintage Book of Fathers.* London: Trafalgar Square, 1998.

Hamlet Lives in Hollywood: John Barrymore and the Acting Tradition Onscreen. Edited by Murray Pomerance and Steven Rybin. Edinburgh: Edinburgh University Press, 2019.

Hampton, Howard. "BULLSEYE: Howard Hampton on Vincente Minelli's *The Bad and the Beautiful* (1952)." *Artforum,* November 21, 2019. https://www.artforum.com/film/howard-hampton-on-vincente-minnelli-s-the-bad-and-the-beautiful-1952-81335.

Haynsworth, Leslie, and David Toomey. *Amelia Earhart's Daughters.* New York: William Morrow and Company, 1998.

Hill, Donna L., Christopher S. Connelly, and Joan Myers. "Biography, Act 3: Marriage, Later Years." https://web.archive.org/web/20150524094442/http://nitanaldi.com/biography-2/act-3-marriage-later-years/.

Hopper, Hedda. "Diana Barrymore Has a Long Road to Go Before Hitting Top, Says Hedda." *Fort Worth Star-Telegram,* July 27, 1942.

Hopper, Hedda. "Hollywood." *New York Daily News,* October 18, 1942.

Hopper, Hedda. "Looking at Hollywood." *Chicago Tribune,* June 27, 1942.

Jefferson, Miles. "The Negro on Broadway, 1955–1956: Pits and Peaks in an Active Season." *Phylon* (1940–1956) 17, no. 3 (1956): 227–37. https://doi.org/10.2307/272873.

Jessel, George. *Elegy in Manhattan.* New York: Holt, Rinehart & Winston, 1961.

Johnson, Erskine. "Hollywood Newsreel." *Hollywood,* January 1943.

Kerr, Adelaide. "Another Acting Barrymore Goes Her Own Sweet Way." *Oakland Tribune,* September 11, 1941.

Kobler, John. *Damned in Paradise: The Life of John Barrymore.* New York: Atheneum, 1977.

Kotsilibas-Davis, James. *The Barrymores: The Royal Family in Hollywood.* New York: Crown, 1981.

Kupcinet, Irv. *Kup's Chicago.* Cleveland and New York: World Publishing Company, 1962.

Kupcinet, Irv, and Paul G. Neimark. *Kup: A Man, an Era, a City.* Los Angeles: Bonus Books, 1988.

"Ladies Courageous (1944)." *AFI Catalog of Feature Films: The First 100 Years, 1893–1993.* https://catalog.afi.com/Catalog/moviedetails/24031.

Lafer, Lawrence, and David Quirk. "Death Stills the Storm for Diana Barrymore." *New York Daily News,* January 26, 1960.

Lahr, John. *Tennessee Williams: Mad Pilgrimage of the Flesh.* New York: W. W. Norton & Company, 2014.

Lake, Veronica, and Donald Bain. *Veronica: The Autobiography of Veronica Lake.* New York: Citadel Press, 1969.

Lambert, Gavin. *The Ivan Moffat File: Life Among the Beautiful and Damned in London, Paris, New York, and Hollywood.* New York: Pantheon Books, 2004.

Lanning, Ray. "Movie Reviews: 'Between Us Girls,' Palace." *Cincinnati Enquirer,* September 18, 1942.

Leavitt, Richard F. *The World of Tennessee Williams.* New York: G. P. Putnam's Sons, 1978.

"Len Thomas Gay." *New Haven Morning Journal-Courier,* March 23, 1908.

"Let's Go Bowling!" *Modern Screen*, June 1942.

"'Lillie' Martin's Younger Sister." *New York Press*, May 10, 1904.

Little Hut, aka *Bamboo Bed*: claim against Diana Barrymore and other company correspondence, 1955–1957, Actors' Equity Association Records, WAG 011, box 295, folder 1, Tamiment Library/Robert F. Wagner Labor Archives, New York University.

McHarry, Charles. "Diana Remembers Daddy." *Florida Magazine*, July 29, 1956.

McReynolds, Bill. "Entertainment Capers." *Amarillo Globe-Times*, April 16, 1957.

Mank, Gregory William, Charles Heard, and Bill Nelson. *Hollywood's Hellfire Club: The Misadventures of John Barrymore, W. C. Fields, Errol Flynn and the Bundy Drive Boys.* Port Townsend, WA: Feral House, 2007.

Mantle, Burns. "John Barrymore, as Actor, Lover, Playboy, Completes a Chapter." *New York Daily News*, June 3, 1942.

Martin, Joseph. "Diana Back with Mate; Next Act Anybody's Guess." *New York Daily News*, June 11, 1953.

Martin, Joseph, and Neal Patterson. "So, 10 Drinks or So Later, Diana Shows Her Husband the Door." *New York Daily News*, June 10, 1953.

Martin, Mildred. "Aldine's 'Ladies Courageous' Is Film Tribute to Wasps." *Philadelphia Inquirer*, May 31, 1944.

Mavity, Nancy Barr. "Life and Wild Times of Diana Barrymore." *Oakland Tribune*, April 7, 1957.

Maxwell, Gilbert. *Tennessee Williams and Friends*. Cleveland and New York: World Publishing Company, 1965.

Michael Strange Papers, *T-Mss 1994–009, Billy Rose Theatre Division, New York Public Library for the Performing Arts.

Morrison, Michael A. *John Barrymore, Shakespearean Actor*. Cambridge: Cambridge University Press, 1997.

Nesbitt, Cathleen. *A Little Love and Good Company*. London: Faber & Faber, 1975.

"Nightmare (1942)." *AFI Catalog of Feature Films: The First 100 Years, 1893–1993.* https://catalog.afi.com/Catalog/moviedetails/27378.

O'Hanlon, Michael. "Between Us Girls." *Kay Francis' Life and Career*, August 3, 2013. https://kayfrancisfilms.com/between-us-girls-1942/.

O'Malley, Sheila. "'Make voyages!—Attempt them!—there's nothing else. . . .' Happy Birthday, Tennessee Williams." *Sheila Variations*, March 26, 2022. http://www.sheilaomalley.com/?p=66317.

Othman, Frederick C. "Hollywood Film Shop." *Chico Record*, August 30, 1942.

Parsons, Louella O. "Cooper Stays in Demand At Studios." *Rochester Democrat and Chronicle*, January 29, 1943.

Parsons, Louella O. "Diana Barrymore Selected for Lead in 'Eagle Squadron.'" *Camden Courier-Post*, December 22, 1941.

Peak, Mayme Ober. "So Profile Will Tutor." *Buffalo Evening News*, February 7, 1942.

Pennington, Lee. "Eagle Squadron (fiction version)." *Photoplay*, June 1942.

Peters, Margot. *The House of Barrymore*. New York: Simon & Schuster, 1990.

Power-Waters, Alma. *John Barrymore: The Legend and the Man*. New York: Julian Messner, 1941.

Preminger, Otto. *Preminger—An Autobiography*. New York: Doubleday, 1977.

"Preview Set for Tonight At Orpheum." *San Francisco Examiner*, October 20, 1942.

Purple Parrot, Northwestern University (Evanston, IL), February 1943.

"Radio: Balcony Scene." *Time*, February 9, 1942.

Reuters. "Diana Sings Salty Song—Gets Gate." *New York Daily News*, February 13, 1952.

"Reviews of the New Films: Frontier Badmen." *Film Daily*, August 11, 1943.

Robb, Inez. "John Barrymore Touchy on Question of Reform." *Louisville Courier-Journal*, January 20, 1939.

Scheuer, Philip K. "Barrymore Biography Ill Advised." *Los Angeles Times*, May 16, 1958.

"Science [*sic*]: The New Pictures." *Time*, October 5, 1942.

Shuler, Marjorie. "Girl with Knuckle Dusters." *Philadelphia Inquirer,* June 29, 1947.

Shulman, Terry Chester. *Film's First Family: The Untold Story of the Costellos.* Lexington: University Press of Kentucky, 2019.

Sikov, Ed. *Dark Victory: The Life of Bette Davis.* New York: Henry Holt & Company, 2007.

Skolsky, Sidney. "Skolsky's Hollywood." *Cincinnati Enquirer,* April 20, 1943.

Smart-Grosvenor, Vertamae. *Vibration Cooking: Or, the Travel Notes of a Geechee Girl.* New York: Doubleday, 1970.

Smith, Dinitia. "Gerold Frank Is Dead at 91; Author of Celebrity Memoirs." *New York Times*, September 19, 1998.

Smith, H. Allen. "From the Gutter to TV." *New York Times*, May 8, 1960.

Spoto, Daniel. *The Kindness of Strangers: The Life of Tennessee Williams*. London: Bodley Head, 1985.

"'Squadron' and 'United' Open." *Motion Picture Herald*, July 4, 1942.

Stack, Robert, and Mark Evans. *Straight Shooting*. New York: Macmillan, 1980.

Stolier, Muriel. "Important Pictures." *Hollywood*, February 1943.

Strange, Michael. *Who Tells Me True*. New York: Charles Scribner's Sons, 1940.

Strauss, Theodore. "Again the Ten Worst." *New York Times*, December 27, 1942.

Sullivan, Ed. "Little Old New York: The Jack of Barrymores." *New York Daily News*, June 1, 1942.

Terkel, Studs. *The Spectator: Talk About Movies and Plays with the People Who Make Them*. New York: The New Press, 1999.

Thompson, C.V. *Trousers Will Be Worn*. New York: G. P. Putnam's Sons, 1941.

"Timely Observations." *St. Joseph News-Press*, April 29, 1957.

T. M. P. "At Loew's Criterion." *New York Times*, March 16, 1944.

"Too Much, Too Soon (1958)." *AFI Catalog of Feature Films: The First 100 Years, 1893–1993*. https://catalog.afi.com/Catalog/moviedetails/52776.

T. S. "'Between Us Girls,' With Diana Barrymore, Kay Francis and Robert Cummings at Capitol—'Busses Roar' at the Palace." *New York Times*, September 25, 1942.

United Press International. "Diana Barrymore's Mate, Blonde Raided." *New York Daily News*, March 12, 1950.

The World of Tennessee Williams. Introduction by Tennessee Williams. Edited by Richard F. Leavitt. New York: G. P. Putnam's Sons, 1978.

United Press International. "Barrymore Buried to SRO Audience." *Miami News*, January 29, 1960.

United Press International. "Diana Barrymore Returns." *New York Times*, April 29, 1955.

United Press International. "Diana Barrymore Rites Conducted in New York." *Los Angeles Evening Citizen News*, January 29, 1960.

United Press International. "Hold Diana Barrymore's Ex as N.Y. White-Slaver." *New York Daily News*, October 29, 1950.

United Press International. "Michael Strange, Author, 60, Dead." *New York Times*, November 6, 1950.

United Press International. "Socialites, Actors Jam Diana Barrymore Rites." *Boston Globe*, January 30, 1960.

United Press International. "Vice Charges Ruin His Game." *New York Daily News*, March 17, 1950.

"What Killed Diana Barrymore?" *Modern Screen*, May 1960.

"What Will Happen to This Union of Geniuses?" *Philadelphia Inquirer*, September 19, 1920.

Wheelock, John Hall. *The Last Romantic: A Poet among Publishers—The Oral Autobiography of John Hall Wheelock*. Edited by Matthew J. Broccoli with Judith S. Baughman. Columbia: University of South Carolina Press, 2002.

Whitaker, James. "Barrymores' Brother and Sister Act, 'Clair de Lune,' Is Pretty, But a Mess." *Chicago Tribune*, April 24, 1921.

Williams, Tennessee. *Memoirs*. New York: Bantam Books, 1976.

Williams, Tennessee. *Sweet Bird of Youth*. New York: New Directions Publishing Corp., 1975.

Wilson, Earl. "It Happened Last Night: Diana Barrymore Gets Shiner in Lovers' Tiff." *Winona Daily News*, August 10, 1953.

Wilson, Earl. "It Happened Last Night: Diana Barrymore and Others Getting Unemployment Pay." *St. Louis Star and Times*, January 6, 1949.

Wilson, Earl. *The Show Business Nobody Knows*. Spokane: Cowles Book Company, 1971.

Wright, Cobina, Jr. *I Never Grew Up*. Hoboken: Prentice-Hall, 1952.

York, Cal. "Inside Stuff: Cal York's Gossip of Hollywood." *Photoplay*, July 1957.

INDEX

Page numbers in *italics* indicate images.

ABOUT THE AUTHOR

Photo by Roy Mauritsen

JENNIFER ANN REDMOND'S PASSION FOR WRITING IS MATCHED ONLY BY her love for classic Hollywood, especially the silent and pre-Code era. Her work has been featured in *Classic Images*, *Atlas Obscura*, and the Library of Congress website, as well as three previous books: *Silents of the Vamps: Bad Girls You Don't Know—But Should* (2019), *Southern Belle to Hollywood Hell: Corliss Palmer and Her Scandalous Rise and Fall* (2018), and *Reels & Rivals: Sisters in Silent Film* (2016). She resides in her childhood home on Long Island, where a typical evening involves chai, cats, and a black-and-white movie.